Managing
THE Monster

MANAGING THE MONSTER

Urban Waste and Governance in Africa

Edited by
Adepoju G. Onibokun

INTERNATIONAL DEVELOPMENT RESEARCH CENTRE
Ottawa • Cairo • Dakar • Johannesburg • Montevideo • Nairobi • New Dehi • Singapore

Published by the International Development Research Centre
PO Box 8500, Ottawa, ON, Canada K1G 3H9

© International Development Research Centre 1999

Canadian Cataloguing in Publication Data

Main entry under title :

Managing the monster : urban waste and governance in Africa

Includes bibliographical references.
ISBN 0-88936-880-5

1. Refuse and refuse disposal — Africa.
2. Urbanization — Environmental aspects — Africa.
3. Environmental policy — Africa.
I. Onibokun, Adepoju G., 1943-   .
II. International Development Research Centre (Canada).

TD790.M36 1999   363.72'8'6'096   C99-980242-9

IDRC Books endeavours to produce environmentally friendly publications. All paper used is recycled as well as recyclable. All inks and coatings are vegetable-based products.

CONTENTS

v

vi

FOREWORD

This book presents the results of the African component of a global project on sustainable cities. In 1993, it successfully competed for support from a limited, special initiatives fund of Canada's International Development Research Centre (IDRC). At that time, program specialists argued that the project offered "great potential for an extensive and well-coordinated research network to pool scarce funding and conduct high-quality research, by senior specialists in renowned institutions, which would focus on priority urban social, environmental, and economic issues for a more sustainable management of Southern cities." The reader will no doubt find that this promise has been fulfilled by the research presented in this book. More importantly, we hope that you will concur that *Managing the Monster* is nothing less than a benchmark contribution to our knowledge on governance and waste management in major urban centres of Africa.

The authors are senior experts from a wide range of entities involved with waste management. They have served as advisers or directors of United Nations agency offices, research-oriented nongovernmental organizations, metropolitan council departments, and university schools and institutes in Africa. Both the proposal and project benefited from discussion between the team and a larger group of experts from around the world, assembled under the Global Urban Research Initiative coordinated by Richard Stren of the University of Toronto.

Ably coordinated by Adepoju G. Onibokun, chief executive of the Centre for African Settlement Studies and Development in Nigeria, this team assigned itself the daunting task of tackling comprehensively a notoriously underreported and mismanaged urban service: waste management. The published literature on the subject was very limited and the researchers had to rely heavily on the gray literature, documents either unpublished or with limited circulation. Adding to their burden, the team undertook to investigate waste management through a governance perspective. At the time, this was a very new approach and, today, remains highly demanding and innovative, for the type of information it requires, the relationships it needs to address, and the recommendations it is expected to deliver.

Managing the Monster highlights new directions on policy and technology that are highly relevant to IDRC's current focus on urban development research in the South. In a number of urban sectors (water, housing, utilities, open-space management, etc.), better governance is central to improving the effectiveness of service provision. As shown in this book, better governance implies redressing inequitable access to resources and services, confusion and conflict over responsibilities, top-down decision-making, and lack of accountability and transparency. Resource utilization by cities cannot be made more sustainable without increasing waste and by-product recovery; this is needed to reduce urban demands on rural areas and to make cities themselves more viable and liveable. A more equitable, viable, and sustainable use of urban resources can only be enhanced by better governance.

Further, the positive experiences and local capacities discussed in this book point to the real potential for much greater Africa–Africa exchange and cooperation. Greater societal participation, a more decentralized administration, locally appropriate legislation and technologies, and a more integrated approach to managing urban resource flows are all needed to reduce costs and to increase incomes of increasingly poorer city populations and deficit-ridden urban governments.

Luc J.A. Mougeot
Senior Program Specialist
International Development Research Centre
Ottawa, Canada

PREFACE

This work is the product of comparative research on governance and urban waste in Africa carried out by four teams of researchers in four major cities in Africa: Abidjan, Côte d'Ivoire, in francophone West Africa; Ibadan, Nigeria, in anglophone West Africa; Dar es Salaam, Tanzania, in East Africa; and Johannesburg, South Africa, in southern Africa. The study was funded with a grant from the International Development Research Centre (IDRC), of Canada. The coordinators of the research are members of the African Research Network for Urban Management, which has for more than 10 years embraced most of the leading urban researchers and urban-research institutions on the African continent.

This book attempts to characterize waste-management systems in Africa within the framework of governance. It pursues the governance debate and how it helps us to deepen our understanding of urban problems in Africa. It has six chapters. Chapter 1 is an overview of the governance debate in Africa, focusing on the various ways governance is conceptualized. It concludes that to move the debate forward, we need to operationalize the concepts by applying them to a specific aspect of urban management in Africa — in this case, urban waste. This chapter also discusses the scope and the objectives of the studies carried out in the selected African cities and the methodology adopted by the research teams. Chapters 2–5 contain analyses of the waste-management systems and approaches in the four key African cities. Chapter 6 is a synthesis chapter, presenting an analytical overview of the key governance themes raised in Chapter 1. Chapter 6 assesses the efficiency and effectiveness of different modes and modalities (for example, public, private, and community sectors) of managing urban waste, as typified by the selected cities, in political, sociological, economic, and environmental terms. The chapter also recommends policy options for waste management in urban Africa on the basis of what worked or did not work in the four cities.

Many people, too numerous to list, contributed to the research for this book. I am immensely grateful to Dr Koffi Attahi, Mark Swilling, and Lusugga Kironde, who worked with me to coordinate the research. They ably responded to constant demands for review meetings, updates of data, and revisions of draft reports. Special mention must be made of IDRC, which supported the research and is publishing this book. IDRC has had a tremendous impact on human-resource development and capacity-building in Africa through its research-support activities. The Centre for African Settlement Studies and Development is a living example. IDRC's support for this and other initiatives is highly appreciated. I am also grateful to Richard Stren of the University of Toronto, who is the Coordinator of the Global Urban Research Initiative. Professor Stren made useful comments on the study methodology and arranged for the presentation of the first draft of this work in Mexico City and in Istanbul before wider audiences of researchers, policymakers, and donor agencies.

This work is meant to spur concerted action on the endemic problem of urban-waste management in Africa. It is our hope that this publication will further our understanding of the issues and help us achieve a more liveable urban environment in Africa.

A.G. Onibokun

Chapter 1

GOVERNANCE AND WASTE MANAGEMENT IN AFRICA

A.G. Onibokun and A.J. Kumuyi

THE URBANIZATION PROCESS IN AFRICA

Every society wishes to grow in knowledge, population, and value. However, a peak is always reached in the management of this growth, at which point additional development becomes counter-productive. It must also be said that values and production can diminish even before this peak is reached. This might be a result of poor management, poor programs, inadequate facilities, and so on. This is perhaps best illustrated by the positive and negative impacts of the urbanization process in Africa.

Urbanization introduces society to a new, modern way of life, an improved level of awareness, new skills, a learning process, and so on. However, when the rate of urbanization gets out of control, it poses a big challenge to governance — optimizing forces become

1

weakened, institutional capabilities become inadequate and ineffective, and, with these, the problems of urbanization are compounded.

Urbanization is not necessarily a new phenomenon on the continent of Africa, as shown by centres like Addis Ababa, Cairo, Kano, and Timbuktu. What is noteworthy about contemporary urbanization in Africa is its fast pace. Although Africa is presently among the least-urbanized regions of the world, it is recording the highest rates of urbanization. For example, Africa and Asia recorded urban growth of 4.9% and 4.2%, respectively, between 1990 and 1992. However, urban growth in Europe and North America in this period was only 0.7% and 1.0%, respectively (United Nations 1995). Furthermore, it has been observed that only two cities in Africa (Cairo and Lagos) attained populations of 1 million in 1950; by 1970, the number of cities in this category had increased to eight. By 1990, it had increased to 24. It is projected that by the turn of the century, two of these cities will have passed the 10 million mark.

An examination of the growth rates of individual African cities shows a rate of 33% for Swaziland, which in 1950 had an urban population of only 1%. This is expected to rise to 63% by 2025. Similarly, Mauritania's urban population may grow from 3% in 1950 to 70% in 2025, and the population in most major cities will have quadrupled between 1950 and the mid-1980s. In some cities — including Abidjan, Dar es Salaam, Khartoum, Lagos and Nairobi — populations have increased more than sixfold within four decades.

THE WASTE-MANAGEMENT PROBLEM

The rapid rate of uncontrolled and unplanned urbanization in the developing nations of Africa has brought environmental degradation. Indeed, one of the most pressing concerns of urbanization in the developing world, especially in Africa, has been the problem of solid-, liquid-, and toxic-waste management. Recent events in major urban centres in Africa have shown that the problem of waste management has become a monster that has aborted most efforts made by city authorities, state and federal governments, and professionals alike. A visit to any African city today will reveal aspects of the waste-management problem such as heaps of uncontrolled garbage, roadsides littered with refuse, streams blocked with junk, disposal sites constituting a health hazard to residential areas, and inappropriately disposed toxic wastes.

The high rate of urbanization in African countries implies a rapid accumulation of refuse. Social and economic changes that most African countries have witnessed since the 1960s have also contributed to increases in waste generated per capita. For example, the Nigerian Environmental Study/Action Team estimated that 20 kg of solid waste is generated per capita per annum in Nigeria (NEST 1991). This amounts to 2.2 million t/year, given Nigeria's estimated population of more than 100 million. In individual cities in Nigeria, there are indications of rapid increases in the rate of waste generation. In Lagos, an estimated 625 000 t of wastes was generated in 1982. This, according to the Federal Ministry of Housing and Environment, is projected to rise to 998 000 t by 2000. Likewise, an estimated 258 000 t of waste was generated in 1982 in Kaduna, and this is expected to increase to 431 000 t by 2000. These are clear indications of the need for adequate management services, which are typically not found in African cities.

3

The sheer volume of waste does not actually constitute the problem — it is the inability of governments and waste-disposal firms to keep up with it. The situation in Nairobi aptly illustrates this. Although between 1977 and 1983 the population of this city was increasing at an estimated annual rate of at least 6%, the amount of refuse collected fell from 202 229 t in 1977 to 159 974 t in 1983 — a decline of 21% over 6 years. Thus, over the late 1970s and early 1980s, the municipal authority in charge of waste was collecting, on average, almost 10% less refuse per capita every year (Stren and White 1989). A similar situation was observed in Malindi (a secondary town in Kenya), where increasing population is a major constraint. In 1991, in Malindi, an estimated 36 000 t of solid waste was produced, but only 7 300 t was transported to dumping sites by the municipal collection service.

Refuse removal provided by the Dar es Salaam city council is plagued by the same difficulties (Stren and White 1989). In this city, only 24% of daily refuse is collected. Also, in Kinshasa, household waste is only collected in a few residential areas. In the rest of the city, household waste is put on the road, on illegal dumps, or in storm-water drains or is buried in open sites (Hardoy and Satterwaite 1992).

THE IMPLICATIONS OF URBANIZATION PROBLEMS FOR GOVERNANCE

The problems generated by rapid urbanization in Africa threaten the governance of urban centres. The diverse and complex problems facing towns and cities in Africa, especially the problem posed by urban waste and by grossly inadequate urban infrastructure and social services, call into question the capacity for governance of African countries.

What do we mean by *governance*? An increasing volume of published and unpublished material is available on "problems of governance." Governance embraces the role of the state in society; the management or mismanagement of socioeconomic activities in the public, private, and community sectors; and the involvement or lack of involvement of civil society in the management of society as a whole. The World Bank perceives governance as "the manner in which power is exercised in the management of a country's economic and social resources for development" (World Bank 1992). Depending on the way in which that power is exercised, governance can be either good or bad. Good governance can be defined as the presence of a government with good and legitimate leadership, a lawful claim to power and authority (based on a mandate derived from the people's will), vision, and a progressive sociopolitical agenda acceptable to, and accepted by, the people and implemented with honesty, transparency, and accountability. Good governance requires a government to draw its legitimacy from, and be accountable to, the governed.

The leadership's vision, transparency, accountability, legitimacy, credibility, predictability, and reliability, combined with society's confidence and stability, are the hallmarks of good governance. Good governance also emphasizes effective and accountable institutions, democratic principles, a reliable electoral process, representative and responsible structures of government, and the need to ensure an open and legitimate relationship between civil society and the state. Good governance will lead to the institutionalization of appropriate policies, programs, and strategies for urban management that help to eliminate or ameliorate the problems posed by rapid urbanization. Governance in the African context therefore needs to be examined to determine the extent to which it responds to the challenges of urbanization and urban growth. Much of the discussion on governance has been at a general (and often abstract) level. There is a need to operationalize some of the new concepts with reference to a set of concrete relationships.

Although the body of literature and practical knowledge about the technical, administrative, and institutional dimensions of waste management in Africa is large and growing, policy frameworks and implementation strategies must be accompanied by new forms of governance to increase efficiency and effectiveness and maximize popular participation in service provision. An increasing interest in public–private–community partnerships is evident in the sector, but this is often related to a concern with technical or financial issues, rather than with the political, sociological, and environmental relationships involved. Technicofinancial approaches have failed to develop the kinds of organizational and institutional approaches needed to empower citizens to comprehend the service and participate effectively, as they have no clear conceptual and strategic framework to allow an understanding of what this involves.

The conclusion we draw is that the governance debate has been insufficiently informed by the practical problems of service provision, and the debates about improved governance in the waste-management sector (and, indeed, the service sector as a whole) have lacked a clear conceptual and strategic framework to empower the citizens organizationally and institutionally.

THE CONCEPTUAL FRAMEWORK

A study of governance and urban waste must examine not only the formal structures of government but also the informal structures created by the society, such as community-based institutions, associations, and organizations; their relationships; and the relationship between the formal and informal structures for collection, transportation, and disposal of waste. Such a study should have four main components:

- Intergovernmental relations;

- Fiscal mobilizations and allocations;

- Planning activities; and

- The participation of the people.

Efficient and effective service delivery depends on several key elements, the most important of which are managerial and organizational efficiency, accountability, legitimacy, and responsiveness to the public, transparency in decision-making, and pluralism of policy options and choices.

Many reasons have been advanced for the prevailing circumstances in African cities, but researchers have yet to ascertain where the problems really lie and what can be done to address them. A cursory look at cities and countries in Africa reveals that this is a heterogeneous continent and that many systems to address the waste problems are in place. Only some of these systems have achieved a measure of success. A cursory analysis of cities in the francophone countries shows that they are cleaner than those in the anglophone countries. Within the anglophone countries, some cities have managed their waste more efficiently than others. Understanding of the factors influencing the performance of the various waste-management systems in Africa can provide useful lessons for all these countries.

THE STUDY

The researchers at the African Research Network for Urban Management (ARNUM) considered it desirable to look at the problems and the challenges posed by solid-waste management in Africa, with a view to examining what has gone wrong and which systems have worked and to making recommendations for developing appropriate management systems aimed at solving the problem of urban-waste management in Africa. Our view, however, is that we cannot realistically examine this problem without examining governance.

In our definition of governance, we referred to transparency, accountability, creditability, and stability of government; the definition also emphasizes public–private–community partnership in urban management. The question is, to what extent are these key elements considered in the management of urban wastes in Africa? A satisfactory answer to this question calls for a more systematic understanding of the relationship between governance and waste management in African cities. In recognition of this, in 1994 the International Development Research Centre approved a grant for comparative research on waste-management systems in Africa. The project was to be executed by a selection of researchers from ARNUM, as part of ARNUM's contribution to the Global Urban Research Initiative (GURI) project. Four cities were selected for study — Abidjan, Dar es Salaam, Ibadan, and Johannesburg, and a governance paper was prepared for each region.

The objective of the study was to describe, compare, and appraise the typical forms of governance that major African cities apply in the management of their waste (including liquid, solid, organic, nonorganic, toxic, and nontoxic waste), with a view to recommending policy options, generally advancing the understanding of this service delivery in urban Africa, and providing a basis to develop an agenda of actionable programs. The specific objectives were

- To describe and analyze the nature and function of the institutional arrangements for waste management in four urban-governance settings, with a view to establishing country profiles;

- To assess and compare the efficiency and effectiveness of diverse combinations of partnership between the public, private, and community sectors in managing urban waste in the selected cities in political, sociological, economic, and environmental terms;

- To recommend policy options, where desirable, to improve waste management in specific urban settings; and

- To advance our knowledge of governance strategies for urban-waste management in Africa.

Four cities were selected for study, representing anglophone and francophone countries, a variety of governance settings, and various sizes of towns (Table 1). These four cities also reflect diverse colonial histories and diverse subregions of the continent. In each country, the researchers identified the institutional arrangements (existing administrative, regulative, execution–delivery, and funding–financing arrangements). They characterized and evaluated the role of the private and public sectors and the community-based organizations in various phases of waste management (collection, transportation, disposal, reuse, etc.).

Table 1. Waste governance in four African cities.

Country	City	Waste-governance setting
Anglophone		
Nigeria	Ibadan	State run and privatized
Tanzania	Dar es Salaam	State run and community based
South Africa	Johannesburg	Community based and privatized
Francophone		
Côte d'Ivoire	Abidjan	State run and privatized

The researchers adopted measures and indicators of performance to evaluate the efficiency of the system. The first assignment of the research team was to identify and agree on performance indicators. They interviewed managers and selected community leaders and a sample of public- and private-sector functionaries to document their informed opinion on the efficiency of existing modes of governance. The goals of this exercise were to determine which waste-governance systems have been efficient and the factors responsible for the efficiency or otherwise of the systems in use and to recommend the governance systems worthy of emulation, adaptation, or adoption by other cities.

To recommend policy options to improve waste management in specific urban settings, the research team relied on the study findings. The research team established which systems or modes of governance were working and why and which were not working and why, on the basis of which the team recommended policy options and waste-management models.

The research team accomplished the following more specific tasks:

- *Task 1* — In each country, it reviewed existing reports pertaining to baseline information generally about the country and more specifically about the sampled city, in terms of location, recent history, the economy, demographic conditions, utilities, and services.

- *Task 2* — It designed and pretested a guideline format for collecting data from the institutions responsible for waste management. These include organogram data and data on personnel, equipment, environmental laws, and funding.

- *Task 3* — In each city, it collected data from available past studies on refuse-generation rates and refuse composition, density, and volume. In each city, the team also documented the existing modes of storage, collection, and transfer of refuse, including frequency of pick-up, efficiency of collection and transfer, routing, and citizen participation in the overall system. The study included an examination and assessment of existing disposal facilities with respect to the location and capacity of landfill sites and other environmental issues.

9

- *Task 4* — It assessed tasks 1–3 in terms of degree of success or failure and the factors that may have been responsible.

- *Task 5* — It provided basic management recommendations on ingredients necessary to improve the particular city's model; and noted what the model has to offer to other cities (if any).

- *Task 6* — Meetings of research associates from the four countries (intercountry workshops) were arranged to consider progress and to draft results. Two meetings were held during the study: the first meeting was held in Dar es Salaam at the beginning to work out and agree on methodology, forms, format, and outline; and the second meeting was held in Ibadan at the end to discuss field experiences, draft final reports, and consider a synthesis report. The GURI regional and final meetings in Mexico City in 1995 and in Istanbul in 1996 provided the team with other opportunities to compare notes on the progress of the research in each city.

In 1996, ARNUM organized the Urban Forum international workshop in Nairobi, which brought together researchers, practitioners, and donor and development agencies for a 3-day dialogue on urban research in Africa. The reports of the research on governance and waste in four African countries were among the papers presented at the workshop. Following the various workshops and review meetings, the authors revised their country reports, which are published in this volume.

Chapter 2

ABIDJAN,
CÔTE D'IVOIRE

Koffi Attahi

THE PROBLEM AND ITS THEORETICAL BASIS

Today, the questions of urban waste management and, by extension, those of urban environmental planning and management represent some of the major challenges facing urban managers, as a
consequence of their effects on human health, sustainable development, and urban finance. If, in the past, waste management in
African cities has been perceived solely as a technical, organizational, and financial operation, today the realization is dawning
that waste management has an important cultural dimension and
gives leverage for power of the highest order.

In the Abidjan metropolis in 1994, the removal of some
500 000 t of household refuse, out of a total of about 920 530 t,
consumed a little in excess of 5 billion XOF, or 61 % of the city's

total budget (Table 1) (in 1998, 610.65 CFA francs [XOF] = 1 United States dollar [USD]). The amateurism of the contracted company, the frequent crises in the city's waste management, and people's overt or covert desire to partake in managing the substantial financial resources involved have attracted a number of new competitors for influence in the city's waste management. This has greatly politicized waste management, to the extent that a patrimonial system of management has been installed, overseeing both the visible and the hidden networks to the detriment of the quality of service. The appearance of new actors on the scene over the years has complicated the organization of waste management. Today, we have a hybrid system of management: although it lays claim to the techniques of privatization, decentralization, and recentralization, it has assembled actors from civil and political societies with ill-defined and often controversial responsibilities and very often maintains informal and noncontractual relations.

In this setting, it is illusory to attempt to use a classical approach to the analysis of the problem of waste management, with stress on description of structures, means, and results. The governance approach seems appropriate because it emphasizes the political analysis of the stakes, relations, and strategies of the various actors participating in the management system and applies the criteria of transparency, efficiency, efficacy, feasibility, and responsible participation, among others, in assessing performance.

It should be clarified that this study covers only three components of urban waste management: liquid waste, solid waste, and industrial waste. The management of liquid waste involves the

Table 1. Financial indicators of solid-waste management in Abidjan, 1990–94.

Year	A Population	B Waste collected (t)	C Cost of collection and sweeping (XOF)	Expense per capita (C/A) (XOF)	Expense per t (C/B) (XOF)
1990	2 050 858	452 440	3 999 537 268	1 950.17	8 839.92
1991	2 143 240	—	4 142 777 642	1 932.95	—
1992	2 228 970	441 970	3 368 038 460	1 511.02	7 620.51
1993	2 318 129	436 234	4 286 626 676	1 849.17	9 826.43
1994	2 410 354	508 847	5 186 643 034	2 151.81	10 192.93

Source: Directorate-General for Technical Coordination, Abidjan, Côte d'Ivoire.
Note: In 1998, 610.65 CFA francs (XOF) = 1 United States dollar (USD).

evacuation and treatment of waste water of domestic origin: household water or sewage water (feces and urine) and industrial waste water (Table 2). The contractual agreement for the removal of household refuse distinguishes three categories of urban solid waste:

- All types of household refuse, ash, broken glass or crockery, and all sweepings and residues that are deposited in individual or collective dustbins placed in front of residences or along public roads;

- Residues from schools, barracks, hospitals, hostels, prisons, and public buildings, assembled in designated locations in prescribed receptacles; and

- Objects discarded in public places and carcasses of small animals.

According to the Classified Installations Inspectorate of the ministère d'Environnement (MOE, Ministry of Environment), which is responsible for industrial waste-management policy, there are two types of industrial waste:

- Industrial waste equivalent to household refuse: paper, plastics, canteen wastes, saw-mill waste, etc.; and

- Dangerous or toxic waste, including hydrocarbons, phytosanitary products, catalysts used in the petroleum industry, polychlorinated biphenyls, chlorine oxides, lead and arsenic used in the treatment of metals, and cyanide.

Table 2. Composition of solid-waste in Abidjan, 1987 and 1994.

Nature of elements	1994 (%)	1987 (%)
Fines	25.7	37.6
Fermentescibles	52.8	44.2
Wood	9.5	4.6
Glass, stones	1.2	1.1
Minerals	0.9	1.14
Textiles	1.3	1.0
Paper, carton	4.18	5.3
Rubber	4.7	1.0

Source: Ministry of Environment, Abidjan, Côte d'Ivoire; CRI (1987).

13

A good reference study of the management of urban waste identifies four levels of intervention: planning, budgeting, execution, and control. Our analysis of each of the three main categories of waste will successively review

- The brief history of the management of liquid, solid, and industrial waste;

- The components of sectoral policies and management mechanisms;

- The actors and their responsibilities, the perception and exercise of these responsibilities, the competition for influence, the points of friction and their impact on the service rendered, the resources, and the results; and

- The evaluation of the management system in place and recommendations.

Before embarking on the actual study of the issue, however, it is pertinent to present the setting.

THE SETTING OF ABIDJAN

Data and physical constraints

Abidjan, the economic capital of Côte d'Ivoire, is situated in the south of the country, bordering on the Atlantic Ocean and straddling the Ébrié lagoon. The site of the city has four distinct morphological components: the coastal belt, the Petit-Bassam peninsula, the Ébrié lagoon, and the plateaux running from south to north over a distance of about 30 km.

The coastal belt is a sandy, low-lying zone linked to the sea by a beach washed periodically by huge dangerous waves, locally called the barrier waves. This zone is made up of sand deposits from the sea and is very marshy. Today, it accommodates the suburbs of Vridi and Port-Bouet and the airport. Its development entailed extensive sanitary work and drainage. The Petit-Bassam peninsula is made up of extremely marshy alluvial soil. This low-lying zone, where the water level is often less than a metre underground, is the location for the suburbs of Treichville, Marcory, and Koumassi. Prone to frequent floods during the rainy seasons, it has undergone extensive landscaping and drainage. But despite all these efforts, the risk of the spread of waterborne disease is very high.

The lagoon divides the city into two zones (North and South), linked by two bridges. It is a vast body of brackish water with a sandy and muddy bottom, varying in depth, and linked to the sea since 1951 by the Vridi channel. The lagoon, which has become the natural dumping ground for the greater part of the city's liquid waste, is very polluted. Its two bays, situated in the industrial zones of Brietry and Koumassi, receive the highest amount of effluent and are very poorly linked to the rest of the lagoon network. They have reached a very advanced stage of pollution, with the emission of nauseating odours.

The plateau zone, which stands out because it is higher than the other zones, presents two features: the lower-plateau zone bordering on the lagoon, where the suburbs of Cocody, Yopougon, and Riviera are located, and the high-plateau zone, rising up to 110 m, where the suburbs of Adjame and Abobo have been built. The plateau zone, which is better ventilated, offers a healthier environment.

The climate of Abidjan is influenced by four seasons: two dry seasons (from December to March and from August to September) and two rainy seasons (from April to July and from October to November). Temperatures vary very little, with a maximum of 32° in April and minimum of 28° in July. Abidjan is within the wettest zone of Côte d'Ivoire, recording an average of 2 800 mm of rain annually. Humidity is very high, with an average higher than 80%.

Land area, population, and socioeconomic data

Land area — Abidjan, created around 1912 along the Abidjan–Niger railway line, has undergone spectacular development, spread over three phases.

- In the first phase, which took place between 1912 and 1960, when Abidjan was a colonial city and harbour serving the old centre (comprising Treichville, Marcory, Adjame, and the Plateau), the city recorded an average growth rate of 12%.

- In the second phase, corresponding to the period when Abidjan acquired the status of political and economic capital of the new state of Côte d'Ivoire, the city consolidated

15

and modernized its structures, launched its expansion into the outlying areas, and recorded an average growth rate of 11% between 1960 and 1980.

- In the third phase, that of the economic crisis that began at the end of the 1970s, the city has experienced a sudden slowdown of expansion in area and population and has had an annual average growth rate of 4%.

The metropolis is a semicircle spread within a radius of 30 km on the waterfront and covering an area of 57 735 ha.

The town-planning workshop on Abidjan, in its atlas on the types of land occupation (DCGTx and AUVA 1990), differentiates five types of land use: natural spaces, urban land, human settlements, areas for human activity, and installations:

- *Natural spaces* — These cover 36 003 ha, or 62% of the area of the metropolis, and make up 8 981 ha of the lagoon and 22 302 ha of undeveloped space (bushes, woodland, forests, plantations, water banks, embankments, and natural spaces). Land set aside for agricultural purposes (extensive agriculture) takes up more than half of the natural spaces, that is, 56.99%.

- *Urban land* — This second type of land use covers 3 396 ha, or 5.88% of the metropolis, and comprises three distinct categories: allotted but unserviced urban plots, urban land serviced for human settlement, and urban land serviced for economic activity, particularly the industrial zones.

- *Human settlements* — These occupy 5 652 ha, representing about one-tenth of the area, and this type of land use comprises four distinct categories:

  - Compound houses accommodate the majority (that is, 53.7%) of the inhabitants of Abidjan and cover 40% of the settled area; 90% of these dwellings are to be found in the populous neighbourhoods of Abobo, Adjame, Koumassi, and Treichville.

  - Individual households also occupy 40% of the settlement areas; these are scattered individual houses (19.7%) and grouped individual houses (20.3%).

❑ Blocks of flats take up 6.3% of settlement space; 4% of these flats have been constructed by real-estate companies; and 2%, by individuals.

❑ Unauthorized dwellings represent 13% of settlement area and shelter 16.4% of the urban population.

In all, 15.2% of the residential area, built on unplanned land, is difficult to reach by car and is serviced through the existing networks:

■ *Human activities* — These occupy 1 778 ha, or 4.9% of the city area; 67% of these spaces have been assigned to artisanal and commercial activities of a precarious kind.

■ *Installations* — These, excluding road networks, cover 2 825 ha; roads, which occupy about one-fifth of the city area, consist in total of 2 042 km of network, with 272 km of primary tarred roads, 940 km of secondary tarred roads, and 830 km of dirt roads.

Population and socioeconomic data — Abidjan currently has a population of 2.5 million inhabitants, spread over about 375 000 dwellings. The population of the city is very young, with 51% aged less than 20 years and 43% aged 20–45 years. The last population and human-settlement census (GOCI 1980) indicated that 3.2% of the city's population was living in individual homes (in groups or blocks); 26.7%, in blocks of flats; 53.7%, in compound houses; and 16.4%, in unauthorized settlements. The percentage of children in full-time education was 72% out of a population largely of new city dwellers. The average monthly household income was 76 920 XOF.

Management structures of the city

Since 1980, within the framework of the drive for the decentralization, Abidjan has been managed by 10 basic districts, which are divided into neighbourhoods and into 112 sectors. The mayors and municipal councillors elected in their respective districts are responsible for managing their local communities and exercising their authority according to the law on decentralization. This same law, which also established the city of Abidjan, has taken from these districts the control of a certain number of services considered "urban" or "regional" and assigned them to the supra-municipal structure.

17

Notable among these services are public lighting; household refuse, sanitation, and drainage; road traffic; parks and gardens; slaughterhouses; fairs and markets; cemeteries; district roads, the enforcement of land regulations, town planning, and urban development; and the naming of roads, public squares, and buildings.

Although the city of Abidjan has, in theory, authority over these urban services, the enforcement of this authority, along with the management of markets, has always remained in the hands of the districts; the same is true of household refuse, the effective management of which is carried out by several institutional actors, to the extent of actually marginalizing the city of Abidjan.

Abidjan has the status of an urban community and functions according to the rules governing the districts. It is administered by the General City Council, which has 50 members elected for a period of 5 years on the basis of 5 grand councillors per district. The city mayor is elected by the 10 district mayors, who are required by law to choose one of their colleagues elected in the Abidjan metropolis. The winner immediately resigns his or her post as district mayor and assumes the new responsibility. The 10 mayors of the districts making up Abidjan are automatically deputies to the city mayor. Because the city of Abidjan is the economic capital and the showcase of modern-day Côte d'Ivoire, its development and management are handled by four types of institutional actors — the ministries, the city, the districts, and the actors from the civil society — despite the theoretical attribution of authority to the city. Faced with dwindling and insufficient resources and the emergence of other factors, the city authorities seem somewhat resigned. They continue to dream of a powerful city at the forefront of development but do not envisage any change in their roles.

MANAGEMENT OF LIQUID, SOLID, AND INDUSTRIAL WASTE IN ABIDJAN

BACKGROUND TO URBAN WASTE MANAGEMENT IN ABIDJAN

The organization of urban waste management in Abidjan has undergone a lot of changes in recent decades, owing particularly to the instability of the government team and the volatility of the executing agencies. In fact, each reduction or enlargement of the government team has entailed a redefinition of competencies and of ministerial organizational charts and very often the appointment of new persons to head the structures. Moreover, the institutional landscape for the management of solid and liquid waste has been greatly affected by the concentration of development studies and the monitoring of major state projects in the hands of a single structure attached to the President's Office and, later on, in the Prime Minister's Office. That unit is called the Direction et contrôle des grands travaux (DCGTx, department of major public works).

The management of liquid waste partly set in motion changes similar to those of World Bank projects in the 1970s and 1980s. At the end of the 1980s, when the sector for the management of liquid waste was emerging from difficulties with feasible management structures, the sector for solid-waste management confronted, in its turn, a crisis that persists to this day.

Liquid waste

In the early years of independence, the modest city of Abidjan had very little sanitary and drainage equipment. Most household waste water, drainage water, and industrial waste were disgorged into the lagoon. During this period, the rainy seasons, with their numerous floods in the low-lying and marshy areas of the Petit-Bassam peninsula and the coastal belt, were highly dreaded. The self-cleansing power of the Ébrié lagoon had been overestimated, and the lagoon was showing indications of advanced pollution. But it took the serious cholera outbreak of 1969 to force the authorities to draw up a sanitation and drainage policy. The two products of this policy are the Société d'équipement des terrains urbains (SETU, state land-development agency) and the Fonds national pour l'assainissement (FNA, national sanitation fund).

SETU, created by administrative order 71-672 of 29 December 1971, is a state-owned company under the dual authority of the Ministry of Economy and Finance and the Ministry of Public Works, Construction, and Town Planning (more recently renamed the MOE). Its purpose was to procure and service areas of the city through surveys and the execution of drainage and road works and the provision of network services (water, electricity, and gas). Another law, No. 75-95 of 31 December 1975, extended these functions to include the maintenance of the drainage network and other completed projects. At the same time, the FNA, fed by a 10 %

tax imposed on net income from landed property, was instituted to meet the financial needs of the sector. Following on the heels of this, an emergency program (1975–78) and an extraordinary one (1977–82), amounting to 12.5 billion XOF, were launched to reinforce the existing equipment base and to create new infrastructure.

Funding from the United Nations Development Programme and the World Health Organization enabled the city to draw up a drainage master plan to establish a coherent approach within the sector. The plan opted for the construction of a system of primary and secondary collectors, making it possible to centralize the collection and marine evacuation of waste water of all types after preliminary treatment. Following the administrative reorganization of the waste-water sector, a central drainage project and the FNA assumed responsibility for partial funding of infrastructure and debt repayment. The FNA subsequently replaced the Fonds national de l'eau (FNE, national water fund). The latter was fed by a levy of 38.40 % on the selling price of water, the total amount of drainage tax levied on landed property, state subsidies, and loans.

At the beginning of the 1980s, management difficulties undermined the smooth operation of the arrangement then in place. In fact, SETU was labouring under the weight of a debt of 9 billion XOF, of which 2 billion XOF was held by private purchasers of land; and 7 billion XOF, by national agencies. In 1986, SETU was dissolved, notwithstanding the reservations of the World Bank, and its functions were transferred to DCGTx.

In 1987, on the initiative and insistence of DCGTx, a new contract that linked the city's water department (that is, the newly created structure to replace the central sanitation department) to the Société des eaux de Côte d'Ivoire (SODECI, Côte d'Ivoire water company) transferred to SODECI the authority to collect the taxes on the sale and maintenance of drainage services.

The implementation of the objectives of the master plan is now complete; investments made in the city total 115 billion XOF. Abidjan has a drainage network of 2 000 km, with 640 km for liquid waste and 955 km for rain water, including 390 km of open drains; 140 km of single-drain network; and 45 special installations (pumping stations, pretreatment stations, depots). The main collector, measuring 22.6 km, was completed, with the construction of a 1.5 km outlet drain to the sea, equipped with a chimney. Today, 40 % of the city's population has access to the sewerage system; 20 % use septic tanks; and 26 % resort to traditional latrines.

Solid waste

The history of solid-waste management in Abidjan covers three distinct stages:

- The period between 1953 and 1990, with management by a private company, La Société industrielle des transports automobiles africain (SITAF, private solid-waste operator);

- The period from 1991 to September 1992, when management was undertaken by the Waste Department of the city of Abidjan, with the support of the state; and

- The period from September 1992 to the present, with management newly ceded to a local private company, ASH International.

The SITAF period (1953–90) — Toward the end of the colonial period, when Abidjan was just an emerging city, it undertook its first experiment in privatization of household-refuse service. The city signed a concessionary contract with SITAF, a subsidiary of the French company, Société industrielle des transports automobiles (SITA, industry group for automobile transportation), specialists in the production of materials for the collection, transportation, and treatment of household refuse. This company later signed contracts to manage household refuse in other large cities in Africa. Under the contract SITAF was to undertake the removal of household refuse and sweep the principal streets of Abidjan. However, the SITAF contract, wrongly designated as a service concession contract, was more or less an arrangement with a state-owned company, as the city assisted SITAF to set up business and paid the company a fee for the services provided. In the event of a deficit, it helped the company to balance its accounts. This was also a long-term contract renegotiated every 5 years. The calculation of the monthly fee was based on a formula combining the tonnage of refuse transported and the distance covered, as declared by SITAF. Abidjan had not considered the possibility of monitoring the activities of its service provider. The whole arrangement therefore was based on mutual trust, until the beginning of the 1980s, when the newly elected mayor of the city, a shrewd, experienced businessman, began to express his anxiety and doubts about the escalating costs of the services.

21

Indeed, at the end of the 1984 financial year, the cost of household-refuse collection represented 39 % of the overall budget and 58 % of the city's operational budget. At the mayor's request, the government asked DCGTx to audit the operations of SITAF. The DCGTx team of auditors, after meticulously examining the collection routes and systematically weighing the tonnage of refuse collected through the year, concluded that the tonnages and kilometres declared by SITAF as a basis for the calculation of fees had been inflated over a long period. In other words, the service was overinvoiced. On the strength of these revelations, Abidjan, with the support of the experts of DCGTx, started to negotiate with SITAF, with the view to lowering the cost of its services. The new contract signed at the end of these negotiations retained as a basis for calculation the actual tonnage of refuse collected and dumped. It also saw the arrival of a third actor, the DCGTx acting as delegated supervisor to monitor the contract on behalf of the city. The DCGTx created its household-refuse unit and decided to maintain a weighing team on a permanent basis (day and night) on the weighing bridge at the dumping site. As a public service organization, it gave its service to the city of Abidjan free of charge. The impact of these new measures on the operations was immediate; indeed, from 47 % in 1985, the costs fell to 40 % in 1986, then to 33 % in 1987, and only rose to 34 % in 1988 (Table 3).

Table 3. Economic indicators of solid-waste management in Abidjan, 1984–94.

Year	A Solid waste collected (kg)	B Cost of collection and sweeping (XOF)	C Budget of Abidjan (XOF)	Ratio B/C	Ratio ($\times 10^{-7}$) A/B
1984	344 054	3 238 103 944	8 300 000 000	0.39	106
1985	408 243	4 475 077 416	9 600 000 000	0.47	91
1986	423 921	3 407 378 357	8 517 000 000	0.40	124
1987	430 234	3 515 945 391	10 614 269 000	0.33	122
1988	481 517	3 526 344 080	10 507 269 000	0.34	136
1989	482 279	3 424 538 885	8 674 460 000	0.39	140
1990	452 440	3 999 537 268	9 239 340 000	0.43	113
1991	—	4 142 777 642	9 415 700 000	0.44	—
1992	441 970	3 368 038 460	9 256 530 000	0.36	131
1993	436 234	4 286 626 676	8 507 483 000	0.50	101
1994	508 847	5 186 643 034	8 451 603 000	0.61	98

Source: Directorate-General for Technical Cooperation, Adidjan, Côte d'Ivoire.
Note: In 1998, 610.65 CFA francs (XOF) = 1 United States dollar (USD).

SITAF, having been held in check in this manner, grudgingly accepted the new contract but did not give up. Under the pretext that its commissions were inadequate for the provision of good-quality service, it decided to lay off almost one-third of its maintenance personnel, thereby politicizing the issue. In fact, as a mark of solidarity for their dismissed colleagues, the staff of SITAF embarked on 3-day work to rule, during which they collected household refuse from only the principal routes of the city. The city, forced to resume negotiations, remained inflexible on the new provisions of the contract but, as a gesture of appeasement, agreed to undertake the cleaning of the streets.

Thereafter, SITAF lost interest in the business, feeling closely watched and under suspicion. During this period (that is, the end of the 1980s), the economic crisis worsened to such an extent that the state, on the verge of suspending payments, decided (in a fit of arrogance) to pay only the salaries of civil servants. The public treasury refused to pay the bills of national companies. Thus, SITAF, which occasionally found itself in 4–6 months' arrears on payments, became incapable of renewing its fleet of vehicles at the beginning of 1988. Faced with the prospect of a deterioration in its services, which would likely tarnish its image, the company decided to withdraw honourably and refused to renegotiate its contract on its expiry at the end of 1989. The city was unprepared for this eventuality, and it appealed to SITAF to stay on for another year while the city tried to find an alternative solution.

The city devised a three-party partnership with SITA and Chagnon of Montréal (a Canadian company), which in the long run enabled the city to get a hand in the business before buying out the shares of the two partners and then managing the business as an autonomous authority, vested with management organs and assigned its own budget. The Ivorian government, which in turn suspected the city of trying to repeat the game played by SITAF, rejected the partnership proposal. By the end of 1990, it was evident that the city was not prepared to lose SITAF. The mayor therefore left for Paris to renegotiate the contract, but the doors of the parent company of SITAF, SITA, were closed to him. He rushed back to Côte d'Ivoire to close the chapter definitively on the SITAF era.

23

The period of management by a stated-owned company (1991–92) — After abrogating the contract with SITAF, Abidjan decided to take up the challenge by providing cleaning services for an interim period, which was to last 21 months. To provide uninterrupted service immediately, the city bought up the equipment of SITAF. But because the average age of the acquired equipment was 12 years, breakdowns proliferated, and as early as November 1991 the city of Abidjan needed to partially replace the collection equipment. The choice was made to replace the tipper trucks (model 6000), which did 50 % of the refuse collection. Contacts were signed with European manufacturers. But faced with the lengthy delivery periods (6–8 months) and very high costs, the city decided to contact Canadian suppliers. The Canadian suppliers proposed more efficient equipment at very competitive prices and easy payment conditions. The city ordered and received from the firm Chagnon, for 822.490 million XOF, six crusher trucks (24 m^3), 3 fork-lift trucks for loading bins of 3–6 m^3, and 360 bins of 3 m^3. Immediately after, the city decided to procure French equipment. In this instance, the city ordered 10 reconditioned SITA 6000 tipper trucks to reinforce its collection capacity. When SITAF was operating at its peak, in June 1986, it owned 84 vehicles and machines, with a collection capacity of 1 606–1 700 t/day. After taking over the service in January 1992, the city council found itself with only 55 vehicles and machines, with a daily collection capacity of 1 090 t. The new acquisitions enabled it to achieve a total daily collection capacity of 1 763 t, with an increase of 1 050 t/day in the capacity of the equipment then in use (Table 4).

Table 4. Performance indicators of solid-waste management in Abidjan, 1990–95.

Year	Population	A Waste generated (t)	B Waste collected (t)	Ratio B/A (%)	Waste generated per capita per day (kg)
1990	2 050 858	786 575	452 440	57.50	1.050
1991	2 143 240	818 330	—	—	1.046
1992	2 228 970	850 815	441 970	51.94	1.045
1993	2 318 129	885 125	436 234	49.28	1.046
1994	2 410 354	920 530	508 847	55.27	1.046
1995	2 507 288	920 895	—	—	1.006

Source: Directorate-General for Technical Coordination, Abidjan, Côte d'Ivoire.

It is worth noting that it was at this time that the household-refuse crisis reached its climax. In 1991, toward the end of the year, the high rate of immobilization caused by the overaged vehicle fleet reduced the collection capacity to about 700 t/day. Faced with a proliferation of unauthorized refuse dumps and the indignant protests of the people, the state mobilized supplementary resources by approving a special grant, managed by MOE, and by requisitioning equipment and machinery from the ministry responsible for public works to carry out periodic refuse-collection campaigns. During this period, the state also sanctioned the arrival on the scene of partners in refuse collection.

In the face of the grave crisis, the President of Côte d'Ivoire, as a first step, requested the Prime Minister to take charge of the dossier on solid wastes in Abidjan. The Prime Minister set up a small crisis-management unit, bringing together the city of Abidjan, the Minister of Environment, the Ministry of Infrastructure, and the DCGTx, headed by the adviser to the Prime Minister responsible for projects and policies, with the mandate to assess the situation and recommend an appropriate solution. But to increase reflection on the crisis and involve all the other actors, the state decided to create a national commission for public health. The commission was created in 1992. But contrary to all expectations, its chairship did not fall to the MOE, which was already chairing the national commission on human settlements; rather, it was given to the Ministry of Interior, which clearly harboured the intention of playing an important role in the waste-management system. As the adviser to the Prime Minister responsible for the coordination of the activities of the household-refuse unit was at this time also performing the functions of Deputy Director-General of DCGTx, this structure progressively consolidated its position within the waste-management system.

Finally, this period also saw the start of precollection and collection activities by young school dropouts in the neighbourhoods. These people created small private or community enterprises for refuse precollection, thereby activating a link in the collection chain that had been dormant. These precollection structures received training from the household-refuse team of the Département d'Assainissement et d'Infrastructure (DAI, department of sanitation and infrastructure) of MOE, which had been reflecting on ways of reactivating this link.

From the beginning of the crisis, the state had requested the DAI, the city of Abidjan, and the DCGTx to carry out a technico-financial analysis of the system of household-refuse management and to propose some options for the decision-makers. The resulting study, entitled "A study of the management of household refuse in the city of Abidjan" (DAI et al. 1991), drew extensively on the data of a previous, more comprehensive study, "Master plan for the collection and disposal of waste in the city of Abidjan," prepared by a Canadian consultancy, Roche International (CRI 1987), with the support of the Canadian International Development Agency. DAI's study set efficiency against cost in the following three types of management:

- Management based on collection by crusher trucks (28 m^3);

- Management based on collection by fork-lift trucks (32 m^3), with loading bins of 6 m^3 or 4 m^3, with or without precollection; and

- Management based on combinations of the two types of trucks.

The data and options proposed in the ministry's study, which was completed in July 1991, provided a basis for defining a strategy for the collection of refuse in the city and for preparing tender documents for a refuse-collection contract.

Having learned a lesson from the monopoly operation of SITAF, the Ivorian authorities decided to put an end to all forms of monopoly and to encourage competition among various companies. Thus, the new scheme for refuse collection proposed by MOE and DCGTx divided the management system into the following eight sections:

- Five sections corresponding to the five geographical zones for precollection, collection, and transport, covering the city of Abidjan;

- One section for mechanical sweeping of the city;

- One section for the management of transfer stations and transportation to the dump; and

- One section for the management of the sanitary landfill.

These authorities also decided that each of the sections should be assigned to a specific small or medium-sized company, preferably a national one, to develop national expertise in the sector and contribute to the fight against unemployment.

At the close of the international tender, five companies had submitted bids. One of these was an international company of Nigerian nationality, Waste Management Ltd, with offices in Lagos and Abuja. When the bids were opened, it was discovered that only two of the five companies satisfied the solvency and bank-guarantee criteria. The companies were

- Waste Management Ltd, to which the Tender Board recommended the allocation of five of the eight sections; and

- Enterprise de transport, construction, bâtiments et electricité (corporation for transportation, construction, trade, and electricity), an Ivorian company without any experience in waste management, but to which the three remaining sections were allocated.

According to some members of the Tender Board, this was an equitable distribution, as Waste Management Ltd, which won the larger part of the contract, had three major assets: experience, a partnership with an American company seasoned in waste management, and the requisite financial cover.

Contrary to all expectations, and as the members of the Tender Board were preparing to publish the results of the tender, instructions came from the Office of the President of Côte d'Ivoire to stop the process, declare the tender inconclusive (unfruitful), and offer the contract to ASH International, an Ivorian bidding company that had not even gone beyond the preselection stage. The instructions were automatically carried out, and the era of ASH began.

The ASH International period (from September 1992) — The award of the contract to ASH International did not surprise either Ivorians or international observers of the Ivorian political scene, as it was in line with the logic of the policy of "mercenary" support, actively pursued by the late President Houphouet Boigny, who never forgot his political friends in difficult times. In fact, one must recall that following the agitation for democracy in 1990, the regime of President Houphouet Boigny was seriously shaken by

27

unprecedented protests. At the peak of the crisis, when he considered relinquishing power and seeking refuge in France, he received unexpected political support from a certain number of opportunist movements, one of which was led by Ahmed Bassam, the future boss of ASH International. All these movements, banking on the absence of a credible political alternative, the inexperience of the opposition leaders, and the anarchy into which the protest movements had thrust the country, took the risk of publicly supporting the President while calling on him to undertake the necessary political changes in an orderly and disciplined manner. Ahmed Bassam's movement, "I Love the PDCI" (Parti démocratique de Côte d'Ivoire [democratic party of Côte d'Ivoire]), had the unique characteristic of regrouping the fringe urban youth, composed mainly of school dropouts and the unemployed youth who had not benefited from favours of the regime but who had chosen to rally to its help. The youth movement openly denounced the hypocrisy and stereotypical language of their militant elders in President Houphouet Boigny's party, who for obvious reasons were hiding the realities in the course of the political power struggle in their regions or constituencies. The youth movement convinced the old President to entrust the organization of the elections to an emerging wing of the party that comprised innovators and youth organized in support groups. The initial movements sparked off others that progressively restored the political weight of President Houphouet Boigny, who won the election of 1990, using much fewer resources than in previous campaigns.

A new partnership agreement for the management of sweeping the major routes and precollection, transfer, control, and dumping of household refuse was prepared by DCGTx, MOE, and the city of Abidjan and signed by ASH International and the city of Abidjan in July 1992.

ASH International commenced work on 2 September 1992. Immediately after pocketing the contract and for reasons that are still unclear, the boss of ASH International decided to terminate the partnership with its American counterpart in the ASH group that had offered the indispensable international guarantee.

Convinced that one did not need any intensive technical know-how to manage the collection of household refuse, Ahmed Bassam set up a family enterprise of close to 2 000 persons, whom he loosely controls. Confronted with a sudden slump in refuse collection, as a result of very frequent breakdowns and poor use of equipment, the city experienced the worst crisis in household-refuse collection, and tongues loosened to denounce the contract. Pressure was put on the city of Abidjan and MOE to denounce the contract and to abrogate it on the grounds of incompetence and noncompliance with its provisions. The major institutional actors rallied to the assistance of ASH International. On their advice, ASH International reduced its work force, recruited professionals, and signed a partnership agreement with the Canadian company Chagnon, which attached one financial expert and one city engineer to set up its accounting system and operational service.

29

Faced with these realities, Ash International was unable to organize the precollection stage and blamed the established precollectors, whom it accused of causing it financial losses by dumping part of the precollected refuse in ravines. The confrontation between ASH International refuse collectors and the precollectors led to the withdrawal of many precollection companies from these activities. Faced with this reduction in collection capacity, ASH International decided unilaterally to close the transfer station and to start moving the refuse directly to the dump at Akouedo.

The uncontrolled tipping of refuse on the dumping site led to its saturation and created environmental pollution in the village of Akouedo, where the football field became the manoeuvring area for ASH International's trucks. The village authorities requested the city of Abidjan to close the dump at Akouedo. They had already been alarmed by various epidemics, the pollution of groundwater, and the abundance of rats, flies, mosquitoes, and cockroaches resulting from the stoppage of the legally required sanitary treatment of the dumping site by ASH International.

To support their request, the villagers organized a sit-in on 4, 5, and 6 November 1994, which blocked the access of ASH International's trucks to the dumping site. The mayor of the city intervened to ease the crisis with the promise to satisfy all the main grievances, especially those regarding the rational use of the dump, the resumption of sanitary treatments, and the burying of biomedical waste. The state sent equipment from work sites to the dump to put it in temporary order. On the insistence of the city authorities, ASH International subcontracted the management of the dump to Y.P. Bejani. Following the failures of this company, the city of Abidjan suggested that ASH International subcontract the work to Motoragri, a state-owned company dealing with agricultural motorization and specializing in excavation works. Since

February 1995 Motoragri has been the latest actor in household-refuse management.

At the beginning of this year (1995), following the increasing unhealthiness of the city as a result of inadequate collection and elimination of household refuse, the Prime Minister gave instructions to the mayor of the city to carry out a financial and technical diagnosis of ASH International, with recommendations to improve its performance. A technical commission formed by the various partners, basing itself on the work and conclusions of two technical and financial committees, submitted integrated reports and recommendations at the end of February. The implementation of its recommendations has led to an improvement in household-refuse management.

Industrial waste

The first alarming signs of uncontrolled discharge of industrial-waste water into the lagoon appeared at the end of the 1960s, with nauseating smells and the impoverishment of the flora and fauna.

The service responsible for the inspection of dangerous installations was at the time tasked by the Ministry of Public Works, Construction, and Town Planning to find ways to limit and eventually neutralize the impact of industrial pollution. To tackle the pollutants at source, it began by updating its lists of industrial establishments that emitted pollution. But the Ministry of Public Works, Construction, and Town Planning, which at the time had the task of promoting industry, held the view that industrial pollution was a price the young nations of the Third World had to pay in the fierce competition to attract foreign investors. It therefore limited itself to a diagnosis of the problem and proposed some directives and exhortations. This lax attitude persisted until 1972, the year of the first Stockholm conference on the environment.

Indeed, the evaluation of the environment made within the framework of Côte d'Ivoire's contribution to the Stockholm conference, as well as the discussions that took place during the actual conference, helped to develop environmental awareness. The periodic appearance since 1973 of water hyacinths on the lagoon and the difficulty of combating this phenomenon have also strengthened environmental awareness and created a political will to preserve the lagoon and marine environment.

In 1973, the service responsible for the inspection of classified installations, attached to the newly created Secretary of State for the Environment, fitted itself out to play an effective role, in collaboration with existing laboratories and research centres. In 1974, to generate resources to meet monitoring costs, it signed two administrative orders (Nos. N 74-525 and N 74-526 of 9 October 1974), setting out, respectively, the apportionment of inspection taxes on petroleum companies and the apportionment of inspection taxes on dangerous establishments. The Abidjan metropolis counted more than 60 industries producing dangerous or toxic waste, with 22 in the textiles and related sector, 14 in the chemical products sector, 11 in the cosmetics and detergents sector, 6 in the paint, glue, and varnish sector, 6 in the petroleum-products sector, and 5 in the phytosanitary-products sector.

The service responsible for the inspection of classified installations currently operates on the basis of the French texts of the regulations of 1926 governing unhealthy, inconvenient, or dangerous establishments. Indeed, the Ivorian law hastily passed in 1988 during the crisis in the transportation of radioactive waste from countries of the North to those of the South has not been followed by an enforcement order. The government has therefore not been able to abrogate the 1926 law. Consequently, the administrative orders and bylaws currently in force in France within the framework of the 1926 legislation are still applicable in Côte d'Ivoire. A committee is currently working to adapt this legislation to the Ivorian setting.

The collection and transportation of dangerous or toxic waste are not subject to official permit. However, the removal and transfer to the dump of dangerous or toxic waste that in principle should undergo pretreatment require the approval of the Service d'inspection des installations classées (SIIC, classified installations inspection service). This organization authorizes the transfer of waste to an appropriate storage area of the dump after ascertaining the admissible level of toxicity. Four specialized private companies — namely, ASH International, SATD, Lassire, and CI Maintenance — as well as other smaller transport companies, are active in the collection and transportation of industrial waste. Used oils and waste from the phytosanitary industry are treated locally.

Since October 1991 Centre ivoirien anti-pollution (CIAPOL, Ivorian antipollution centre) has been providing the necessary technical backup for the SIIC. Its central environmental laboratory is responsible for the systematic analysis of natural-water samples and the evaluation of pollution levels and other nuisances. A subsidiary company, tasked to be interventionist, monitors pollution in the sea and the lagoon to deal with accidental pollution through its rapid-intervention strategy, "the POLUMAR [pollution maritime] plan."

THE POLICIES, METHODS OF FUNDING AND MANAGEMENT, MEASURES IN PLACE, AND RESOURCES

If there is a sufficiently coherent management strategy for liquid waste, using a few dependable tools, the same cannot be said of solid waste, as the city is only just emerging from a grave crisis caused by the extreme politicization of solid-waste management. This section reviews the policies, financial tools and cost-recovery approach, and the legal technical means applied to three types of waste: liquid, solid, and industrial.

Liquid waste

The policies — After the emergency response necessitated by the cholera epidemic and to ensure coherence in infrastructure investment, the city adopted a drainage master plan and is continuing to execute it. It has completed major construction works for the primary collector and the outlet drain to the sea.

Methods of funding — In 1987, the government decided to merge all the financial mechanisms of the water sector into the single entity FNE. This fund fed from the drainage tax, the surtax on water sales, government subventions, and loans and is managed by the autonomous debt-depreciation office, a public financial organ managing public loans and state debt. Its resources help to finance the installation and maintenance of infrastructure in the water sector (including urban and rural water supply and drainage).

Management methods — MOE, which has competence in matters of drainage, has entrusted the maintenance of drainage installations (operation of treatment and pumping stations, etc., and cleaning out certain categories of gutters) to a private company, SODECI. The operational costs in 1995 amounted to 1.5 million XOF, which was to be paid by the FNE on presentation of the bills. Negotiations are in progress to transform the current operational contract into a lease contract.

The operation of the six sludge-dumping sites is handled by the city of Abidjan. The total receipts from monthly fees of 3 000 XOF per cesspool emptier that uses the dumps are not enough to cover the operational expenses, and MOE intends to integrate the operation of these dumps within the new lease contract with SODECI. The MOE is at the same time redoubling its efforts to regain management of the sites.

The legal and regulatory framework — Without a code on sanitation, the sector for liquid-waste management is organized on the basis of a dozen decrees and orders, notably the following:

- Administrative order No. 62-528 of 7 November 1968, fixing the supply, storage, and use of water resources in Abidjan;

- Bylaw No. 6616/CAB of 13 May 1968, setting out the modalities for the transfer to the Abidjan district of the water supply and distribution, as well as drainage installations situated on the territory of a commune and the water-distribution agency;

- Bylaw No. 4/SEM/DE of 29 January 1974, regulating the evacuation of water at car-wash bays;

- Interministerial order No. 4605/mtp of 31 August 1978, approving the provisions for drainage services applicable to the Abidjan metropolis;

- Bylaw No. 573/SP/CAB of 23 October 1985, relating to the creation and organization of a national public- and social-hygiene committee; and

- Administrative order No. 87-1472 of 17 December 1987, setting up a national committee for public health.

Human and technical resources — SODECI currently uses 15 trucks for cleaning out gutters. These trucks are equipped with vacuum pumps and operated by some 30 driver–mechanics.

Solid waste

The policies — A master plan for the retrieval and removal of the solid waste of Abidjan (CRI 1987) exists but has not been adopted. Nevertheless, this document and the study on the management of household refuse in the city of Abidjan (DAI et al. 1991) have provided basic information for preparing a management strategy contained in the tender dossier for the allocation of the contract to manage solid waste in Abidjan. This strategy was not implemented because of political interference, incompetence, and the contract operator's lack of resources.

Methods of funding — A taxe d'enlèvement des ordures ménagères (TEOM, tax for household-refuse removal) is charged at 2.5 XOF per KW/h sold by the electric utility in Abidjan. This tax, created in the 1960s, has never been reviewed, and today it contributes a maximum of 1.5 billion XOF, whereas the operational costs of solid-waste management amount to 5 billion XOF. The rest is made up through the contributions of the 10 districts of the city, which add up to 3 billion XOF/year, as well as the global operational grant provided by the state, which varies between 500 million and 600 million XOF/year.

Proposals for a change in the rate and for reform of the TEOM have been refused by the government on the pretext that the fiscal pressure has been excessive, even though it has authorized the creation of a national television fee, based on the same electricity receipts over the same period.

Management methods — The provision of solid-waste service in Abidjan is assured by a private operator, ASH International, linked to the city of Abidjan by an agreement. By authority of a note from the Prime Minister, dated 30 October 1992, MOE, in conjunction with the DCGTx, monitors the execution of the contract. The service contract for last year (1994) amounted to 5 186 643 034 XOF to collect 508 847 t of refuse.

On the suggestion of the city of Abidjan, ASH International subcontracted the management of the Akouedo dump to Motoragri. This contract is in two parts: one part is related to the opening of tracts by the bulldozers, which generates 20 million XOF monthly, and the other part covers transportation of waste into the valleys, spreading of earth on the piles of refuse, and compaction, which pays at the rate of 1 419 XOF/t.

The legal and regulatory framework — Solid-waste management is regulated by a bylaw and two agreements:

- Bylaw No. 46/CAB-2 of 22 March 1954, concerning the removal of household refuse in Abidjan;

- The agreement of 24 July 1992 between the city and the firm ASH International for the management and operation of the public service, comprising sweeping of the principal routes and collection, transfer, and controlled dumping of household refuse in Abidjan; and

- The agreement linking ASH International to Motoragri for management of the Akouedo dump.

Human and technical resources — ASH International employs a total of 644 people, among them a managing director, a general manager, 2 deputy managers, 2 special advisers, 4 heads of service, 17 team leaders, 16 heads of cleaning sectors, 106 drivers, 231 refuse collectors, 58 loading-bin overseers, 25 mechanics, 8 inspectors, 14 commercial agents, etc.; 577 agents, representing 89.59 % of the personnel, have very few qualifications and are assigned the tasks of sweeping, collection, and transportation of refuse. In February 1995, ASH International had a total of 93 machines and vehicles, with only 30 in working condition, that is, an immobilization rate of 67.74 % and a theoretical collection capacity of 1 710 t/day. ASH International significantly improved this capacity after repairing 11 vehicles in April and acquiring some new trucks in July 1995. Because the amount of equipment in working condition is insufficient, it is overused. Indeed, the company operates a three-shift 24-hour service to collect the maximum of household refuse. The service is organized along 50 routes, equipped with 60 containers of 14 m³, 30 containers of 7 m³, and 300 containers of 3 m³ (Tables 5, 6, and 7).

35

Table 5. Distribution of routes and containers by district, 1993.

District	Routes	Containers 14 m³	7 m³	3 m³
Port-Bouet	3	5	0	57
Koumassi	5	3	0	25
Marcory	5	2	1	28
Treichville	5	6	0	20
Plateau	2	2	6	25
Cocody	7	7	6	35
Adjame	6	12	5	17
Attecoube	1	3	3	33
Abobo	6	7	4	27
Yopougon	8	13	5	33

Source: Directorate-General for Technical Cooperation, Abidjan, Côte d'Ivoire.

Table 6. Composition of ASH International's operating fleet, February 1995.

Structure of the fleet	Vehicles per category (*n*)	Vehicles in working condition (*n*)	Waste collected by category of vehicle (t)
Crusher truck	28	16	960
Fork-lift truck	8	3	300
Ampliroll	7	3	300 + 120
Tipper truck	16	0	0
Container vehicle	5	1	30
Lifter truck	4	0	0
Compactor truck	9	0	
Tractor	7	3	
Loader	4	3	
Grader	5	1	

Source: Directorate-General for Technical Cooperation, Abidjan, Côte d'Ivoire.

The company operates a site of 153 ha, opened in 1965, as an unrestricted dump. For the management of the dump, Motoragri has been assigned three bulldozers, two loaders, two graders, two compactors, four tipper trucks, two hydraulic shovels, and one bascule bridge.

Industrial waste

The policies — There is a coherent policy built around the objective of ensuring pretreatment at the source of pollution, as well as two important implementation mechanisms: the SIIC and CIAPOL. The SIIC monitors activities of polluting industries, and CIAPOL has the task of watching over the lagoon and the sea, systematically analyzing water samples, fighting pollution, and monitoring the enforcement of relevant laws, administrative orders, and national, regional, and international agreements for companies and ships.

Method of funding — SIIC is financed through the inspection tax on dangerous establishments. This tax, which varies according to the category and the surface area of the establishment, generated 380 million XOF in 1995, with a collection rate of 60–70%. The chief inspector thinks that this tax can generate more than 1 billion XOF if all dangerous establishments are classified and if the collection rate is improved. Theoretically, the three main actors share the proceeds of this tax according to the following predetermined formula:

- 70% is allocated to the national budget;

Table 7. Characteristics of ASH International's fleet, 1994.

| Working | Not working | | Availability rate (%) |
	Under repair	Awaiting spare parts	
Tipper truck			56
119	B106	122	
BS10	BS18	123	
118	120	124	
114	103		
Tipper truck			100
106			
102			
115			
121			
BS09			
Crusher truck			100
604			
603			
605			
T06			
T01			
602			
Fork-lift truck			33
F01	F02	F03	
Ampliroll			40
501	505	503	
504		502	
Container vehicle			67
405		403	
402			
Compactor truck			50
305		312	
316		315	
Lifter truck			100
BP07			
307			
309			
304			
Tractor			43
207		201	
Tr03		206	
204			
Loader			50
214		211	
209		240	
212		213	

Source: Directorate-General for Technical Cooperation, Abidjan, Côte d'Ivoire.

- 25% is allocated to the common fund for technical and material assistance for the SIIC and CIAPOL; and

- 5% is shared, as a bonus, among the people on staff at the SIIC and CIAPOL.

Management methods — The inspectorate department for classified installations is a service attached to the Office of the Minister of Environment and Tourism, charged with development and enforcement of policies in this sector. CIAPOL, on the other hand, is a public-sector establishment created by administrative order No. 94-662 of 9 October 1991 and functioning as a national laboratory. In addition to ASH International, the private sector is very active in the management of industrial waste. We have, notably, three licenced small-scale carriers in this sector, handling the transportation of industrial waste to the dump, and five companies licenced to treat dangerous, toxic waste. Some of the waste that cannot be treated locally is transferred to France for adequate and appropriate treatment.

The regulatory and legal framework — The regulatory framework is essentially French in origin and not very well adapted to the Ivorian context. The most significant legal documents cover the following:

- Administrative order of 20 December 1926 regulates dangerous, unhealthy, or inconvenient establishments;

- The general bylaw of 28 April 1927 announces the implementation of the order of 20 December 1926;

- Local bylaw No. 3270, of 20 December 1932, organizes the inspection of dangerous, unhealthy, or inconvenient establishments;

- Administrative order No. 85-949, of 12 September 1985, concerns the organization of an emergency plan to intercept and ensure against accidental pollution at sea, in the lagoon, or in the coastal zones (the POLUMAR plan);

- Bylaw No. 0819 TP/MM, of 3 May 1968, concerns the pollution of water bodies, particularly with hydrocarbons;

- Law No. 88-651 is designed to protect public health and the environment against the effects of toxic industrial and nuclear waste and other harmful substances;

- Bylaw No. 38/MIP/DENT, of 28 June 1990, modifies the nomenclature of the administrative order of 20 December 1926, concerning dangerous, unhealthy, or inconvenient establishments; and

- Administrative order No. 91-662, of 9 October 1991, announces the creation of a public institution, administrative in nature, designated CIAPOL, and sets out its attributions, organization, and mode of operation.

Human and technical resources — The SIIC of the city of Abidjan has, currently, only 20 inspectors, with 13 based in Abidjan, 3 in Bouaké, 3 in Daloa, and 1 in San-Pedro. All the inspectors have secretariat service. The entire inspection department has altogether three microcomputers and four vehicles. The service usually seeks the collaboration of the police to enforce certain decisions.

THE INSTITUTIONAL AND POLITICAL CONTEXT OF MANAGEMENT

This section concerns the actors and their responsibilities, the perception and exercise of responsibility, the struggle for power, and its impacts on service delivery.

Actors, responsibilities, and power relations in the management of liquid waste

MOE — Liquid-waste management in Abidjan involves six main actors with, in principle, well-defined responsibilities. One of the most important actors is the state of Côte d'Ivoire itself, through the MOE. This department, vested with some of the tasks of the Department of Water Resources, is responsible for formulating and implementing policies. It manages SODECI's performance contract and monitors the company's activities on behalf of the state. In this capacity, the department checks the bills of SODECI before they are forwarded to FNE for authorization and payment by the accounts office.

This department also owns, on behalf of the state, all the equipment and drainage installations, although it entrusts the actual operation to SODECI.

SODECI — SODECI is a private company and a subsidiary of the huge French group Bouygues. It has contracts to supply water and maintain the drainage network of the city of Abidjan. SODECI's services do not include cleaning up concrete gutters of district roads, an activity falling within the domain of the districts and households. It also does not manage the six sewage depots, which are operated by the city of Abidjan.

District authorities — The district authorities, represented by the city of Abidjan, manage the urinals, public toilets, and sewage depots. After some unfortunate experiences with public toilets in the city parks and small toilets built in selected areas, the districts are experimenting with some forms of management partnerships or outright privatization. The laxity of the management of sewage depots, noticed by the authorities of MOE, has compelled them to start thinking about integrating the operations of the drainage and sanitation installations in a new lease contract, under negotiation with SODECI.

FNE — The FNE has since 1987 been the financial organization responsible for the management of resources mobilized for the water sector. These resources partly serve to finance the drainage infrastructure and to repay the sector's debts.

Private cesspool emptiers — The operators of cesspool emptiers constitute a little known sector that is beginning to get itself organized. They do not represent a real political force, and their lack of cohesion makes it difficult to control their activities.

Households — Owing to the lack of awareness, as well as the inadequacy of facilities, city dwellers urinate and defecate in public parks and along the walls of isolated buildings and throw waste water into the street, instead of into drains. Landlords very often do not maintain the dry gutters and communal septic tanks used by their tenants.

Conclusion — The management of liquid waste is a modern well-structured sector, in which people assume well-defined responsibilities and in which efficient management mechanisms are in place. The informal sector, however, controlled by the cesspool-emptier operators, needs to be better organized. The power relations between landlords and tenants favour the former, who refuse to fulfil their obligations. Unfortunately, sanitary officials, because of a lack of transportation, no longer carry out inspections. The direct management of infrastructural facilities by the districts has shown its limitations, and forms of indirect management are being developed.

Actors, responsibilities, and power relations in the management of solid waste

A dozen actors intervene in, or have an impact on, the management of solid waste. The state is represented by four institutional actors, and only two of these have responsibilities recognized in legal texts. The four institutions are MOE, the Ministry of the Interior, DCGTx, and the Ministry of Economy and Finance.

MOE — MOE, responsible for policies on public health, has, with the help of the refuse crisis, activism, and a sense of initiative, succeeded in carving a niche for itself in the chain of solid-waste management. Vested by the government with responsibility for mobilizing resources to organize selective operations in support of Abidjan's efforts in this sector and then later to propose a collection strategy, it has become the principal manager of the contract between ASH International and the city of Abidjan. It has also assumed the additional role of training the personnel of the pre-collection companies. Currently, it remains the preeminent actor.

41

Ministry of Interior — The Ministry of Interior has no official status in waste management. But the supervisory role it exercises over local governments has given it access to this sector. In this capacity it authorizes and stamps the major contracts linking the districts to suppliers or companies. Its chairship of the national commission on public hygiene consolidated the ministry's role, even though the commission has never worked.

DCGTx — DCGTx offers technical support to MOE in monitoring ASH International agreements. Its political influence has considerably diminished over the years, after the departure of its powerful Deputy Director-General from the Prime Minister's Office. This explains why the city of Abidjan is in no hurry to respond to DCGTx's new request for the payment of its services. The reason is the latter's diminished political clout.

Ministry of Economy and Finance — The Ministry of Economy and Finance, through its treasury services, is responsible for regularly meeting the city's financial obligations to ASH International. It has a crucial influence in the provision of services, as only the treasury can decide on the amount and period of payment, owing to the principle of the unity of accounts, which demands that the resources of the state, local government, and public institutions be lodged in the treasury.

A second category of actors — the local authorities — comprises the city of Abidjan and the districts.

City of Abidjan — After creating additional services needed to manage (under a state-owned company) the household-refuse collection, the city is unhappy with playing the role of financier. Although it has no role in monitoring the agreement, the subdepartment for household refuse of the Department for the Environment, alongside DCGTx, provides weighing and monitoring services. It feels that it now has the means to monitor the agreement without recourse to any external body, not even DCGTx.

The districts — The districts are of the view that their compulsory contributions to the running costs of Abidjan are too high. Because the removal of household refuse is a municipal responsibility in the interior towns, the districts of Abidjan want to retain their contributions and carry out the task in their respective territories.

Other actors in the sector responsible for solid-waste management include ASH International, the precollectors, the households, the scavengers and recyclers, the Akuedo community (next to the Akuedo dump), and the Office of the Prime Minister.

ASH International — After the death of President Houphouet, ASH International, the company contracted for household-refuse removal, still enjoyed the hidden support of certain influential people in the Office of the Presidency, by way of respect for the memory of the former president. Subsequently, in the face of the gravity of the crisis and threats to suspend the contract, the company resorted to developing and maintaining a network of informers and key pawns, both within the circle of official actors in the system and in the high echelons of power, to eliminate, unilaterally and without concern for the consequences, two important links in the collection chain: the precollectors and the transfer stations. Despite the shortcomings of management and the persistence of the refuse crisis in Abidjan, ASH International is, surprisingly, competing for the contract for household-refuse management in Yamoussoukro. The majority of actors in the household-refuse collection chain today think that the situation has improved, following their mobilization to assist in the collection of household refuse on the recommendation of the Prime Minister. But nobody either in the city of Abidjan or at MOE expects a review or renegotiation of the contract with ASH International, on the grounds of non-compliance with any of its obligations.

Precollectors — The precollectors came on the scene because of the shortcomings of ASH International. They receive training from MOE and technical support from districts such as Yopougon, Abobo, and Koumassi that are responsible for issuing authorizations for this profession on their territories. Faced with the hostility of ASH International, the precollectors are forming associations to increase their negotiating power. But the associations confront many difficulties.

Today, the general association of household-refuse precollectors of Abobo, created in 1993 with 15 members, is down to 9 members. The Union of Pre-collectors of the District of Yopougon, created on 20 March 1991, has since 26 June 1994 become the Ivorian Organisation for Public Cleanliness, led by a director-general, instead of a chairperson as in the past. It brings together 15 companies employing a total of 70 people. Despite all these attempts to organize, the precollectors still lack the necessary credibility to gain the confidence of banks. Their ardent desire is to be recognized as partners of ASH International and be offered contracts by it. The negotiations are in progress.

Households — The households have no influence in the system. Indeed, despite their acceptance of the initiatives of the precollectors and their financial contributions, they are still not consulted by the central authorities. The central authorities see their role in relation to the households as one of creating awareness but do not see the households as effective participants in the system of government. It seems that the state, ASH International, and the districts hesitate to tread in areas where the precollectors have succeeded. Thus, the initiative to introduce refuse bags, undertaken unilaterally by ASH International in July 1995, did not receive a favourable response from households, even though the idea is laudable and householders really desire to contribute.

Scavengers and recyclers — The recovery network is not recognized or organized. A recent study (CFD 1995), financed by a French development fund, made it possible to estimate the number of scavengers at 800, with 280 operating at the Akouedo dump alone. They are not adequately equipped and are exposed to frequent fatal accidents, which no longer attract the attention of the public (scavengers are buried under the refuse or crushed to death by the bulldozers and trucks on the sites). The study also brought into relief the economic importance of retrieval and recycling in the metal and plastics sectors of industry. The study insufficiently emphasized the serious risks posed by the uncontrolled resale of retrieved products to consumers (households). As a result of this study, a law is being examined to regulate the management of refuse dumps.

Akuedo community — Akuedo, the village community situated next to the dump, has on two occasions demonstrated its power by blocking access to the dump when the community felt it was necessary. After the last crisis, an ad hoc committee on the dump was set up, with representatives from the city of Abidjan, the Ministry of Health, MOE, ASH International, and Motoragri. The excavation works and the work on opening lanes, which have now been completed, have reduced the tension. The new project for the development of the dump, proposed by the committee, is being examined. This will lead to the specialization of the quays and eventually to controlled dumping.

Office of the Prime Minister — The Office of the Prime Minister intervenes only in the event of a crisis and to coordinate ideas and settle differences about sharing and meeting responsibilities.

Actors, responsibilities, and power relations in the management of industrial waste

Industrial-waste management involves three main actors with well-defined responsibilities:

- MOE, represented by the SIIC, is responsible for developing and implementing policies. Its main task is tracking all dangerous establishments operating in the country and monitoring the extent to which their activities are conducted in accordance with the law. Finally, it is charged with the evaluation and billing of the inspection tax on dangerous establishments.

- The second actor is CIAPOL, which carries out the function of the central laboratory for the Inspection Department and the private sector.

- The Ministry of Finance is responsible for collecting and sharing the inspection tax. Faced with financial constraints, this ministry is unwilling to honour the dispositions of the sharing formula. As a consequence, the poorly equipped SIIC cannot satisfactorily discharge its responsibilities. The chief inspector contends that more than one-third of dangerous establishments are still not classified.

EVALUATION OF WASTE MANAGEMENT IN ABIDJAN

The evaluation of waste management is done according to the type of waste: liquid, solid, and industrial. Keeping in mind the four levels of intervention — planning, budgeting, execution, and control — I systematically evaluate the main elements, particularly the policies, methods of funding and management, the legal and regulatory framework, and human and technical resources. This evaluation is based on the criteria of good governance particularly transparency, efficacy, efficiency, feasibility, and the participation of, and respect for, the rights of city dwellers.

LIQUID WASTE

In the sector responsible for liquid-waste management, a coherent policy has been defined within the framework of a drainage master plan for the city. To accelerate private connections to the network, SETU launched a campaign of social connections and enabled 1 550 low-income landowners in residential areas to link up to the drainage network. Unfortunately, despite the success recorded, the campaign has not been repeated, owing to management difficulties and the premature abolition of SETU. The system of funding and infrastructural cost recovery, based on receipts from water sales and lodged in the autonomous treasury, is a feasible and flexible arrangement.

The management chain comprises very few actors, and the responsibilities are well defined. The main operator, SODECI, is highly motivated and has adequate equipment and qualified staff. However, a few cloudy areas exist in the system:

- The private cesspool emptiers' sector is still not formally organized and is, consequently, little known and difficult to monitor.

- With the decline in the frequency of home visits by sanitary inspectors, many owners of compound houses no longer carry out their responsibilities of emptying their septic tanks. This creates a nuisance for the tenants.

- Insufficient toilets and urinals in working condition and open to the public, coupled with the absence of urban culture and the inadequacy of awareness campaigns, have left many city dwellers with no other choice but to defecate and urinate in inappropriate places in the city.

- The management system for sludge-dumping stations is not feasible; and

- The majority of public or private operators of public toilets encounter difficulties in technical and financial management.

SOLID WASTE

Drawing on the lessons in refuse management during the period of SITAF, the Ivorian authorities equipped themselves with the elements of a refuse policy for the city of Abidjan during the interim management period under a state-owned company. Unfortunately, rash intervention by politicians prevented the implementation of some of the principles and components of this policy.

There are too many actors in the chain of household-refuse management. Their responsibilities are poorly defined and sometimes challenged. Currently, the city of Abidjan, which is supposed to be at the top of the chain, appears marginalized. The city questions the active role of MOE and DCGTx. A general malaise hangs over relations among the actors.

The monopoly position of ASH International, a deviation from the new policy, gave it a strategic position of financial power, enabling it to organize its political survival. This company, the principal operator, has very little experience in the sector and works with old equipment that is insufficient and overused. The absence of a maintenance culture (building up of spare-part stocks, routine maintenance) accounts for a high immobilization rate of the fleet (see Table 7). Despite the provisions of the policy in force, the company has made no effort to integrate the precollectors and the scavengers and recyclers into the collection chain. The proposed sanitary landfill is not yet in place. The households, which are barely consulted in decision-making, have developed an apathy, which explains the failure of the recent initiative to introduce household-refuse bags. The legal and regulatory framework has become obsolete, and the system of funding has become outmoded and incapable of covering the costs of the sector.

INDUSTRIAL WASTE

Although the legal and regulatory framework in force in France and adopted by Côte d'Ivoire is irreproachable with regard to norms, it needs to be adapted to the specific realities of the Ivorian context. An industrial-waste policy is partially in place, with clearly defined responsibilities for the actors and an adequate financing mechanism, but this policy is not fully implemented and does not take account of the waste generated by the informal sector (tanneries, jewellery manufacture, artisanal dyeing) or that created by used nonrecoverable industrial products (scrap yards, abandoned garages, etc.). The absence of incinerators in the hospitals, the closure of treatment stations for used water in hospitals, and the nonimplementation of the policy of sanitary landfill pose serious problems for the management of medical waste. The absence of regulations for the collection and transportation of industrial waste comparable to those for solid waste (rubble, sawdust, cartons, papers, etc.) and inadequate monitoring encourage the development of unauthorized dumps. The two main executing agencies lack material and financial resources. Indeed, the proceeds of the inspection tax are not fairly shared.

RECOMMENDATIONS

A laudable effort has been made to develop management policies for the three areas of waste in Abidjan. However, the weaknesses in these policies, especially with regard to industrial waste, must be corrected. The policy options must be applied without undue interference from politicians. Feasible funding mechanisms and cost-recovery measures must be developed on the model of the FNE for solid wastes.

The sharing formula for the proceeds of the inspection tax needs to be reviewed, with a view to allocating more resources to the SIIC and CIAPOL. The state and local authorities should disengage themselves from the delivery of services and concentrate their efforts more effectively on planning and monitoring. The obsolete legal and regulatory framework of the three components of urban waste must be revised to take account of all types of wastes generated and the specific context of Côte d'Ivoire. The institutional framework, particularly that of solid-waste management, must be reviewed, with a view to reducing the number of institutional actors and to clarifying their responsibilities. The institutional actors and the operators and managers ought to integrate the views of city dwellers into waste management; in this connection, a participatory approach should be introduced. Finally, simple technical- and financial-management mechanisms must be made available to small-scale operators of equipment and providers of sanitation services.

Chapter 3

IBADAN, NIGERIA

A.G. Onibokun and A.J. Kumuyi

INTRODUCTION

Governance has been described as an approach or perspective that
"focuses on state and societal institutions and the relationships
between them, as well as on how rules are made in a society which
are accepted as legitimate and enhances values that are sought by
individuals and groups within the society" (Olowu and Akinola
1995, p. 23). Governance has also been identified with the "founding values and constitutional metapolicies, that constitute the
nature of governing institutions, guide their actions and shape the
complex relations between them and the society" (Swilling et al.
1995, p. 78). Stren et al. (1992, p. 541) described public management based on principles of governance as one that "attempts to
improve the system of government, to emphasize efficiency and
responsibility for all institutions, to promote democratic principles
and electoral processes and to establish a new organic relationship
between government and civil society."

According to Swilling et al. (1995), the growing literature on governance is an attempt to capture a shift taking place across the globe in thinking about the nature of the state and its relationship to society:

> *The shift from a noun ("government") to a verb ("governance"), from structure to relations, from dependence to interdependence, from linearity to (feedback) loops, from rational structuration to chaos as process is influenced by the combined universal disillusionment with the nature of the state and the impact of the postmodern imagination that has abandoned the myth of human self-unification and the vision of a utopian end-state.*

The debate was triggered off by the World Bank's (1992) report on sub-Saharan Africa, which emphasized that the root problem in Africa is bad governance — that is, personalization of power, denial of human rights, corruption, undemocratic government, low levels of participation, etc.

As Onibokun and Faniran (1995) pointed out, governance has two faces: first, the leadership, which has responsibilities derived from the principles of effective governmental organization; second, the governed, that is, the citizens, who are responsible for making relevant inputs to the socioeconomic and political affairs of their society. In other words, governance is a relationship between rulers and the ruled, the state and society, the governors and the governed. It is important that the two principal actors be as close as possible to ensure the legitimacy, accountability, credibility, and responsiveness of the rulers and the effective participation, cooperation, and responsiveness of the ruled.

Hyden (1992) posits that the effective functioning of these interactions hinges on four main principles:

- Trust within and between groups about the nature, purpose, and rules of sociopolitical interaction and practice;

- Reciprocity, which can only exist if associations and parties are allowed to organize themselves and to defend and promote the stakeholders' interests via political competition, pressure, negotiations, and conflict resolution;

- Accountability, which means that governors can be held accountable by the governed through procedures and processes (such as elections, referenda, etc.); and

50

- The governors' capacity to rule, that is, an ability to make policies and implement them in ways that resolve the problems of ordinary citizens and promote the legitimacy of the public realm.

There are many levels of leadership and many components of the governed. Governments are national, state, local, and municipal. These different levels of government interact among themselves, and the interactions are backed by laws or legal instruments of power and governance, including constitutions, Acts of Parliament, and military decrees. These levels also compete for power, which in many cases is won by the higher tiers, engendering strife, distrust, and envy and impairing not only the relationships among the various tiers but also their ability to perform their duties. The types of interaction vary from those of highly centralized governments to those of democratic, decentralized states. The extent of powers at the higher levels determines the amount of resources at the disposal of leaders at each tier, but the lowest tiers often are the poorest. For instance, the power of the federal government in Nigeria in revenue mobilization and allocation has made the lower tiers of government almost totally dependent on it, and this detracts significantly from their needed autonomy and active participation in governance. The lowest tiers, particularly the municipal and local governments, are the worst hit, as they have hardly any revenues of their own.

Also, the ruled have socioeconomic differences and different backgrounds in terms of income, wealth, education, enlightenment, and political awareness. These differences not only determine their interactions among themselves but also the ways they perceive problems, proffer solutions, and otherwise respond to issues.

An important aspect of the relationships within and between the two components of governance is the change that usually occurs. For instance, laws regulating certain behaviours and activities may change after some time. Where these changes become too frequent, without well thought out appraisal, instability results, and this may paralyze operations. Successive governments at various levels often castigate their predecessors and abandon their programs (irrespective of the relevance or appropriateness of such programs), and this disrupts operations.

Governance applied to waste management incorporates not only the formal structures of government but also the informal structures created by society, such as community-based organizations (CBOs), institutions, and associations, as well as the ways formal and informal structures interact in the collection, transportation, and disposal of waste. It involves intergovernmental relations, fiscal mobilizations and allocations, planning, and citizens' participation. The efficiency and effectiveness of delivery depend most importantly on managerial and organizational efficiency, accountability, legitimacy, responsiveness to the public, transparency in decision-making, and pluralism of policy options and choices.

One needs to ask to what extent these elements are present in Nigerian urban-waste management. To answer this question and to understand the problem of urban-waste management in Nigeria, a study was carried out, focusing on Ibadan. This chapter is the report of that study. The emphasis is on the politics, economics, and sociology of waste management.

URBANIZATION AND URBAN PROBLEMS IN NIGERIA

Available data reveal that Nigeria's urban population has been growing at an alarming rate. Nigerian towns and cities are exploding — growing in leaps and bounds. A little more than 50 years ago, fewer than 7% of Nigerians lived in urban centres (that is, settlements with populations of 20 000 or more). This proportion rose to 10% in 1952 and 19.2% in 1963. It is now estimated at about 40% and is expected to be as high as 45% by 2000. In fact, Nigerian cities are among the fastest growing in the world. Nigeria now has 7 cities with populations at 1 million; 18 cities, at more than 500 000; 36, at more than 200 000; and 78, at more than 100 000. As well, there were 5 050 towns with more than 20 000 people (Onibokun and Kumuyi 1996).

Mainly political and economic factors have been responsible for this rapid growth in urban population in Nigeria. The colonial era influenced the growth and pattern of urbanization in many ways, including the creation of new towns, principally along the transportation routes and at the ports and mining camps; modernization of the physical structures of existing towns; introduction of modern utilities; and changes in the economic base that led to the emergence of modern commercial–industrial centres outside the traditional town centres. The recently created state level of government has had perhaps the most significant impact by introducing new poles of political and economic growth. Consequent on all these pull factors in towns and cities, the city centres became attractive and rural–urban migration began to occur on a vast scale. The World Bank estimated the average annual growth rate in Nigerian towns for 1970–75 at 7%, of which the rural–urban migration accounted for 84% (World Bank 1993).

The problems and challenges posed by this rapid urban growth are immense. Very frightening and perhaps more easily observable are the human and environmental poverty, the declining quality of life, and the untapped wealth of human resources that they represent. Housing and associated facilities (water, electricity, etc.) are similarly inadequate, such that millions now live in substandard and subhuman environments, plagued by slums, squalor, and similarly inadequate social amenities, such as schools and health and recreational facilities. The gradual decline of social values and the breakdown of family cohesiveness and community spirit have resulted in increased levels of juvenile delinquency and crime. The level of provision of infrastructural facilities has declined, and intracity mobility is greatly hindered by poorly planned and inefficiently managed land use and a sharply reduced network of roads.

The municipal service that has seemed to fail most strikingly is waste collection and disposal. The service is frequently inadequate, with a preponderant proportion of the refuse generated remaining uncollected and with large parts of cities, particularly the low-income areas, receiving little or no attention. In most towns, the service is unreliable, irregular, and inefficient. The onus is often on the local government to provide a service for solid-waste management, but a fundamental deficiency of this system is the failure of governments to assume basic responsibility in raising sufficient funds to provide acceptable levels of service (Olowu 1981; Koehn 1992; Stren et al. 1994). Often, the local governments act alone, rather than in concert with the public, which has a negative impact on good governance.

53

GOVERNANCE OF WASTE MANAGEMENT IN IBADAN

GEOGRAPHICAL CHARACTERISTICS

Ibadan, at long. 7°2′ and 7°40′E and lat. 3°35′ and 4°10′N, was founded in 1829. It was initially occupied by immigrants, who moved into the city in search of security from intertribal wars. It is now the largest indigenous city in tropical Africa and is the capital of Oyo state, one of the 30 states in Nigeria. As the crow flies, it is 128 km northeast of Lagos and 345 km southwest of Abuja, the federal capital.

The city has grown particularly through the establishment of certain institutions and the construction of roads and the railway line. The convergence of the two major trade routes (through Ijebu and Abeokuta) on Ibadan, coupled with the arrival of the railway, accelerated the growth of the city. European traders were attracted and granted leasehold to land in 1903. Today, five primary roads and an expressway from Lagos radially converge on Ibadan from different directions. Most of southwestern Nigeria (excluding the Lagos area) is its hinterland for the procurement of specialized goods and services.

Since its founding the city has had rapid growth, both in area and in population. Developed land increased from only 100 ha in 1830 to 12.5 km² in 1931, 30 km² in 1963, 112 km² in 1973, 136 km² in 1981, and 214 km² in 1988. Similarly, in 1856, the population was estimated at 60 000; by 1890, it had increased to about 200 000; in 1963, it was 625 000; and today, it is almost 2 million (NISER 1988). Measured from the General Post Office in the central business district, the city has sprawled out to a radius of 12–15 km along the primary roads. The city's metropolitan region covers about 4 200 km², with boundaries varying from 17 km in the southwest to 44 km in the northeast. It comprises 11 local-government areas, with 5 in the inner city and 6 in the outer areas.

The city can be classified into seven morphological regions, varying in their housing–population densities, types and levels of infrastructural facilities, and environmental and sanitary characteristics: the core area, the older suburb, the newer eastern suburb, the newer western suburb, the post-1952 suburb, the government-reserved areas (GRAs), and the government-planned residential estates (at Bodija and Oluyole).

54

The major sources of employment are, in descending order of importance, retail trade, public administration, service and repair industries, and education. The issues of great and pressing concern, which are also germane to our subsequent discussion are

- The city's unplanned growth since its foundation in 1829;

- Poorly managed solid-waste and drainage systems;

- Poor transportation facilities;

- Grossly inadequate public utilities and social infrastructure;

55

- Poor and inadequate housing, as well as environmental pollution; and

- Mismanagement.

These issues have all been compounded by political instability and an absence of informed and effective political leadership (CASSAD 1994).

WASTE GENERATION IN IBADAN

Solid waste

Although it is generally agreed that enormous quantities of solid waste are generated in Ibadan daily, the exact figures have not been determined, probably owing to the use of diverse methods of calculation. Maclaren International Ltd (1970) found that the average per capita quantity of solid waste generated was 0.37–0.5 kg/day for the traditional areas of the city and 0.53 kg/day for the newer areas. Oluwande (1983) estimated the average solid waste generated and its mean production rates per head for three distinguished areas of Ibadan: 0.420 kg/day in the GRA; 0.377 kg/day in outlying areas; and 0.35 kg/day in the old city.

According to Egunjobi (1986), 38 million kg of solid waste was collected in the suburbs of Ibadan in 1986. The suburbs constitute about 21% of the city. On this basis, it can be estimated that 181 million kg of solid waste was generated in the city as a whole in 1986. This gives a per capita waste-generation rate of 0.31 kg/day, using the 1986 estimated population of 1.6 million for the city.

In 1982, PAI Associates recorded the volume and weight of solid waste generated per household per day in Ibadan. The study revealed that waste generation varied according to land use, with residential land use taking the bulk of the share. The generation rates were 3.4 kg/household per day in the traditional areas, 3.2 kg/household per day in the newer areas, and 3.3 kg/household per day in the whole city (altogether giving a per capita generation rate of 0.33 kg/day).

Several researchers have studied the volume of refuse generated in the city. For example, Maclaren International Ltd (1970) estimated this volume at 182 900 t. The latest study, conducted by Haskoning and Konsadem Associates (1994), estimated the per capita rate at 0.6 kg/day, with a density of 300 kg/m³. The projections are based on an annual growth rate of population per year (Table 1).

The solid-waste composition in Ibadan comprises leaves, paper, food waste, tins, glass, and rags (Maclaren International Ltd 1970). This is because Ibadan is located in the heart of a rich agricultural land and has a large old and unplanned section. PAI Associates (1983) made a comparative analysis of the composition of solid waste from two acres of Ibadan in 1970, which showed that residential land use accounted for 70.1% of the waste generated, followed by commercial land use (18.8%) and industrial land use (9.7%). Institutional and other land use accounted for 0.7% each.

The mean percentage composition of solid waste in Ibadan in 1982 for different parts of the city is summarized in Table 2, which shows that in the newer areas (GRA, Bodija, and Mokola and Sango), food remnants and tins and metals constitute the largest proportion of solid waste, whereas in the traditional areas (Agugu,

Table 1. Population and solid-waste generation estimates for Ibadan, 1992–2000.

Year	Population (×10³)	Waste generation per year (t × 10³)
1992	3 430	751
1994	3 620	754
1996	3 638	797
1998	3 748	821
2000	3 860	845

Source: Haskoning and Konsadem Associates (1994).

56

Table 2. Solid-waste composition in Ibadan, 1983.

	GRA	Bodija	Mokola and Sango	Oke Ado	Agugu	Traditional core (Ojaba)
	Mean % composition by weight					
Leaves	7.5	4.3	33.2	23.5	32.6	26.5
Food remnants	35.5	19.2	9.1	3.6	5.4	6.9
Paper	15.1	26.2	10.7	19.4	15.2	16.6
Cartons and rags	1.3	1.5	4.8	6.8	4.5	10.9
Plastics and polythene	4.1	8.9	3.7	11.6	4.8	6.1
Tins and metals	20.8	11.4	16.4	16.4	7.7	12.8
Bones, ash dust, and stones	5.9	16.7	19.1	18.1	28.8	21.0
Miscellaneous	0.8	11.8	3.0	0.5	1.0	2.2

Source: Compiled from PAI Associates (1983) and Sridhar (1996).
Note: GRA, government-reserved area.

57

Table 3. Changes in solid-waste composition in Ibadan, 1969–82.

	1969		1982	
	Old town (GRA)	New town (Bodija)	Old town (Oke Ado)	New town (Agugu)
Leaves	80.7	9.7	34.4	5.6
Food remnants	9.0	70.3	6.7	27.4
Paper	3.4	10.0	15.9	20.7
Cartons and rags	4.1	1.6	7.7	1.4
Plastics	—	—	5.5	6.5
Tins and metals	2.3	5.9	10.3	16.1
Bones, ash dust, and stones	0.5	2.5	6.1	10.9
Miscellaneous	—	—	18.4	11.1

Source: PAI Associates (1983).
Note: GRA, government-reserved area.

Ojaba) leaves and bones, ash dust, and stones constituted the bulk. The composition by weight of the various constituents of solid waste has also changed, with the leaves' share declining over time and the shares of tins and metals, paper, and bones, ash dust, and stones increasing (Table 3).

Liquid waste

The Ibadan metropolis has a lot of problems with the management of its liquid waste. PAI Associates (1983) estimated the magnitude of liquid waste within Ibadan at 22 650 million L (an average of 6.2 L per household), and Akintola and Agbola (1989) projected the amounts of liquid waste for 1990 and 1995 at 113.7 million and 126.5 million L, respectively.

Liquid waste in Ibadan also contains tins, sticks, excreta, oil, pieces of iron scrap, and refuse. Outside of large institutions, such as the University of Ibadan's Teaching Hospital and the International Institute of Tropical Agriculture, Ibadan has no sewerage system. The city's human waste is disposed of largely by means of septic tanks, pit latrines, and buckets.

The uncontrolled disposal of liquid waste into open gutters, open spaces, along roads, etc., poses serious health hazards. Bodies of stagnant water produce bad odours, breed mosquitoes, and sometimes obstruct the movement of people and goods. For instance, the 1983 study by PAI Associates revealed that 50 % of the stagnant pools emitted bad odour, 70 % bred mosquitoes, 24 % obstructed the movement of people, and 12 % bred worms and other germ-breeding pests.

Poor practices for liquid-waste disposal are responsible for waterborne diseases that are common in the city, particularly in its inner core. The unwholesome environment forces the populace to spend appreciable portions of their low income and time on improving their personal health, with adverse consequences for general economic well-being.

Industrial waste

The industries in Ibadan generate a lot of waste, particularly chemical and toxic waste, explosives, and ash, but the exact quantities have not been measured. The industries make private arrangements for disposal of their waste, with little or no monitoring. Groundwater pollution is a possibility, as companies do not take precautions at disposal sites to supervise and ensure proper sanitary conditions.

GOVERNANCE OF WASTE MANAGEMENT
IN PERSPECTIVE

Although waste removal is one of the most pressing problems in
Nigerian cities, it is not a new problem. As Onibokun (1989)
observed, the history of urban management (including waste management) in Nigerian cities is closely tied to that of local governments, which went through four evolutionary periods.

59

THE PRECOLONIAL PERIOD

In the precolonial period, the areas of the north and the west that
had substantial urban populations had a hierarchy of emirs or
obas, chiefs or community heads, area heads, and compound
heads, with defined areas of jurisdiction for the administration of
each community. The inhabitants of these communities lived by a
system of well-defined rules and functional differentiations. In the
east, where agglomerations of settlements were less pronounced,
the different kinship groups were informally and loosely controlled
through the lineal heads. As the urban communities were fairly
simple, the indigenous system of administration was appropriate
for the rudimentary management of these folk-urban communities. Public places were swept in rotation by groups of women;
household and other refuse was deposited in surrounding bushes,
where it decomposed. However, the native physical-planning
methods were inadequate to handle the extent and rate of future
developments and thus inadvertently sowed the seeds of later
chaos.

THE COLONIAL PERIOD

In the colonial period, the colonial masters adopted a policy of indirect rule. They introduced ordinances to strengthen city administration, including

- The *Public Health Act* of 1909, which laid the foundations
  for improved health management; this period also saw the
  introduction of sanitary inspectors, who went house to
  house to ensure that the houses and their surroundings

were clean and, for recalcitrant residents, applied appropriate sanctions;

- The *Township Ordinance* of 1917, which classified townships into three categories and set up different municipal arrangements for first-order cities; and

- The *Town and Country Planning Act* of 1947, which recognized the need for a separate establishment to complement the local-government councils in the south and native administrations in the north, to handle town and country planning functions; this led to the establishment of city and town planning authorities in all the larger urban areas, which had powers to regulate the use of land, prepare development plans and schemes, approve new building plans, and implement development-control measures.

Despite these measures and the creation of the GRAs, which have remained the best parts of Nigerian cities, the major shortcoming of the colonial era was that the British colonial masters treated Nigeria as primarily a rural country and regarded the urban centres as accidents of area development. They therefore made no effort to solve the emerging urban problems, particularly of sanitation. Wraith (1964, p. 68) observed that in the west, which had six cities of more than 100 000 inhabitants, "the chaotic urban communities presented a challenge which should have been met ... . They now present almost insoluble problems of planning and sewage and lack any normal civilized amenities."

Another cause of the ineffectiveness of city administration during the colonial period was that the towns administered by town councils were subordinate to the native authorities, which were constituted and controlled by obas and chiefs, people who were mostly "old men by the time they attained office, with interest in another age" (Wraith 1964, p. 94). Their main interest was "ancient law and custom," and it was left to the Health and Public Works Department of government to deal with the most urgent and compelling of municipal problems" (Wraith 1964, p. 95).

THE IMMEDIATE PRE- AND POSTINDEPENDENCE PERIOD

The third phase in the evolution of the local governments was the transition to independence, or the immediate pre- and postindependence period. One of the important landmarks of this period was the introduction of the *Local Government Ordinances* of 1950/54, which were subsequently amended in 1955, 1957, 1958, 1967, and 1973. The ordinances introduced a three-tier system of administration: county councils, urban and rural district councils, and local councils. Furthermore, in the three regions, the ordinances recognized the special needs of the metropolitan areas and urban centres and created specific local-government types, namely, municipal councils for the big cities and urban councils for the smaller towns, each with a single tier, different in function and composition from other local governments. These councils were assigned specific functions, including removal of night soil, maintenance of other forms of sanitation, and personal health services.

A town planning authority (in Lagos, a development board) was established in each of the urban-council areas. These were independent of municipal government (although the latter had representatives on them) and were accountable to the regional governments. In addition, each of the regional state governments established certain parastatals to handle special functions, and some of these duplicated the functions of both the urban councils and the local planning authorities. Among such parastatals were the states' wastes-management boards. The regional state ministries also had among their defined functions those of maintaining parts of the municipal roads and handling certain municipal services, including solid-waste management.

These setups resulted in duplications, conflicts, inefficiency, and wastage. A number of factors crippled the performance of urban functions in this period:

- The local-government structure was unstable because the setup, financial allocations, administrative machinery, composition, headship, etc., changed with the whims and caprices of the higher authorities;

- Greed, corruption, and lack of accountability were promoted by the transience of the performers at the local-government level;

61

- Resources were inadequate, including money, skills, and materials;[1] and

- Local governments had too much interference, particularly from the regional state governments, too much politics among councillors and other politicians, and too many councillors and committees, and all these constituted a drain on finances and a cog in the wheel of progress.

THE 1976 LOCAL-GOVERNMENT REFORMS

The fourth and final phase of local-government evolution started with the introduction of the local-government reforms in Nigeria in 1976. The *Local Government Edict* of 1976 established a unified and common local-government system; 301 single-tier local-government councils were created (their number has since been increased to 589), and each was expected to function as an effective third tier of government. The local-government councils were empowered to exercise substantial control over local affairs, as well as being given staff and financial powers. The 1976 *Local Government Edict* was latter entrenched in the 1979 Constitution of the Federal Republic of Nigeria.

The role of the federal government

Under the new system, the 1979 Constitution limits the responsibilities of the federal government in urban management to setting broad guidelines and national policies for local-government structure, number, functioning, and management. Such broad policies may also include, by convention, setting up national standards (building codes, subdivision regulations, environmental-quality protection, etc.) to guide urban planning and management.

Worried about the increasing deterioration of the environment, in 1988 the federal government of Nigeria pursued its mandate to set up the Federal Environmental Protection Agency (FEPA) and in 1989 formally launched the National Policy on the Environment. Both FEPA and the National Policy on the Environment emphasized sanitation and waste management, "as part of an

---

[1] Lack of funds and professional staff turned many of the urban councils and municipal planning authorities into purposeless bodies and a drain on the regional state governments. They were managed by people who had inadequate experience or training.

integrated, holistic, and systematic view of environmental issues" (FEPA 1990, p. 6). Among the important tasks specified by the National Policy on the Environment, for sanitation and waste management, are the following:

- Conducting a study of the most reliable systems appropriate for local domestic and industrial waste;

- Specifying waste-disposal and -treatment systems that consider the geological and environmental setting and encourage recycling;

- Specifying waste-disposal sites that guarantee the safety of surface- and groundwater systems;

- Setting up and enforcing standards for adequate sanitary facilities for the disposal of human and other solid waste in dwellings, estates, and public facilities in both urban and rural areas;

- Establishing monitoring programs, including periodic surveillance of approved waste-disposal sites and their surroundings and waste-water systems; and

- Establishing monitoring stations for control of the disposal of leachate from dump sites into surface- and groundwater systems.

The federal government has also taken other positive measures to improve environmental management:

- The National Urban Development Policy of 1989, with the role of developing a dynamic and sustainable system of urban settlements, fostering economic growth, promoting efficient regional development, and ensuring improved standards of living and well-being for all Nigerians;

- The Environmental Impact Assessment Decree No. 86 of 1992, giving legal muscle to the various policy provisions on the need for environmental-impact assessments (EIAs) of both public- and private-sector projects when such projects are planned; and

- The Urban and Regional Planning Decree No. 88 of 1992, providing general and specific guidelines for development and focusing on the quality of the environment by requiring EIAs for specified categories of development.

Similarly, since its establishment FEPA has led to the enactment of the following important laws on environmental management:

- The National Effluents Limitation Regulation S.I.8. of 1991, which makes it mandatory for industries to install antipollution equipment and to provide primary treatment of effluents and chemical discharges;

- The Hazardous Wastes Criminal Provision Decree 42 of 1988;

- The Pollution Abatement in Industries and Facilities Generating Waste Regulation S.I. of 1991; and

- The Management of Solid and Hazardous Wastes Regulation S.I.15 of 1991.

To complement the efforts of FEPA, a state Environmental Protection Commission (EPC) was established for each state in 1989. Edict No. 17 describes the tasks and responsibilities of the EPC. The most important of those concerning solid-waste management are

- To advise the state government on environmental policies and priorities;

- To formulate and enforce policies, statutory rules, and regulations on waste collection and disposal;

- To render advisory services and support to all local governments;

- To prepare master plans on solid-waste collection and disposal;

- To monitor discharges and the environmental impact of these discharges;

- To enforce applicable laws on activities related to the environment; and

- To establish environmental criteria, guidelines, specifications, or standards for environmental protection.

The federal government has therefore taken adequate legislative steps to tackle environmental problems, including solid-waste management. However, much success is yet to be achieved, largely because of the weakness of the enabling legislation and the inability of the relevant agencies to enforce some of the laws. The implementation strategies for such laws leave much to be desired. As Maxime Ferrari of the United Nations Environment Programme Regional Office in Kenya once remarked, "the painful reality is that [although] African governments still pay lip service to environmental issues, actual action still lags behind resolutions and declarations of governments in many parts of Africa" (Ferrari 1988, p. 12). The situation has not been helped by the public's lack of voluntary compliance with the laws. As Ola (1984, p 74) remarked, "though a good law is necessary and useful, voluntary compliance with the law is still a long way off in this country and so all the innovations contained in the law need to stand the test to time." The powerful people in the country, whom the general populace should normally emulate, are the first to flout the laws, and other citizens take their cue from them.

The roles of the state and local governments

The Ministry of Local Government (at present, the Department of Local Government Affairs in the state governor's office) monitors the activities of local governments and passes directives and instructions to them as may be determined by state legislation. However, the local governments have full constitutional responsibility for management of sewerage and solid-waste disposal. This is underlined in Table 4, which lists the functions exclusive to the local governments and those they share with the state governments under the 1976 local-government reforms and the 1979 Constitution of the Federal Republic of Nigeria.

It needs to be pointed out that in 1989, for a number of reasons, most municipal and local governments could not perform many of the functions imposed on them by the Constitution. Furthermore, waste management did not feature among the few functions that these tiers of government performed. (The reasons for this situation were treated in detail by Onibokun [1989].) However, as a consequence, in many parts of the country, the state governments have had to intervene in solid-waste management from time to time. But such interventions have not been permanent, so

Table 4. Functions of local governments under the 1976 local-government reforms and the 1979 Constitution of the Federal Republic of Nigeria.

Category A — exclusive functions
  Markets and motor vehicles
  Sanitary inspection
  Slaughter houses and slabs
  Regulation of food establishments
  Registration of births, deaths, and marriages
  Collection of local taxes
  Cemeteries and burial grounds
  Control of animals
  Sewage or refuse disposal, or both
  Public conveniences
  Grazing grounds
  Community and recreation centres
  Control of private forest estates
  Parks, gardens, and open spaces
  Regulation of self-propelled vehicles

Category B — functions shared with the state government
  Medical services
  Agricultural services
  Information and public enlightenment
  Primary and adult education
  Support for arts and culture
  Road construction and maintenance
  Public health education
  Rural and semiurban water supply
  Town and country planning
  Fire protection
  Public housing
  Operation of commercial enterprises

Source: FGON (1978, 1979).

the responsibility for waste management has shifted several times from the municipal and local governments to the state governments and vice versa.

CURRENT INSTITUTIONAL ARRANGEMENT FOR WASTE MANAGEMENT IN IBADAN

In no city are the problems of waste management better illustrated than at Ibadan, Africa's largest indigenous settlement. The spectacular failure of many programs and machineries for waste disposal in this city has led to a continuous shift in responsibilities between agencies and the various tiers of government, as well as prompting some degree of privatization. For instance, between

1988 and 1989, responsibility for solid-waste management was with the Environmental Sanitation Board. However, following an institutional directive in 1989, responsibility was again transferred to local governments. In this new dispensation, collection facilities and other equipment were shared among the five local governments that occupy the city's core, namely, the Ibadan North, Northeast, Northwest, Southeast, and Southwest local governments.

Since 1991, however, these five local governments have entrusted responsibility for solid-waste collection and disposal to the Ibadan Urban Sanitation Committee (IUSC). The IUSC is governed by the Ibadan Urban Sanitation Board (IUSB), which comprises representatives from the five local governments and the state EPC. In Nigeria, we have the Sanitation Committee at the local level, the EPC at the state level, and the FEPA at the federal level. The members of the IUSB are the five health officers of the five local governments, representatives of the Ministry of Health and the EPC, and the project manager of the IUSC. There are two subcommittees, namely, Operations and Technical. Apart from solid-waste collection, transportation, and disposal, the committee also maintains the vehicles. The operations of the IUSC are subsidized by the five local governments, which contribute equal amounts, irrespective of their populations or the amounts of waste they generate. For instance, in 1993, the budget of 5 million NGN was contributed at the rate of 1 million NGN per local government (in 1998, 86.8 Nigerian naira [NGN] = 1 United States dollar [USD]). In 1994, the local governments budgeted 6.5 million NGN from their share of the federal-government statutory allocation and 3 million NGN from their own purse, making a total of 10 million NGN. This was far below the estimated 70 million NGN the IUSC needed to perform its functions more effectively. Internally generated revenue during the year was a meagre 200 000 NGN. Table 5 shows the allocation of funds to the IUSC for 1992 and 1993. The main advantage in using this system is that it removes the problems of sanitation at the boundary areas of local governments. Local governments retain responsibility for cleaning markets, sweeping streets, and cleaning drains.

Every week, the Project Manager of the IUSC and the five chief environmental health officers of the local governments discuss the collection schedule. In each local-government area, one skip eater is available to collect the skips. The five trucks were donated by the EPC. It is unclear why they should be based at the

Table 5. Ibadan Urban Sanitation Committee waste-disposal unit allocations, 1992 and 1993.

No.	Classification and experience	Estimate 1993 ($\times 10^3$ NGN)	Approved 1992 ($\times 10^3$ NGN)
1.	Maintenance of refuse vehicles; purchase of material, tools, spare parts; operations of battery charging and vulcanizing unit	1 200	500
2.	Maintenance of heavy plants and machines	1 200	400
3.	Purchase of lubricants and oils	500	200
4.	Purchase of sanitary materials and equipment	250	50
5.	Maintenance of office furniture and equipment; electricity and water bills	160	10
6.	Stationery and printing	40	6
7.	Training staff; workshop	150	5
8.	Environmental sanitation day exercises	720	150
9.	Provision of new vehicles	600	—
10.	Miscellaneous expenses	300	25

Source: Oyo State Environmental Protection Commission, Ibadan.
Note: Estimates for 1992 were for 6 months only. NGN, Nigerian naira (in 1998, 86.8 NGN = 1 United States dollar [USD]).

local-government premises when there is a main yard at Agodi and this arrangement may lead to conflicts and confusion between the local governments and the IUSC. The IUSC currently has five divisions, sections, and units, each headed by a chief who supervises other junior officers. The administrative setup is shown in Figure 1.

The EPC is the state arm of FEPA. It is administered by a Board of Directors and is headed by a general manager referred to as an executive secretary. Under this person are three directors (research and planning; personnel, finance, and supplies; and environmental management and works services). The EPC has at present a work force of 200. In addition to its functions listed earlier, the EPC is mandated to undertake the following assignments that are crucial to solid-waste management:

- Providing grants to appropriate authorities and bodies with similar functions to enhance their capacity for environmental management (for example, the EPC donated one skip eater to each of the five local governments);

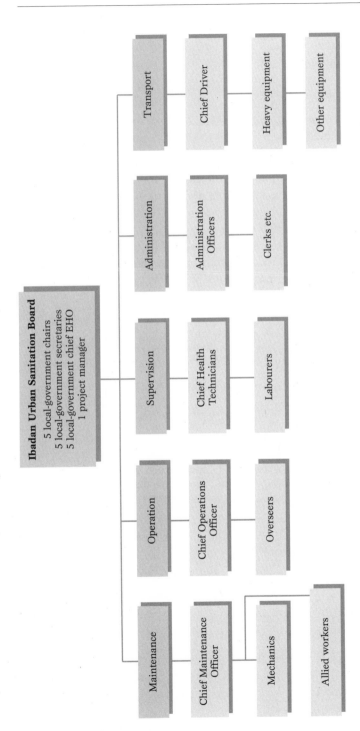

Figure 1. Organogram of the Ibadan Urban Sanitation Committee. Source: Oyo State Environmental Protection Commission, Ibadan, 1996.

- Collecting and making available through publications and other appropriate means, in cooperation with other public or private organizations, basic scientific data and other information; and

- Contracting with public and private organizations and individuals to help fulfil the EPC's functions and responsibilities.

The EPC covers the whole of the state and handles waste-related matters in all the urban areas. It took inventory of all areas needing attention in environmental matters in all the local governments and established an EPC in each of them. It started a program of environmental education.

In Ibadan, the EPC is involved in the physical execution of both the Ibadan Flood Control/Storm Drainage and the Ibadan Waste Management components of the World Bank-assisted Oyo State Urban Project, for which it is an implementation agency. It awarded contracts for the following projects:

- The Ibadan Flood Control and Storm Drainage;

- Rehabilitation of the old ring-road refuse depot;

- Rehabilitation of the eroded areas of upper Ogunpa; and

- Rehabilitation of the IUSC–EPC workshops at Agodi.

There are also proposals for improving the collection system, including promoting and rationalizing the involvement of private contractors. The EPC has also begun to identify new sanitary landfill sites at the periphery of Ibadan. Eight sites have been identified, and the studies and designs are expected to commence soon. The sites are along the major roads entering Ibadan from Oyo, Iwo, Akufo, Abeokuta, Old Lagos, Olojuoro, Akanran, and Ife. The EPC has also embarked on the local fabrication of skips. The first products have been received, and they cost half as much as the old skips.

IUSC's CURRENT WASTE COLLECTION AND DISPOSAL

Solid waste is collected by skip eaters from the available 50 skips located at major roads and markets in different parts of the city and transported to the ring-road disposal site. The locations of the skips have a few flaws.

- They are too few and inadequately scattered. Too few skips are allotted per depot, and when these are full, people dump refuse in the surrounding areas.

- Many of the dumps are located far from the intended users. One consequence is that residents resort to dumping their refuse everywhere, such as on vacant lands.

- The skips located beside the major roads are aesthetically offensive.

IUSC has no organized system for collecting the waste from house to house and transporting it from the houses to the skips. This is the responsibility of the residents, and in places where the skips are far from homes, particularly in the inaccessible core areas of the city, people are tempted to dispose of the waste before they reach the skips. At each of the skip points, two overseers are employed to clean the surrounding area. The skips are located in the residential areas. Some of the tipped solid waste is usually blown into the surrounding residential areas, as well as along the street between the dumping and disposal sites. This is a major cause of environmental pollution in the city.

The skips are collected in two shifts, day and evening. But operations are seriously hampered because these shifts coincide with the peak traffic periods. Each truck collects between 6 and 12 skips per day, that is, 3–6 skips per shift, depending on the season, as activities are also considerably slower during the rains.

The waste is deposited at the ring-road disposal site. Ibadan used to have three sites, namely, the ring-road disposal site in Ibadan Southwest, Oniyere in Ibadan Southeast, and Ijokodo in Ibadan North. However, the Oniyere and Ijokodo sites have been closed down, leaving the ring-road site, which is encircled by residential areas and has degenerated into open dumps breeding flies, harbouring rodents, and leading to potential major health hazards, which may hamper human productivity. This site has became grossly inadequate, and its operational costs have mounted because of the long distances separating it from many parts of the city.

Early in 1995, Nigeria was preparing for the Junior World Cup. The ring-road disposal site was abandoned because it is very close to Liberty Stadium, one of the four venues for the competition, and two new refuse-disposal sites were chosen outside the city, namely, Ajakagan and Aba-Eku. These sites were prepared with the assistance of the World Bank. Even though Nigeria's right to host the World Cup was later withdrawn, operations did not return to the ring-road site, and the two new depots remain in use.

In addition, when the state government realized that the two new landfills would be inadequate, it identified four others along the major roads linking Ibadan with other towns:

■ Bode-Igbo village, along Ibadan–Abeokuta road, with an area of 21.6 ha;

■ Lapite village, along Ibadan–Oyo road, with an area of 23.6 ha;

■ Elesingodogbo village, along the Ibadan–Iwo road, with an area of 21.4 ha; and

■ Alomaja village, along the Ibadan–Ijebu–Ode road, with an area of 22.5 ha.

Additional sites have been identified along other roads outside the core of the city where the IUSC operates. It is left to be seen what management arrangement will be made with the six fringe local governments where the new sites are located.

At the ring-road disposal site, two bulldozers are available to move the waste from the entrance road to the actual site. Whenever one or both bulldozers malfunction, which quite frequently happens, or the entrance road is bad, the trucks have to dump the waste far from the site, often obstructing the highway.

Facilities are limited at the central workshop where vehicles and other equipment are parked and maintained. Operational and nonoperative vehicles clog the site. For a number of financial, technical, and other reasons, the vehicles are not always functional. This accounts for the IUSC's meagre contribution (estimated at not more than 10 %) to waste collection in the city.

The facilities for waste collection in Ibadan in 1994 are shown in Table 6. Few vehicles and equipment were always functional. Only one of the two bulldozers at the ring-road disposal site was functional. Only 2 of the 7 tippers and none of the 18 compactors were in operation. On the whole, only 57 of the 93 available pieces of equipment were working.

Table 7 shows the total number of workers available in the waste-management system at Ibadan in 1993. As noted earlier, the IUSC has 200 workers, contributed by the five participating local

72

Table 6. Current facilities for waste collection, Ibadan, 1993.

Type	Model	Available	Operational
Bulldozer	—	2	1
Payloader	Kamatsu	1	0
Tippers	Bedford	7	2
Skip eaters	Leyland	15	9
Skips	—	50	45
Compactors	Ford	18	0

Source: Haskoning and Konsadem Associates (1994).

Table 7. Human resources for waste collection, Ibadan, 1993.

Post	Number
Project manager, Urban Sanitation Committee	1
Supervisors	4
Superintendent	12
Foreperson	6
Drivers	17
Collectors (operate with trucks)	50
Sweepers (street sweeping)	60
Labourers (overseers)	70
Mechanics (at workshop)	14
Others (cleaning of public toilets, other sanitation activities)	110

Source: Haskoning and Konsadem Associates (1994).

governments. The other 144 workers are the direct contribution by local governments to such waste and sanitation activities as street sweeping. Nonetheless, it is apparent that the waste-management system in Ibadan is generally understaffed. It is estimated that between 400 and 500 staff are needed for the effective performance of the IUSC functions. A major reason for the lack of staff is the dearth of funds. Also, employment in waste-collection and -disposal activities is looked down on, and the salary structure is not enhanced to compensate for this.

In 1993, the IUSC spent 2 million NGN on fuel and oil and 3 million NGN on maintenance, spare parts, and administration, making a total of 5 million NGN (the amount contributed by the local governments). During that year, the cost of efficient solid-waste management (involving 1–15 trucks, without new equipment) was estimated at 6 million NGN for administration and 5 million NGN for maintenance, making a total of 11 million NGN. In other words, the IUSC had less than 50 % of the resources it needed for optimum performance in 1993. Since then costs have gone up astronomically, following the increase in fuel prices (from 0.70 NGN/L to 3.25 NGN/L, and then to 11.0 NGN/L) and the deregulation of the foreign-exchange market. But the contribution of each of the five local governments remained stagnant at 1 million NGN. Although this increased slightly more recently, it still falls short of the requirement.

PRIVATE WASTE COLLECTION

The private waste collectors in Ibadan are all members of the Association of Environmental Contractors. In 1994, they served an estimated 10 000 households in the Ibadan urban area. At present, 28 private firms are registered with IUSC, but only 10 of these are functioning. The criteria for registering are office accommodation, available equipment, staff strength, and financial capability. Although the registration is free of charge, if the applicant meets the conditions, it pays a dumping fee of 5 000 NGN/year to use IUSC depots. No particular part of the city is allocated to any contractor, and they are free to make their own arrangements. Many companies and institutions in the city make use of these private collectors.

Some small-scale operators use wheel barrows to collect over short distances. They operate in the Sabo area and in some markets and motor parks and charge their clients agreed sums of money. However, they dispose of the refuse they collect in refuse depots within the neighbourhood. These are often not cleared regularly and therefore constitute both an environmental hazard and an impediment to traffic.

A report of the Nigerian Institute of Social and Economic Research (NISER), the *Socio-Economic Survey of Ibadan City* (1988), covering the 15 conveniently delineated zones of the city revealed that 35.9 % of the sampled households used private collectors. The degree of use was highest in the newer well laid out and accessible parts of the city, such as the Oluyole Estate, where 79.1 % of households used their services; Felele–Challenge, 89.5 %; Agodi GRA, 67 %; and Mokola, 79.8 %. But they were least used in the old, indigenous parts of the city, such as Agugu (3.8 % of households), Oranyan (3.6 %), Kobomoje (9.15), and Gege (1.1 %). Most private collectors rent tipper trucks for their operations; one owns a compactor truck; and some own their own tipper trucks. Households pay 20–50 NGN per month for their services.

Frequency of refuse collection by agencies

The 1988 NISER survey revealed that for households using government agencies the most common interval for solid-waste collection was more than once per week (31.9 % of respondents). The next most common was weekly (5.2 %), followed by biweekly (2 %). Daily and triweekly collections were uncommon. The intervals for waste collection by private firms employed by the government were similar. Such firms most commonly collected refuse at an interval of more than 1 week (32.7 %). Collection once a week was the second most common (5.8 %), followed by collection biweekly (2.8 %). Daily collection occurred in only one case (Sawmill–Onipepeye), and triweekly collection occurred in 0.4 % of cases (Table 8).

75

These figures are very different for refuse collection by firms employed by residents. Weekly collection was the norm (29.2 %). Biweekly and triweekly collections also occurred more commonly than in the cases of government agencies or private firms employed by government (Table 9).

THE POPULACE

People bear responsibility for manually carrying wastes generated in their households to the skips (that is, in cases where households do not have refuse bins or drums). This responsibility is particularly great in many parts of Ibadan, particularly the inner core, which is not accessible to trucks, thus making it necessary to place the skips far away at the main roads. This demands a lot of cooperation from people — because when they decide to throw away the refuse before they get it to the skips, the pollution problems persist. But for reasons elucidated later, this cooperation has not been forthcoming.

Payment by residents for refuse collection

Table 10 shows that in 1988, apart from the 9.5 % of respondents who could not indicate how much they paid for refuse collection, an appreciable proportion of residents did not pay for refuse collection (41.3 %). This indicates that refuse collection in many areas was a voluntary community undertaking. This is underlined by the fact that the highest proportions of those who did not pay

Table 8. Frequency of refuse collection by private firms employed by the government in Ibadan, 1988.

Zone	No response		Daily		Weekly		Biweekly		Triweekly		Irregularly		Not applicable	
	n	%	n	%	n	%	n	%	n	%	n	%	n	%
1. Agugu	25	9.5	0	0.0	3	1.1	0	0.0	0	0.0	90	34.1	146	55.3
2. Mokola	86	35.4	0	0.0	19	7.8	13	5.3	0	0.0	52	21.4	73	30.0
3. Yemetu	105	43.2	0	0.0	14	5.8	7	2.9	1	0.4	17	7.0	99	40.7
4. Oranyan	13	6.7	0	0.0	3	1.6	1	0.5	0	0.0	92	47.7	84	43.5
5. Kobomoje	41	22.0	0	0.0	8	4.3	0	0.0	1	0.5	32	17.2	104	55.9
6. Ayeye	47	25.1	0	0.0	5	2.7	3	1.6	3	1.6	43	23.0	86	46.0
7. Gege	8	4.3	0	0.0	0	0.0	0	0.0	0	0.6	155	82.9	24	12.8
8. Felele–Challenge	26	10.1	0	0.0	1	0.4	2	0.8	0	0.0	85	32.9	144	55.8
9. Monatan–Iwo Road	4	2.6	0	0.0	3	2.0	3	2.0	0	0.0	111	72.5	32	20.9
10. Oke Ado–Oke Bola	44	17.5	0	0.0	54	21.5	25	10.0	6	2.4	22	8.8	100	39.8
11. Agbowo–Orogun	14	7.7	0	0.0	16	8.8	28	15.4	0	0.0	28	15.4	96	52.7
12. Sawmill–Onipepeye	66	22.1	1	0.3	5	1.7	10	3.3	0	0.0	133	44.5	84	28.1
13. Alamu–Apata	3	1.3	0	0.0	39	17.0	0	0.0	0	0.0	57	24.9	130	56.8
14. Oluyole Estate	6	4.7	0	0.0	3	2.3	0	0.0	0	0.0	66	51.2	54	41.9
15. Agodi GRA	6	4.1	0	0.0	10	6.9	6	4.1	0	0.0	48	33.1	75	51.7

Source: NISER (1988).
Note: GRA, government-reserved area.

Table 9. Frequency of refuse collection by firms employed by residents, Ibadan, 1988.

Zone	No response		Daily		Weekly		Biweekly		Triweekly		Irregularly		Not applicable	
	n	%	n	%	n	%	n	%	n	%	n	%	n	%
1. Agugu	25	9.5	1	0.4	6	2.3	2	0.8	2	0.8	91	34.5	137	51.9
2. Mokola	20	8.2	0	0.0	183	75.3	13	5.3	3	1.2	10	4.1	14	5.8
3. Yemetu	98	40.3	1	0.4	36	14.8	5	2.1	3	1.2	11	4.5	89	36.6
4. Oranyan	14	7.3	1	0.5	1	0.5	4	2.1	1	0.5	90	46.6	82	42.5
5. Kobomoje	42	22.6	0	0.0	16	8.6	0	0.0	1	0.5	27	14.5	100	53.8
6. Ayeye	45	24.1	0	0.0	18	9.6	5	2.7	5	2.7	44	23.5	70	37.4
7. Gege	7	3.7	2	1.1	1	0.5	0	0.0	0	0.0	154	82.4	23	12.3
8. Felele–Challenge	2	0.8	0	0.0	152	58.9	76	29.5	2	0.8	6	2.3	20	7.8
9. Monatan–Iwo Road	4	2.6	1	0.7	47	30.7	12	7.8	0	0.0	66	43.1	23	15.0
10. Oke Ado–Oke Bola	23	9.2	0	0.0	124	49.4	8	3.2	1	0.4	24	9.6	71	28.3
11. Agbowo–Orogun	22	12.1	0	0.0	64	35.2	8	4.4	0	0.0	30	16.5	58	31.9
12. Sawmill–Onipepeye	56	18.7	1	0.3	51	17.1	14	4.7	1	0.3	108	36.1	68	22.7
13. Alamu–Apata	0	0.0	0	0.0	96	41.9	7	3.1	5	2.2	37	16.2	84	36.7
14. Oluyole Estate	0	0.0	0	0.0	93	72.1	9	7.0	0	0.0	18	14.0	9	7.0
15. Agodi GRA	3	2.1	0	0.0	74	51.0	18	12.4	0	0.0	23	15.9	27	18.6

Source: NISER (1988).
Note: GRA, government-reserved area.

Table 10. Amounts people paid for the refuse collection per month, Ibadan, 1988.

Zone	No response		Free		NGN								
					≤5.00		5.01–10.00		10.01–15.00		15.01–20.00		>20.00	
	n	%	n	%	n	%	n	%	n	%	n	%	n	%
1. Agugu	14	5.3	237	89.8	0	0.0	7	2.7	5	1.9	0	0.0	1	0.4
2. Mokola	5	2.1	2	0.8	39	16.0	177	72.8	18	7.4	1	0.4	1	0.4
3. Yemetu	82	33.7	75	30.9	12	4.9	68	28.0	6	2.5	0	0.0	0	0.0
4. Oranyan	4	2.1	176	91.2	2	1.0	8	4.1	1	0.5	1	0.5	1	0.5
5. Kobomoje	93	50.0	68	36.5	4	2.2	20	10.8	0	0.0	0	0.0	1	0.5
6. Ayeye	18	9.6	121	64.7	13	7.0	34	18.2	1	0.5	0	0.0	0	0.0
7. Gege	15	8.0	167	89.3	1	0.5	2	1.1	1	0.5	1	0.5	0	0.0
8. Felele–Challenge	7	2.2	18	7.0	39	15.1	182	70.5	11	4.3	1	0.4	0	0.0
9. Monatan–Iwo Road	9	5.9	64	41.8	15	9.8	51	9.8	13	8.5	1	0.7	0	0.0
10. Oke Ado–Oke Bola	8	3.2	10	4.0	7	2.8	225	89.60	1	0.4	0	0.0	0	0.0
11. Agbowo–Orogun	4	2.2	32	17.6	20	11.0	100	54.94	26	14.3	0	0.0	0	0.0
12. Sawmill–Onipepeye	19	6.4	173	59.5	10	3.3	81	27.1	10	3.3	1	0.3	0	0.0
13. Alamu–Apata	6	2.6	62	27.1	1	0.4	108	47.2	52	22.7	0	0.0	0	0.0
14. Oluyole Estate	0	0.0	18	14.0	0	0.0	93	72.1	18	14.0	0	0.0	0	0.0
15. Agodi GRA	0	0.0	27	18.8	6	4.1	83	57.2	28	19.3	1	0.7	0	0.0

Source: NISER (1988).
Note: GRA, government-reserved areas; NGN, Nigerian naira (in 1998, 86.8 NGN = 1 United States dollar [USD]).

for refuse collection were in the areas inhabited by the indigenous population, such as Agugu (89.8%), Oranyan (91.2%), Ayeye (64.7%), and Gege (89.3%).

Of those who paid for refuse-collection services, the majority (37.9%) paid between 5.01 and 10.00 NGN/month. The parts of the city with high proportions of residents who paid the most popular charges were Mokola (72.8%), Felele–Challenge (70.5%), Oke Ado–Oke Bola (89.6%), and Oluyole Estate (72.1%). In the city as a whole, 5.3% of the residents paid 5.00 NGN/month or less, 5.6% paid between 10.01 and 15.00 NGN/month, and 0.3% paid more than 15.00 NGN/month. On the whole, the proportion of people who made payments in the highest brackets (more than 10 NGN/month) was highest in Alamu–Apata (22.7%), Agodi GRA (19.3%), Agbowo–Orogun (14.3%), and Oluyole Estate (14%), with an average of 5.9% for the whole city.

79

Despite the trend of price inflation in the country, payment for refuse-collection services has only increased slightly. For example, the charges now range from 20 to 50 NGN/month. However, many residents of the city expressed their willingness to pay more if service was improved.

Degree of satisfaction with refuse-collection services

At the time of the survey (NISER 1988), the majority of residents of Ibadan were satisfied with the refuse-collection services; 26.6% were quite satisfied; and 41.7% were just satisfied. However, 8.1% were not so satisfied; 15.0% were dissatisfied; and 0.8% were utterly dissatisfied. High figures of residents who were satisfied occurred in areas where more reliance was placed on private firms paid by residents such as Felele–Challenge (89.1%), Oke Ado–Oke Bola (87.6%), Agbowo-Orogun (88%), Alamu–Apata (81%), and Agodi GRA (84.1%). At the other extreme, more people were either not so satisfied, dissatisfied, or utterly dissatisfied in Oranyan (50.2%), Agugu (44.7%), and Gege (44.9%).

Residents who were dissatisfied gave a number of reasons: 6.9% complained of the great distances that separated their houses from the refuse depots; 4.1% of the respondents were dissatisfied because the agents employed did not come regularly; 1.6% complained about high charges; and 3.1% complained about the inadequacy of refuse collection and disposal facilities, a complaint that was loudest in the indigenous sections of the city. A small proportion of residents, 1.2%, were dissatisfied because of the indiscriminate way the collectors dumped the refuse. In particular, where the method of burning was adopted to dispose of refuse, some people complained about the unhygienic and unsightly nature of such depots. Many residents were reluctant to cooperate with their neighbours in matters of environmental sanitation.

Other waste-disposal methods employed by the populace

Because of a lack of institutionalized waste-disposal facilities or the inability or unwillingness of people to use them, people employ a variety of other methods to dispose of their waste, with severe repercussions on the environment. For instance, the illegal dumping of refuse in open spaces, along the roads, in open gutters, etc., blocks drains and sewer holes, disrupts business in commercial areas, reduces road space, and holds up traffic. In addition, as solid-waste services are unable to cope with the volume of refuse, it is usually burned in households, zones, depots, and disposal sites, which causes air and general environmental pollution. In fact, the 1988 NISER study revealed that burning refuse and disposing of the ashes in drainage channels was the method for disposal of refuse used by 26.8% of surveyed inhabitants of Ibadan. Burning and disposing of ashes in open dumps, often unauthorized and with little chance of being cleared, represents the preferred method of 35.8% of the surveyed inhabitants.

There are about 40 markets in Ibadan and a lot of street trading. The unguided increase in the activities of the informal sector in the city has led to the invasion of all available spaces in all land-use types. Petty traders block access roads and disobey planning set-back regulations. These factors not only increase the generation of waste but also complicate collection mechanisms. The nonchalant attitude of people toward the local governments and their members has much to do with this situation.

Nonetheless, the same study revealed that people are very willing to pay for solid-waste removal and disposal if the service is improved. The people need to be mobilized to contribute both in cash and in kind toward improving the environment.

After the military regime was established, on 31 December 1983, it organized environmental days on the Saturday of every second week. This initiative has increased people's participation in waste management. Residents collect solid waste from their homes, and trucks are available to transport it to the disposal site. In some cases, the trucks are donated by individuals and organizations such as the National Association of Road Transport Workers and the National Association of Road Transport Owners. But a lot still needs to be done to get people fully mobilized to make environmental sanitation a way of life, rather than a burden to be endured on specific days of the month.

NONGOVERNMENTAL ORGANIZATIONS, CBOs, AND ACADEMIC AND RESEARCH INSTITUTES

The major areas of intervention for nongovernmental organizations (NGOs), CBOs, and academic and research institutes have been public enlightenment and research. The Nigerian Society of Engineers recently organized a community-based discussion on waste management within the local governments in Ibadan. The Centre for African Settlement Studies and Development (CAS-SAD) has consistently promoted waste management through policy-oriented research, discussions, lectures, and seminars. A lot of research has also been done in the universities and research institutes, but the findings have not always been available to the waste-management service in Ibadan.

EVALUATION OF GOVERNANCE OF WASTE MANAGEMENT

The previous summary has revealed that the inadequacies in the governance of waste management in Ibadan are largely reflected in the waste-management system. The following characteristics of governance hamper effective waste management:

PROBLEMS WITH THE INSTITUTIONAL FRAMEWORK

At all levels of government, Nigeria has institutions and agencies for waste management. That there is so much waste in Nigerian cities is therefore not due to a lack of relevant institutions but to inadequacies in the ways the institutions function. In particular, the various agencies and institutions act in an independent, fragmented manner, and whenever they interact, they are likely to be on a collision course. The general tendency among Nigerians is to want to carve out miniempires for themselves whenever they head any institution, and they would rather drift along than take advice from, or cooperate with, institutions performing similar functions. For this reason, it is always difficult to know which government agency is doing what in waste management, and at which level of government. The interaction of institutions in waste management with other development agencies is even worse, particularly with those concerned with land development, housing, transportation, and other infrastructures. The tendency is for each of the institutions to act independently, regardless of the needs of others.

As we observed earlier, most municipal and local governments in Nigeria cannot perform many of the functions imposed on them by the Constitution. But more important, from the point of view of our present focus, is the fact that most of these governments do not accord high priority to waste management. This is well illustrated by a study conducted by Koehn (1992) of local governments in northern Nigeria. Koehn's results are shown in Tables 11 and 12. As Table 11 reveals, education, tax collection, agricultural services, and rural and semirural water supply received most attention. Furthermore, the functions reported to be among the five accorded the most importance by local governments were, in descending order of importance, education, agricultural services, collection of local taxes, medical services, and rural and semirural water supply. Others were community development, road construction and maintenance, maintenance of law and order, and markets and motor-vehicle parks (Table 12). Needless to say, sanitation and waste management are not in either of these tables. Other studies confirm that Koehn's findings about local governments in northern Nigeria apply to most local governments across the country (Onibokun 1989). Although the statutory roles of the various tiers of government are stated in the Constitution, officials at the local government level, because they do not hold themselves responsible or accountable to the people, clearly do not consult with the general populace in fixing their priorities. In fact, most of the problems of administration at this level stem from this, particularly the inability of government to mobilize the people and elicit their trust and confidence.

Table 11. Functions accorded most importance
by local governments, northern Nigeria, 1979.

Function	% of respondents from local governments who ranked this function as "most important" [a]
Education	43
Tax collection	33
Agricultural services	9
Rural and semiurban water supply	7
All others	8

Source: Koehn (1992).
[a] $n = 138$.

Table 12. Functions reported to be among the five accorded the
most importance by local governments, northern Nigeria, 1979.

Function	% of respondents from local governments who ranked this function in top five [a]
Education	88
Agricultural services	74
Collection of local taxes	61
Medical services	48
Rural and semiurban water supply	46
Community development	33
Road construction and maintenance	31
Maintenance of law and order	28
Markets and motor-vehicle parks	21

Source: Koehn (1992).
[a] $n = 138$.

Institutions at the local level are very unstable. Agencies are created and abolished at random. Those in place are not given sufficient technical or financial support to perform their duties, and because of this they are replaced, but without any correction of the factors that hindered their performance. The situation is well illustrated in Table 13. In Ibadan, before 1972, household-refuse removal was the responsibility of the Ibadan municipal government. Between 1973 and 1978, it became the responsibility of an Ibadan Waste Disposal Board, a creation of the Oyo state government. This period was followed by a reversion of the function to the Ibadan municipal government, in collaboration with the Ministry of Housing and Environment. The takeover of the national

83

Table 13. Temporal changes in the organization of solid-waste management, Ibadan, Kaduna, and Enugu, 1940–85.

City	Period	Management agency
Ibadan	Before 1972	Ibadan municipal government
	1973–78	Ibadan Wastes Disposal Board
	1978–83	Ibadan municipal government; Ministry of Housing and Environment
	1984 – Dec 1985	Sewerage and Refuse Matters Department; Oyo State Environmental Sanitation Task Force; Ibadan municipal government
Kaduna	1940–67	Kaduna Native Authority
	1967–71	Kaduna local government
	1971–85	Kaduna Capital Development Authority
	1985 – Dec 1985	Kaduna State Urban and Development Board
Enugu	Before 1977	Enugu urban council
	1977–84	Enugu local government
	1984–85	Anambra state task force
	1985 – Dec 1985	Anambra State Environmental Sanitation Authority

government by the military, on 31 December 1983, led first to the transfer of waste-management matters to the Sewerage and Refuse Matters Department in the State Ministry of Works and later to the creation of the Oyo State Environmental Sanitation Task Force, which worked in collaboration with the Ibadan municipal government. Later shifts in responsibilities were highlighted in the earlier parts of the paper.

The tenure of political and public officials is tenuous and very unstable. Holders of political office at the local-government level, to whom most responsibility for waste management devolves, are appointed and removed at will by people in higher tiers of government. Because they are unsure of their tenure, a lot of their time is spent currying favour from, and trying to please, the people who hold the reins of government at the higher levels. Therefore, they pay scant attention to long-term sustainable programs or the interests of the people whom they serve. Many of them try to make hay while the sun shines by enriching themselves. There is therefore a high level of corruption and a total lack of transparency. Between 1976 and 1994, the administration at the local-government level (including municipal government) changed more than six times. For instance, Lagos Island Local Government had, between January 1990 and May 1991, worked under four state–federal administrations. New governments are notorious for discrediting previous administrations and abandoning policies and programs on which previous administrations spent vast amounts of money. Successive governments pursue their own fancies in a rather flippant and ad hoc manner, rather than being motivated by a desire to leave lasting legacies. Institutions are created, then merged with other institutions, then made independent again, and later merged. Officials are appointed casually and removed even more casually.

85

This situation ensures that established rules, regulations, and relationships between and within state and societal institutions are flouted and that society can accept no values as legitimate and defensible.

Political differences between the various governments and tiers of government, particularly during civilian regimes, when administration of state and local (municipal) government belonged to different political parties, meant that the roles ascribed to different tiers of government were taken over by others with scant consideration of their ability to perform them.

Governance is also fragmented. Rather than taking a holistic view of governance, the governors force or allow development agencies such as those involved in land-use, transportation, housing, and waste management to pursue their different programs and execute their own projects without consideration of or reference to those of others. However, good governance can only be achieved if relationships, interactions, and feedback are well established and coordinated among the different performers and stakeholders. Without these connections, people tend to lack trust in the governors, which reduces their capacity to rule.

The result of fragmented governance is the confusion one observes, particularly in waste management. For instance, areas of dense population are provided with inadequate roads, which hampers refuse collection. In the past, some sanity came from the Ibadan Metropolitan Planning Authority, which had the mandate to sanitize, regulate, control, and monitor all ramifications of development in Ibadan. This institution was later dissolved, and no similar institution has taken its place. The tendency for fragmented development has thus been given a free rein. Intergovernmental conflicts have led several observers to call for a coordinating body to be established to initiate and coordinate urban programs at the federal, state, and local levels. According to these observers, this body should also provide a forum for public participation in the management of urban problems in the country, which has hitherto not been achieved because of the fragmentation of governance (Uyanga 1982; Gboyega 1983; Olowu 1994).

86

A major deficiency of current waste-management governance in Ibadan is that it incorporates only 5 of the 11 local governments that make up the Ibadan region. Although the five local governments account for about 67 % of the total population of the Ibadan region (Table 14), large sections of the city are administered by the other local governments. Again this is a clear case of exclusion, which does not promote good governance. The six fringe local governments are left to devise their own systems, without consultation or collaboration with IUSC. None of these six local governments has the requisite technical, financial, or managerial resources to effectively cope with waste management in their areas of jurisdiction, and therefore waste collection and disposal are inadequate in their own sections of the city. Furthermore, the recently identified new refuse-disposal sites, which are in the process of study and design by IUSC and EPC, are located in these fringe local-government areas. Without adequate consultation and a mutually beneficial arrangement, the seeds of future collisions are being sown.

Table 14. Provisional population statistics of local-government areas, Ibadan region, 1991.

Local-government area	Male	Female
Ibadan Northwest	72 489	74 270
Ibadan North	151 838	149 101
Ibadan Northeast	133 370	139 370
Ibadan Southeast	112 144	115 721
Ibadan Southwest	137 084	136 944
Akinyele	69 576	70 011
Lagelu	32 895	35 837
Egbeda	64 110	64 888
Ona–Ara	59 789	62 598
Oluyole	45 418	45 602
Iddo	27 918	27 975
Percentage of total population	49.57	50.43

Source: NPC (1992).

PROBLEMS WITH ADMINISTRATION AND MANAGEMENT

Closely linked to problems with the institutional framework are those with administration and management. As we noted earlier, waste-management institutions are grossly understaffed, in terms of both quantity and quality. For instance, about 200 personnel are on the ground, but between 400 and 500 are needed for effective performance. One of the major reasons for this has been the dearth of funds. But even at the best of times, the service has been unable to attract the right calibre of people (particularly at the technical level). This is partly due to the fact that people generally hold the administration at the local-government level in low esteem. Because it is the level of government closest to the people, they tend to hold it responsible for the failure of government in general. Indeed, the local governments' style of administration often lacks consultation and responsiveness to the needs of people. Their style of administration has done little to remove the stigma of inefficiency, corruption, and irresponsibility. Therefore, to a large extent, local-government appointments have hitherto been regarded as last resorts in many parts of the country.

87

This situation is exacerbated by poor conditions of service. Historically, local-government staff have been less well paid than their state (regional) and national (federal) counterparts, and even among the local-government staff, the waste-management section attracts the least pay. Therefore, although local-government staff (despite the harmonization of salaries) feel inferior to their state and federal counterparts, they exhibit an attitude of superiority toward their colleagues in the waste-management section. This situation considerably lowers morale and promotes slothfulness.

As Obadina (1995) observed, the period of 1973–78, when the Ibadan Wastes Disposal Board was in charge of waste management in Ibadan, saw the highest level of achievement to date. This is because of the high proportion of technical personnel available at that time. Technical personnel comprised the general manager (an engineer), the chief design and construction engineer, and six other engineers in charge of operations, planning, design, and construction. The best technical personnel that the management agency has had either before or after that period consisted of two, one, or no engineers, thus making the operation ineffective and grossly inefficient.

Furthermore, the management of the IUSB is dominated by the local governments, whereas actual operational responsibility lies with the IUSC. However, abundant evidence shows that little or no consultation takes place between the two bodies or between these bodies and the populace in determining responsibilities for waste management or making financial allocations to the IUSC. This has greatly impaired the governance of waste management. In most cases, therefore, the responsibilities are unclear. For instance, both local governments and the IUSC have collection vehicles, and the skip eaters donated by the EPC to each of the local governments are stationed at the local governments. It is unclear why the local governments should retain collection vehicles, as the responsibility for waste collection has been entrusted to the IUSC. Local governments have differences of opinion, particularly about budgetary allocations to IUSC and the performance of the institution. In fact, some local governments would prefer to organize waste collection themselves, instead of making use of the IUSC. It should also be noted that the present arrangement lacks proper legislative backing. The required levels of trust, interdependence, and reciprocity are clearly lacking between the two institutions and between these institutions and the populace. The present arrangements for waste management can, therefore, be regarded as being as unstable as the local governments themselves.

PROBLEMS WITH FINANCE

The inadequacies of governance at the urban level (particularly the lack of an organic relationship and mutual trust between the rulers and the ruled), the inadequacies of intergovernmental relations, and the lack of capacity among the rulers have adversely affected the ability of most urban governments to mobilize the resources — money, skill, and materials — needed for good administration.

As Onibokun (1997) demonstrated, "lack of funds and professional staff turned many of the urban councils and municipal planning authorities into purposeless bodies, and a drain on the regional/state governments." Since the 1976 reforms the tendency of local governments has been to look to the federal government for funds, instead of accepting the challenge and advantages that go with financial autonomy, that is, noninterference by the higher tiers of government in their affairs. Quoting various sources,

Onibokun revealed the following characteristics of most local governments in Nigeria:

- They are in debt;

- They are basically underfinanced;

- The fiscal burden is unfairly distributed (that is, large potential areas of taxation, such as property as a basis for tax, are neglected);

- Patterns of expenditure do not reflect a defensible set of priorities;[2]

- The local governments have little concern for cost-effectiveness and avoidance of waste;

- Their financial controls are ineffective; and

- Their financial information often comes too late or is too obscure to be useful.

Thus, the five participating local governments are unable to effectively back up the activities of the IUSC. The IUSC is unable to generate revenue internally. As noted, the federal government remains the principal source of revenue for the local governments, as only a small proportion of total revenue is generated internally. The budget of the IUSC is supplied by the five participating local governments. At present, these contributions (1 million NGN per local government in 1993) are deducted at source and given directly to the IUSC. For this reason, the IUSC is subject to political instability. Furthermore, the contributions are not calculated on any economic basis, as the IUSC is not involved in drawing up its own budget. They are based neither on population figures of the different local governments nor on the particular amounts of waste generated in their areas.

The IUSC's capacity to generate internal revenue is hampered in a number of ways. At present, the only source of revenue from its operations is that received from institutional customers, such as schools, hospitals, and some private institutions. Even here, the IUSC has no organized system for collecting fees. In most

---

[2] For example, spending on civil and administrative overhead is overwhelmingly at the expense of service to people. It is estimated that more than 80 % of available revenue is spent on recurrent expenditure, which puts spending on the increase and leaves only 5 % – 15 % of total revenue for capital expenditure.

cases, people who wish to pay go to one of the revenue offices to settle their bills. Usually, bills are only paid if the client needs continued service or if payment is made a condition for receiving some other service. In other words, what is needed to generate revenue is a system of mutual reinforcement, based on citizen participation and cooperation.

At present, no penalties or sanctions are levied for refusal to pay for services. The markets, which should have been substantial sources of revenue for IUSC, have not been tapped, for lack of a suitable machinery to determine and collect levies. Revenue from waste collection is, therefore, very low, estimated at only 80 000 NGN in all five local governments in 1993, compared with a total expenditure on solid-waste management of 11 million NGN. This revenue increased to 0.2 million NGN in 1994. But this is a pittance compared with current expenditures, which are estimated at 70 million NGN/year.

Capital costs have continued to rise and have become prohibitive. The capital investments for civil works and equipment in 1988, according to Haskoning and Kosandem Associates (1994), were at an estimated 20.8 million USD (or 94 million NGN at the 1988 exchange rate of 4.50 NGN/USD). At the 1995 exchange rate of 82.00 NGN/USD, disregarding the additional waste-collection needs resulting from the continued growth of the city, the cost would be about 1.7 billion NGN. As a matter of fact, Obadina (1995) put the total capital-investment needs at about 5.0 billion NGN, which is clearly beyond the capacity of the management authorities.

PROBLEMS WITH TECHNOLOGY AND INFRASTRUCTURE

Lack of good governance is also reflected in various technical and infrastructural problems, particularly if the equipment is unavailable in the desired quantities and the existing ones are difficult to maintain. As earlier noted, in 1994 only 57 out of the 93 pieces of available equipment were working. At the time of the study, only about one-third of the 43 pieces of equipment were working. Although the IUSC has a central workshop for vehicle maintenance, the facilities are very limited. Operational and nonoperational vehicles are parked at the workshop, which gives it an untidy appearance and severely hampers operations. The main maintenance problems are

- Insufficient funds for maintenance in general but particularly for the procurement of essential spare parts, as some are not locally available;

- Insufficient facilities at the workshop;

- Poor condition of the access roads at the workshop (also at the disposal site);

- Short-comings in the management of maintenance procedures; and

- Problems with maintenance and procurement of spare parts because equipment is sourced from various manufacturers.

However, the officials at the IUSC and the EPC were convinced that the maintenance problems could be solved with adequate funds. Nonetheless, it needs to be stressed that these problems remain crippling, mainly because of the wrong approach taken to the governance of waste management. As the United Nations Centre for Human Settlements (Habitat) (UNCHS 1989, p. 14) pointed out, many municipalities see solid-waste management as a problem of equipment, that is, how to obtain and maintain sophisticated equipment when

> *waste management systems which include community participation and do not require high technology and inappropriate machinery might prove to be sustainable at the community level, since income-generating waste-management systems can be maintained by low-income communities.*

LACK OF PARTICIPATION AND COOPERATION FROM THE PEOPLE

The cooperation of the people, which is a necessary ingredient of good governance, cannot always be taken for granted. On the one hand, most segments of the population believe that they should not bear any responsibility whatsoever for waste collection and disposal, as they consider it a social service and the responsibility of the local governments. On the other hand, people generally have an attitude of nonchalance toward local governments and their members. This is largely because, with the military's frequent and long interventions in governance, the councillors and chairs of local governments are appointed by the state government, rather than elected by the people, and are therefore not the true representatives of the people. In fact, residents in most parts of the city do not know who their representatives are in the local government.

A recent study by CASSAD (1994), carried out in one of the local governments, revealed that 80 % of the people interviewed (mostly people from urban elites) did not know which local-government area they belonged to; 76 % did not know the names of either the chair of the local government or the councillors representing their wards in council. The reasons they gave for this apathy, included the following:

- The local government had not been relevant to their survival;

- The members of the local government did not represent them (rather, they represented the military government that appointed them); and

- The impact of the local government had not been felt in any way (people had to source their own water through wells and boreholes, provide their own roads, and organize their own security).

For these reasons, people saw the officials as inept, inefficient, corrupt, and insufficiently committed to their welfare. They were therefore ill-disposed to cooperate with them. The fact that, despite the efforts of institutions to tackle the waste problem, the streets were still littered with refuse is taken as a measure of the ineptitude of officials and proof that they did not deserve cooperation or assistance. Apart from taxes deducted at source, under the Pay-As-You-Earn system, very rarely do people pay other forms of rates, not even property rates. This situation severely aggravates the financial problems of local governments and increases their dependence on the higher tiers of government, particularly the federal government, for their financial support.

On the other hand, local governments have made little or no effort to mobilize or educate people. In fact, because they depend heavily on allocations from the federal government, the councillors do not feel or behave as if they are accountable to the people or need their support or cooperation. Realizing the insecurity of their tenure, they aspire to please nobody but themselves and those who put them in office. As a result, even the community-based associations, such as landlord–tenants associations, are left out completely, although they play crucial roles in other areas of development, such as the provision of infrastructure and support for security agents. These associations could be made to play even greater roles in waste management. Many such CBOs have donated vehicles for police crime-prevention and patrol operations and, with adequate information, education, consultation, and mobilization, could do the same for waste management.

93

Thus, the lack of participation from people's organizations in the governance of waste management in Ibadan has had the following effects:

- Lack of confidence in the activities of government;

- Apathy and a nonchalant attitude toward government programs;

- Muddled activities of government and lack of accountability of government functionaries;

- Insensitivity and unresponsiveness of government to the needs and aspirations of the people;

- Citizens' lack of a sense of belonging in the operations of government; and

- Absence of useful feedback that would enhance governance.

TOWARD THE IMPROVEMENT OF THE GOVERNANCE OF WASTE MANAGEMENT

Our discussion so far has revealed that a lack of good governance is at the root of most urban-management problems, particularly those of waste management. The existing system of waste-management governance in Ibadan exhibits the following deficiencies:

- It is unrepresentative and undemocratic. The current rulers are appointed or selected by the military dictatorship, rather than elected by the people. It cannot therefore be held accountable for its actions through institutionalized procedures and processes, such as elections.

- It is exclusive and discriminatory. Because the rulers are not elected, they are not in a position to promote other stakeholders' interests through competition, pressure, negotiation, and conflict resolution. Like the military, which put them in power, they strive to monopolize their restricted power to the exclusion of others. Other stakeholders reciprocate by refusing to give them cooperation or trust. The organic and symbiotic relationship needed between the rulers and the ruled is therefore lacking.

94

- Most of the rulers lack the capacity to rule; that is, they are unable to seek or find ways to resolve people's problems. Consequently, the rulers lack legitimacy and relevance.

- The rules and regulations that should determine the relationships between institutions are often lacking, and where they exist, they are ill-defined and flouted with impunity. This leads to conflicts or an apathy that often promotes inefficiency, ineffectiveness, and corruption.

There is therefore a need to redress this situation and to put good governance in place. The most important way to do this would be to accelerate the ongoing democratization process. It is therefore hoped that the current pressure being mounted by the international community and prodemocracy groups, among others, will hasten the return of full democracy in Nigeria. However, in view of the long period of military intervention in governance, there is also an urgent need to reawaken the people's commitment to democracy. This can be achieved through

- Cultivation of a new political culture that emphasizes commitment, honesty, dedication to duty, and service to humanity;

- Education of the people on the need to participate fully in the electoral processes and show more interest in the ways their elected representatives govern; and

- Putting in place appropriate mechanisms to ensure that high-quality leaders are elected and installed for purposeful government.

To further enhance the quality of governance, there is also a
need to consider the following areas of revenue mobilization:

- Self-governance and financial autonomy of urban centres
  might be increased. In many countries, revenue derived
  from property taxes constitutes a major component of the
  internally generated revenue of urban governments, but
  Nigeria has only scratched the surface of this source of
  revenue. There is need to review current practices and
  achievements and set up an appropriate machinery to
  mobilize revenues from property tax.

95

- In some developed countries, a waste-management tax is
  making it possible to achieve a cost-recovery level of 90 %
  in waste-management operations. At present, in Nigeria,
  cost recovery is almost nil and therefore this practice
  should be emulated for better revenue generation. The legislation for this would include appropriate sanctions for
  default. Happily, surveys revealed that people in Ibadan
  would be willing to pay if the services were improved.

- Present methods used by the waste-management services
  for collecting stipulated rates, even from institutional
  clients, are by and large ineffective and inefficient. A system for collection of rates that depends on the goodwill of
  customers cannot work in Nigeria, where people tend to
  cut corners. The rate-collection machinery should therefore be overhauled. In addition, a workable mechanism
  should be put in place to impose and collect levies from the
  markets, as they generate a substantial portion of the solid
  waste.

- Doubtless, the local-government contributions (particularly financial) to waste management would grow if an
  acceptable level of efficiency was achieved. To do this,
  local governments need to strengthen their revenue base,
  largely by emphasizing their internal revenue-generating
  capabilities, particularly the collection mechanisms. In
  addition, it is necessary to emphasize again the fact that
  urban government is largely intergovernmental, involving
  many lateral and vertical relations between different governments. The design of a system to collect rates should be

based on consultation and negotiations among these governments and between the government and the governed.

Another major step in improving governance of waste management would be changing the present lukewarm attitude of the majority of the population toward waste-disposal activities. Increased cooperation and participation from the populace, particularly at the community level, would have positive impacts, such as

- Reduced capital and operating costs;

- Adoption of appropriate (small-scale) technology;

- Reduction in the levels of unemployment in the communities;

- Reduction in the quantity of wastes to be transported and disposed of through a system of thorough sorting and recycling;

- Increased revenues as a result of property monitoring;

- Protection of the environment through prevention of flooding and air pollution;

- Enhanced property values; and

- Greater cleanliness and a generally improved level of sanitation and health in the city.

Increased participation from people and communities can be achieved in the following ways:

- Education campaigns on sanitation and solid-waste management can be developed. Such campaigns could be undertaken by the state and local governments. Also, generous allocations have to be made for this in the improved budgets of the institution responsible for waste collection and disposal. The people have to be informed on how waste is to be collected, the ways it is to be stored and delivered to the collection points, and other responsibilities and benefits. In addition, they should be properly educated in the inherent dangers of inadequate attention to waste removal and disposal — unclean environment, flies, air pollution, diseases, etc.

- The level of consultation can be increased to obtain people's input on various plans and projects concerned with environmental management. Notable citizens and community leaders should be given places on the Board of Waste Management Authorities.

- NGOs should be more involved in the planning and execution of solid-waste disposal.

Our study revealed that one of the problems of governance in Ibadan's waste-management system is the governed's disdain for, and lack of confidence, in the governors, particularly those at the local-government level. Therefore, a more responsive and responsible administrative structure is needed at the local-government level, in terms of resources, personnel, and monitoring of performance. Such an administrative structure should strive to

- Establish and improve budgetary control and proper accountability;

- Discourage the present almost total dependence on external sources of revenue;

- Emphasize institutional capacity-building among personnel; and

- Recruit highly competent technical staff of proven integrity, who can be made accountable and responsible for responding to the needs of the governed.

We have also observed that a major impediment to good governance in Nigeria is the fragmentation of governance, that is, the disposition of various tiers and agencies of government to pursue their various programs and projects with little or no collaboration with others. This has resulted in the confusion, collision, and inconsistencies observed in waste management. To rectify this situation requires a holistic view of planning, including the planning of waste management. All types of land-use activities — housing, transportation, marketing, water supply, waste generation and disposal, etc. — should be regarded as subsystems of a larger planning system, each impacting on the others. It is desirable, therefore, to establish a central planning institution to coordinate and monitor developments in these various areas of land use.

The level of private-sector involvement in waste management has been too low and inconsistent and has, in fact, been on the wane in recent times. Activities of this sector are confined to the newer, well laid out zones of the city, and efforts have been hampered by many factors, such as lack of equipment, poor financing, lack of cooperation within the sector, inconsistencies of government policies, and an absence of a legal and operational framework for private-sector operations. Yet, given the high premium placed on privatization by the structural-adjustment program, one expects a higher level of private-sector involvement. In addition, studies have revealed that private-sector agencies are more efficient than government agencies in the areas in which they both operate. Consequently, efforts should be made to ensure greater private-sector participation. An operational and legal framework, including zoning, should be developed. Incentives should be introduced to encourage the private sector to move into the older parts of the city. Regular training and other capacity-building mechanisms should be put in place. The private firms should come together to share expertise, experience, and facilities to enhance their individual operational capabilities.

Waste recycling is a neglected aspect of waste management. Yet, wastes are known to contain a high proportion of recyclable materials, such as paper, glass, rags, plastics, and metals. The proportion of these materials varies from 35.6% in Mokola to 41.3% in the GRAs, 46.4% in the traditional core areas, and 48.0% at Bodija. Ideally, a significant proportion of these materials should be salvaged at the household level. But because wastes are not sorted out at source, a large proportion is lost because they are so contaminated by the time they reach the dumps that scavengers have difficulty retrieving them. To promote recycling, therefore, it is necessary to

- Promote the segregation of waste materials at source (that is, the household level);

- Streamline the operations of the scavengers, through proper training, upgrading of techniques, and the requisite health-protection mechanisms;

- Promote formalized recycling of waste materials by such modern devices as composting and generation of methane gas through anaerobic decomposition. This would require the cooperation of researchers, the private sector, and the various tiers of government.

The federal government has several policies and programs to monitor and protect the environment, and some of its laws relate to the disposal of industrial wastes. But it is well known that the government, like many other African governments, is high on policies and programs and short on implementation. This trend should be halted. The federal government should strengthen its agencies, particularly FEPA, to meet their obligations more effectively, especially their enforcement of laws on industrial-waste management.

99

Finally, a new and more workable institutional framework is needed for solid-waste management. At present, the relationship between the local governments and the IUSC is too fluid and affected by the instability of the whole political situation in the country; therefore, the IUSC is ill-equipped, both statutorily and in terms of the requisite inputs, to meet the challenges of the future. The Board of Directors administering the IUSC is also too narrow and insufficiently committed to achieving the goals. Although we are aware that an omnibus management authority for waste management is in the pipeline, care must be taken to ensure that it meets the following acid tests of good governance:

- Greater participation of the populace should be achieved, particularly at the community level, through mobilization and education. The existing CBOs could be used or new ones formed specifically for waste management. They should be involved in all deliberations and activities connected with all aspects of waste management in the communities.

- Economic sustainability of operations is important, particularly relating to managerial, technical, and financial aspects. This can be achieved by emphasizing cost recovery of operations and putting in place inexpensive, affordable, and appropriate technology. For instance, in transportation within the vicinity, greater use should be made of carts and wheel barrows, instead of fuelled vehicles, whereas city-wide transportation of refuse should emphasize the use of rolled-up trucks or ordinary tipper vehicles for compactor trucks.

- Greater efficiency of operations is therefore needed to substantially increase the present level of waste collection, which is estimated at less than 10%.

- A high level of recovery and reuse is needed. This should start at the household level.

- A greater portion of the activities connected with waste management should be privatized.

- Well-trained and motivated staff of all cadres are important.

- All people involved in solid-waste management should have a high level of accountability.

- Although emphasis should be on a higher level of revenue from operations, efforts should be made to ensure that the rates are affordable to users.

- The authority should not act in isolation but in concert with other agents of development.

At the root of these structural changes lies good governance. The institutionalization of good governance hinges on democratization and participation. These processes will bridge the existing gulf between the rulers and the ruled and the attendant lack of trust, interdependence, reciprocity, responsiveness, and accountability in governance. Therefore, as efforts are made nationally and internationally to ensure that the country is speedily returned to democracy and that the right people are put in positions of power, the people themselves must be reminded that they will have to demand and obtain power over their own affairs through active participation.

Chapter 4

DAR ES SALAAM, TANZANIA

J.M. Lusugga Kironde

INTRODUCTION

Africa is currently undergoing rapid change. In most African countries, a major population-redistribution process is occurring as a result of rapid urbanization at a time when the economic performance of these countries is generally poor. Besieged by a plethora of problems, urban authorities are generally seen as incapable of dealing with the problems of rapid urbanization. One major area in which urban authorities appear to have failed to fulfil their duties is waste management. All African countries have laws requiring urban authorities to manage waste. Yet, in most urban areas, only a fraction of the waste generated daily is collected and safely disposed of by the authorities. Collection of solid waste is usually confined to the city centre and high-income neighbour-hoods, and even there the service is usually irregular. Most parts of the city never benefit from public solid-waste disposal. Only a tiny fraction of urban households or firms are connected to a sewer net-work or to local septic tanks, and even for these households and firms, emptying or treatment services hardly exist. Industrial waste is usually disposed of, untreated, into the environment.

Consequently, most urban residents and operators have to bury or burn their waste or dispose of it haphazardly. Common fea-tures of African urban areas are stinking heaps of uncollected waste; waste disposed of haphazardly by roadsides, in open spaces, or in valleys and drains; and waste water overflowing onto public lands. This situation was reflected in articles in East African news-papers in 1985 that referred to Dar es Salaam as a "garbage city" (*Sunday News* (Tanzania), 2 Nov 1985, p. 5) and a "litter city" (*African Events,* Nov 1985, pp. 3–5) and to Nairobi as a "city in a mess" (*Weekly Review* (Kenya), 25 Jan 1985, pp. 2–3).

This report looks at the whole problem of the governance of waste management in Dar es Salaam, the largest city in Tanzania. The report is based on a study of various documents related to the question of waste in the city and on discussions and interviews conducted with the general public, central- and local-government officials, politicians, business people, community leaders, formal and small-scale private waste collectors, scavengers, and other individuals, groups of individuals, and institutions connected with waste management. Observations were also made throughout the city.

If waste is unmanaged or poorly managed, it becomes a dan-ger to health, a threat to the environment, a nuisance, an eroding factor in civic morals, and possibly a major social problem. Thus, waste management is an important issue of urban governance. It involves the success or failure of the authorities to deal with this waste, and the response of society to this success or failure.

This report is divided into four sections. The first provides the theoretical framework. The second analyzes the institutional framework for urban-waste management. The third is an evalua-tion of the efficiency and effectiveness of the combinations of part-nerships for waste management in Dar es Salaam, and the fourth gives policy options and recommendations.

THE THEORETICAL FRAMEWORK:
THE CONCEPT OF GOVERNANCE AND ITS
RELEVANCE TO URBAN-WASTE MANAGEMENT

AN OVERVIEW OF THE CONCEPT OF GOVERNANCE

The notion of governance in everyday language refers broadly to
the manner in which a government or state governs the territory
and people under its jurisdiction. However, the current notion of
governance transcends this traditional sense and sees governance   103
as the task of running not only the government but any other public entity. Landell-Mills and Serageldin (1991, p. 14) referred to
governance as

> *the exercise of political power to manage a nation's affairs. ... It*
> *encompasses the state's institutional and structural arrange-*
> *ments, decision-making processes, and implementation capacity,*
> *and the relationship between government officials and the public.*

Although governance so broadly defined clearly covers all aspects
of the complex and myriad relations between a government and a
people, this definition still fails to highlight another aspect of governance, the role of civil society. The current conceptualization of
governance sees it as encompassing the totality of the frameworks
and processes for exercising state powers through official institutions and procedures, the relation between the exercise of these
powers and society at large, and the organizations a society sets up
to respond to the state and promote society's interests. This report
uses Bratton and Rothchild's (1992) concept of governance, a rela-
tional concept emphasizing the nature of the interactions between
the state and the social actors and those among the social actors.

Bratton and van de Walle (1992) argued that the prominence
of the question of governance in recent years is due to a multitude
of factors, including a backdrop of economic malaise; indignation
over internal repression, corruption, and austerity; resentment of
the state's unresponsiveness to popular demands; the collapse of
the communist regimes in Europe; and various donor pressures for
political reform (see also Bratton and Rothchild 1992). In part, the
desire for openness and accountability is reinforced by a new
awareness of the linkages between economic development and
democratic processes (Mbembe 1989). This could be of crucial
importance to urban governance in African cities, given the multi-
plicity of operators on the urban scene, including actors of the civil

society who make urban life tick but whose efforts and contributions are often ignored or even impeded by the state.

At the risk of oversimplification, it is possible to see urban governance at a subnational level in terms of a triadic relationship among central government, including national institutions; local government; and civil society. Civil society includes the private sector, nongovernmental organizations (NGOs), and community-based organizations (CBOs).

104

THE CONCEPTS OF THE STATE AND CIVIL SOCIETY

There is considerable literature and debate on the concepts of the state and civil society, on how the two are related, and how the roles of civil society's constituent groups in democratization should be assessed. Although it is known that state power exists outside government, the state is taken in this report in the sense of central and local governments and public institutions, including political parties.

Chazan (1992) defined *civil society* as that part of society that interacts with the state. This view, however, is considered to be too restrictive, as many associations and groups are informal in character and do not strive directly to influence the state, but they are important in the whole issue of governance. Barkan et al. (1991) saw civil society as comprising those intermediary and autonomous organizations that function and sometimes flourish in the space between the state and the household. In the same vein, Starr (1990) argued that *civil society* refers to a social space distinct from government and that the government is but one of several institutions coexisting in a pluralist social fabric. With a slight reservation, a definition appropriate for this report is the one used by Weigle and Butterfield (1992, p. 1):

> *The independent self organisation of society, the constituent parts of which voluntarily engage in public activity to pursue individual, group, or national interests within the context of a legally defined state–society relationship.*

The reservation is that the status of the civil society and its relationship with the state need not be legally defined or even recognized by the state.

Observers of urban governance (that is, the triadic relationship of central government, local government, and civil society) in

Africa have shown concern with the predominance of central over local authorities. This means that local governments are highly dependent on and controlled by central governments (Stren 1992), particularly in the areas of access to resources and political manoeuvrability.

Furthermore, the relationship between the state and civil society has been an uneasy one, with civil society having gained in importance to some extent as a result of the failure of the state to perform its role. Partly as a result of the failure of the public authorities to perform their duties, alternative systems of urban management, embedded in or part of civil society, have emerged or gained in importance, but with little encouragement from the authorities. The central and local governments show a lack of democracy, transparency, accountability, and cooperation with the public in their operations and processes and in their relationship with civil society. Areas of the failure of the authorities include infrastructure investment and maintenance, provision of services, provision of shelter and land for development, management of the urban economy, and management of the environment (Stren and White 1989). The problem of solid-, liquid-, and industrial-waste management has been a major manifestation of this failure.

105

URBAN-WASTE MANAGEMENT IN A GOVERNANCE PERSPECTIVE

Some definitions

This report concentrates on solid, liquid, and industrial waste. Waste management refers to the storage, collection, transfer, recycling, and final disposal of waste. Solid waste is taken to include refuse from households, nonhazardous solid (not sludge or semisolid) waste from industrial and commercial establishments, refuse from institutions (including nonpathogenic waste from hospitals), market waste, yard waste, and street sweepings. Liquid waste includes nonhazardous foul water and sewage generated by urban households and commercial and industrial establishments. Industrial waste is taken here to comprise liquid or solid waste of a hazardous nature produced by commercial and industrial establishments, including pathogenic waste from hospitals.

The public-good characteristics of urban-waste management

Waste management has importance in a governance perspective. High concentrations of population and economic activity in urban areas means that waste generated cannot be disposed of effectively on an individual basis. Waste has public-good characteristics because it can be disposed of on public or private land and thus cause a nuisance or become an environmental or health hazard affecting society, although the private households and firms that generate waste may consider themselves to have done their duty by removing waste from their private domain. Waste management benefits the whole community, and any resident can enjoy the benefit of the service without diminishing anyone else's benefit. Thus, waste management stands squarely in the public domain as a public good, and therefore citizens expect the governments responsible for waste management to act and keep the environment clean. Here, the divisions of power, responsibilities, and resources between levels of government and the relationships between levels of government and between these levels of government and civil society become important. The success of the authorities in waste management (as well as in other public services) hinges on the availability of resources and good governance, and it creates legitimacy for the state in the eyes of the public. Failure creates hostility and distances the public from the state. This has important implications for resource generation, democracy, transparency, and accountability.

ASPECTS OF URBAN GOVERNANCE IN TANZANIA

The question of waste management is closely tied to the evolution of local government in Tanzania, and this issue has shaped the triadic relationship of central government, local government, and civil society. The evolution of local government in Tanzania can be divided into four phases: the pre-local-government era (that is, before 1949), the predecentralization era (1949–71), the decentralization era (1971–82), and the postdecentralization era (since 1982).

The pre-local-government era (before 1949)

Up to 1946, Tanzania had no local governments in the modern sense. Power was concentrated in the central government and was shared distantly with native authorities. Major urban areas like Dar es Salaam were managed by township authorities, appointed by the governor under the *Township Ordinance* of 1920 and funded directly by the central government. The *Township Ordinance* gave the governor powers to declare an area a township and to make rules for the health, order, and good government of the townships. Soon after the enactment of the *Township Ordinance*, Dar es Salaam and another 29 settlements in Tanganyika were declared to be townships.

In the same year, *Sanitary Rules for the Township of Dar es Salaam* was published, and these rules became effective from 1 September 1920. These gave the Medical Officer of Health powers to ensure the suppression of mosquitoes and deal with sanitary nuisances and insanitary premises (Government Notice No. 39 of 5/8/1920). These rules were later incorporated into the Township Rules made under the *Township Ordinance* of 1920. They are still used by urban authorities to deal with urban waste, despite the repeal of the *Township Ordinance.*

The colonial system of urban management was based on racial segregation. Key public urban services were concentrated in areas set aside for Europeans, whereas areas set aside for Africans received the least service (Kironde 1995). The colonial government strictly controlled the settlement of urban areas, which enabled it to exercise a measure of effective control over urban development, including the provision of services.

Up to the late 1950s, urban management hinged on the issue of public health. Medical officers of health were prominent in urban management. The early Executive Officer of the Dar es Salaam Township Authority, for example, from 1923 to 1930, was a doctor of medicine who also served prominently on the Central Town Planning and Building Committee. This was an advisory body set up to consider most town-development proposals and issues related to urban management, and its recommendations were usually accepted. Medical considerations were usually put forward to justify racial-segregation policies, changes of township boundaries, land-reclamation and drainage schemes, land servicing, differentiated land-use schemes, building regulations, etc.

The predecentralization era (1949–71)

By 1946, the agitation for local-authority status for Dar es Salaam that had been going on since the 1930s was finally translated into the *Municipalities Ordinance*. The central government enacted this legislation with Dar es Salaam in mind and used it to transfer many central-government powers and responsibilities of urban management to the municipal council of Dar es Salaam, which came into existence in 1949. These included powers for solid-waste management and for undertaking and charging for sewerage and other sanitary services.

Lower tiers of local government — that is, town councils, county councils, and district councils — could be formed under the *Local Government Ordinance* of 1953, which was superseded by the *Local Government (District Authorities) Act* of 1982 for rural authorities and the *Local Government (Urban Authorities) Act* of 1982 for urban authorities. Like the municipal council, these authorities were given powers to raise revenue, to make bylaws, and to deal with many matters of local governance, including waste management. At the time of Independence, in 1961, Tanzania had 11 urban councils, but their number grew to 15 by the time of decentralization, in 1971.

Urban authorities of the 1960s had three major problems (Dryden 1968):

- The elected councillors were for the most part ill-equipped to shoulder their responsibilities (in general, they were poorly educated, had little knowledge of the purpose and practice of local government, and were uncertain of their roles as councillors within the system);

- The quality of local-authority employees was in general poor; and

- Local authorities lacked adequate finances to improve and expand the services for which they were responsible.

Besides, corruption and misuse of funds were evident in many councils.

In 1965, Tanzania adopted a one-party political system. The party became very strong and influenced all spheres of life. Local authorities were integrated into the national-party apparatus. All urban-government councillors had to be members of the party. The posts of elected mayor, for municipal councils, and chair, for town councils, were abolished, and the District Party Chair took over their authorities. With such changes, urban councils continued to operate under the guidance and general supervision of the central government through the Ministry of Local Government.

Although local governments were clearly having problems, the central government did little to strengthen them and, if anything, took some steps that undermined local governments. For example, in 1969, for reasons of political expediency, the central government abolished the poll tax, which had been a major source of revenue for local governments. In the light of the continued weaknesses of local governments, the central government was only too glad see them abolished in 1971.

109

The decentralization era (1971–82)

A major change in local administration took place in 1971 with the adoption of a policy of decentralization. What this meant, however, was the abolition of all local governments between 1972 and 1974 and their replacement by central authority.

Essentially, the stated intention of decentralization was to transfer some of the central government's administrative and financial authority to the regions and districts. Although the stated aims of decentralization were to give power to the people, speed up decision-making, and bring about rapid development by stimulating grassroots participation in decision-making and planning, all observers agree that the major achievement of decentralization was to take power away from the people and to concentrate it in the central government. The decentralization policy is largely regarded as having failed for two main reasons:

- Power was usurped by the central-government bureaucracy at the district and regional levels (unlike local authorities, this bureaucracy was accountable, not to the people, but to the central government, and local areas controlled neither the personnel nor the funds they were allocated); and

- Although one of the original goals of decentralization was economic development through greater managerial efficiency, this goal was not achieved, as people felt alienated from the system.

During the decentralization period, the treasury funded the entire budget of urban councils. Nevertheless, major deterioration occurred in urban services and infrastructure. Services like water, power supply, sewage disposal, refuse collection, road and drain provision and maintenance, land-use regulation, fire protection, and malaria control deteriorated badly, and the public raised an outcry over worsening urban conditions. This deterioration was a result of the destruction of existing administrative arrangements, the replacement of experienced human resources in local service by inexperienced people from the central government, and a heavy bias against urban areas in government budgetary allocations (Mbago 1985; Kulaba 1989).

Although it is possible that undue emphasis is put on the deleterious effects of the decentralization policy on urban management (as factors like the poor national economic situation also played a role), decentralization doubtless made a bad situation worse. In 1976, the central government was already showing concern over the deterioration of urban conditions and set up a committee to study the situation and give recommendations. As a result of the committee's recommendations, the local authorities were restored, beginning with Dar es Salaam, under interim legislation in 1978. Permanent legislation restored this and the rest of the councils in 1982.

It has been observed, however, that the restoration of local governments was done hastily, without any clear knowledge of what went wrong earlier with these authorities and with little public debate on the issue. Moreover, restoration was not followed by policies to strengthen urban governments, such as allowing them more autonomy to enhance their revenue-raising capacities.

The decentralization policy promoted the central government's tendency to centralize its authority, and these effects still linger, despite the restoration of local government.

The postdecentralization era (since 1982)

The Constitution of Tanzania stipulates that the national government must establish local-government authorities at all levels, in accordance with laws passed by Parliament. It further stipulates that the primary objective of local government is to devolve power to the people. The Constitution requires all authorities to involve the people in development activities, to provide local-government services, to maintain law and order, and to strengthen democracy.

The current legislation enabling the formation of urban governments and control of their operations is the *Local Government (Urban Authorities) Act* of 1982. According to this law, every urban authority is governed by a council made up of elected councillors, local members of Parliament, and five or six members nominated by the Minister for Local Government. Urban authorities are classified as town, municipal, and city councils. Town councils are headed by a chair, and municipal or city councils are headed by mayors. Both chairs and mayors are elected from among the councillors. Urban authorities govern through standing committees, which are made up of councillors and a number of officials. Committees set up policy and sanction and evaluate implementation. Besides committees, councils have departments. These are usually of a technical nature and are part of the administrative setup of the council. They are made up of technical and administrative staff. Most urban councils in Tanzania have at least seven committees, that is, Administration and Finance, Health and Social Welfare, Education and Culture, Works and Communication, Town/Urban Planning, Trade and Economic Planning, and Human Resources Deployment.

At the operational level, the work of the council is carried out under the guidance of a city director, appointed by the country's president. The city director is the chief executive of the council and is personally accountable for its use of funds. The heads of the various departments form the management team of each urban authority, which is chaired by a director. The relationships between councils and city directors has not been smooth in many urban areas, particularly with the chair or mayors usurping the powers of the city directors and making themselves the chief executives of the councils and with councillors usurping powers of officials. In Dar es Salaam, this sour relationship has resulted into a high turnover of directors: between 1978 and 1994, Dar es Salaam changed city directors 10 times, giving an average tenure of 1.5 years. This has denied Dar es Salaam the continuity in leadership needed to build a stable management tradition.

For administrative purposes, each urban area is an urban district (except Dar es Salaam, which is a both a city and a region and is divided into three districts). An urban district is a part of a larger political district that normally also has a rural component. It is also an electoral constituency with an elected member of Parliament. The district commissioner is the political head of the political district. The urban council is responsible for the "urban area proper," again except in Dar es Salaam, where the council deals with the whole region (including rural wards). The district commissioner is responsible for the administration, planning, and development of villages and the suburban areas of the district. This situation has led to some confusion, and many times the roles of the district commissioners, the regional commissioner, and the local authorities overlap and sometimes conflict. This has been the case particularly in Dar es Salaam.

Currently, Tanzania has 19 urban areas with local authority status, that is, 9 town councils, 9 municipalities, and 1 city council. On top of that, 66 township authorities are administered by district councils. The municipalities of Mwanza, Mbeya, and Arusha are currently seeking city status.

The central–local-government relationship and its implications for the governance of waste management

Under current legislation, the central government has a number of controls over urban authorities. The central government confers local-authority status on any urban area. The central government appoints senior personnel to run urban authorities, and the Minister for Local Government approves the urban authorities' bylaws, budgets, and proposals to tap new sources of revenue or increase existing taxes. The government also occasionally issues directives affecting urban authorities. Of crucial importance is the fact that much of the revenue of the urban authorities comes directly from the central government. Moreover, several central-government ministries and a number of national parastatals have a lot of crucial roles to play in areas under the jurisdiction of urban councils, including road construction, drainage, water and electricity supply, land-use regulations (particularly, land-use planning and land allocation), and environmental management. For example, depending on the status of the road, road construction and maintenance may be the responsibility of the Ministry of Works, the regional engineer, or the urban councils. Responsibility for drainage lies with the Ministry of Communication and Works and with the Ministry of Water, Energy and Minerals (MWEM), as well as with the councils. Water is supplied by a parastatal organization (the National Urban Water Authority [NUWA]) in Dar es Salaam and by the regional water engineer in other towns. Electricity is supplied by a national parastatal organization, and responsibility for land-use planning, allocation, and control lies with the Ministry of Lands, Housing and Urban Development (MLHUD), as well as with councils.

Several observers have decried this situation, pointing out that it denies the urban authorities the autonomy they are supposed to have and leads to confusion, conflict, and problems with coordination, control, and ultimate accountability (Kulaba 1989; Tanzania 1991).

The central–local-government relationship has important implications for the governance of urban-waste management. For example, the central government is responsible for approval of bylaws related to urban management, allocation of land for waste disposal, and a lot of the investment in infrastructure, such as drains, sewers, roads, and treatment plants, although local authorities can easily be blamed if the central government fails to perform its duties.

The problem of financing urban authorities

Two major factors influencing the performance of urban authorities are the types of revenue they can raise and the ways they spend this revenue.

The *Local Government Finances Act* of 1982 gives urban authorities powers to raise local revenue. Sources of local revenue include development levies, market dues, business licences, property taxes, road tolls, and user charges. The central government envisaged that urban authorities would depend on themselves to a large extent, except in the provision of services, in which function they acted as agents of the central government (for example, in the provision of primary education and health services). With very few exceptions, urban authorities in Tanzania have continued to rely heavily on the central government for most of their revenue. Therefore, their ability to manage urban development has depended on how much the central government can allocate to each urban authority, and this has not been much (Tanzania 1992).

Between 1981/82 and 1989/90, for example, the Dar es Salaam City Council (DCC) requested 61.350 billion TZS from the central government but received only 554.2 million TZS (that is only 9 % of the requested amount was granted) (in 1998, 665.8 Tanzanian shillings [TZS] = 1 United States dollar [USD]). Underfunding occurs even where the government is supposed to give the councils the full cost of providing services. For example, it cost 1 200 TZS/year to educate a primary-school child in 1991. The central government was supposed to fully cover this cost. Instead, it allocated to the councils only 200 TZS/year per child (Daily News 1991).

114

The position of the central government on possible efforts by urban governments to raise their own revenue has been ambiguous:

- The central government takes a long time, sometimes several years, to approve bylaws designed to empower urban councils to levy local revenues;

- Many times, the central government has approved rates much lower than those proposed by the urban governments;

- The political will has been lacking to encourage effective local taxes in general and development levies and property taxes in particular (Chaligha 1987; Mkongola 1988; Kulaba 1989; Bukurura 1991);

- The central government sometimes collects taxes that it should share with urban governments but does not give the urban authorities their share (this has been noted in the cases of land rent and road tolls);

- It has been argued that the central government takes for itself the taxes that are lucrative and easy to collect, leaving the difficult ones to local governments (Kulaba 1989); and

- The central government has encroached to some extent on types of tax, such as property tax, that are usually the reserve of local governments.

However, it has also been observed that urban authorities, including Dar es Salaam, have been lax in collecting revenue, even when they have the powers to do so, preferring to rely on government subsidies. This results both in the councils' dependence on central government and in their independence from their area residents. In fact, it is evident that councils, such as that of Dar es Salaam, prefer types of revenue that do not bring them face to face with their area residents, such as road tolls on fuel.

Further examples of DCC's finances illustrate the problem. In 1993, the DCC had a total income of 3.1 billion TZS, of which 2.1 billion TZS (66.8%) comprised subsidies. By September 1994, the DCC had an income of 2.8 billion TZS, of which 2.02 billion TZS (73.2%) comprised subsidies. In 1995, the DCC had a budget of 6.62 billion TZS, of which 4.6 billion TZS (69.1%) comprised subsidies. Thus, it can be seen that the DCC is highly dependent on central-government subsidies.

At the same time, considerable evidence indicates that the DCC does not collect its rightful share of revenue. For example, the development levy is supposed to be paid by every able-bodied person more than 18 years of age, but between 1990 and 1993, the DCC collected a low of 90.4 million TZS (in 1990) and a high of 164.5 million TZS (in 1991). If the population is taken as 2.6 million people and it is assumed that one-half of these people pay the minimum 250 TZS/year levied by the DCC, at least 325 million TZS should be raised through this levy per annum. It must be added that a levy of 250 TZS/year per person is extremely low by any standards. Another example is that of property tax. In the 4-year period 1990–93, the property taxes collected by the DCC ranged from a low of 38.5 million TZS (in 1991) to a high of 128 million TZS (in 1993). Yet, with more than 400 000 properties within its boundaries, the DCC should be able to raise at least 400 million TZS (if a conservative tax of 1 000 TZS per property is assumed). Yet another example is the taxi-registration fee. In 1993, the DCC was able to raise only 0.34 million TZS with taxi-registration fees, although 17.3 million TZS had been raised in 1991 from the same source. The majority of taxis in Dar es Salaam are unregistered and operate without a taxicab licence. It is possible to analyze other sources of revenue and to show that the DCC collects only a fraction of the possible income from the sources available. The reasons for this include inefficiency but also hinge on the lack of accountability and transparency of the DCC to the residents of Dar es Salaam.

Although revenue collection is poor, the pattern of expenditure can also be queried. It has been shown that much of the DCC's expenditure goes to salaries and nonperforming assets like motor vehicles. Thus, out of 3.1 billion TZS spent in 1993, 2.22 billion TZS (72%) was spent on personal emoluments; and out of the 4.42 billion TZS spent in 1994, 2.7 billion TZS (60.3%) went to salaries alone. Outside personal emoluments and allowances, the second highest item of expenditure within each of the DCC's committees was that of plant, vehicles, and craft. An analysis of the value of DCC's assets showed that in 1992 and 1993, 71.5 and 70.9%, respectively, of the fixed assets were accounted for by plant, vehicles, and craft. As will be shown below, performing plant and vehicles, such as those required for waste disposal, form only a small part of this. Of the 133.8 million TZS worth of fixed assets acquired in 1993, 63.9% was accounted for by plant and motor vehicles. The DCC's own funds were used to buy two Toyota™ Landcruisers[1]. The rest of the plant and vehicles, a grader and a loader, were donated by Japan.

It is also noteworthy that the Administration and Finance Committee spent 67.3 million TZS in 1993 on plant, vehicles, and craft but that on the same item of expenditure the preventive section of the Health and Social Welfare Committee, which is responsible for waste management, spent only 38 million TZS. The reverse would have been more logical. Furthermore, it is of interest to note that in 1993, councillors' allowances and transportation accounted for 115.63 million TZS. Assuming 70 councillors, this works out at 137 655 TZS/month per councillor, which is an income very few Tanzanians earn. The Minister for Local Government recently observed that the allowance budget for councillors in Dar es Salaam was greater than that allocated to the city's primary schools (*Sunday News* [Tanzania], 20 Aug 1995).

The central–urban-government relationship in Tanzania is unconducive to local autonomy, particularly in revenue collection. But urban authorities, such as the DCC, do not take full advantage of the revenue sources available to them. Their use of the available sources of revenue does not reflect any priority given to providing the necessary services. This situation adversely affects urban governance in general and waste management in particular. The

---

[1] The use of trademark product names is not intended as an endorsement of any product by IDRC or the author.

central government does not appear to be keen to remedy this problem. One outcome of this is that the central government has considered privatization as an option for the delivery of urban services, as well as considering an increase in the role of civil society in many urban-management functions.

Other problems with urban authorities in Tanzania

In addition to the problems of finances and central-government control of local governments, other problems impede good urban governance in Tanzania. Some of these are the poor quality of councillors, corruption, and citizen apathy.

Poor quality of councillors — Although the situation is changing, several observers have remarked that many councillors in urban authorities have both little income and low levels of formal education. Some are actually unemployed. Therefore, they may not be very articulate or knowledgeable about their roles as councillors.

People have said that some crafty mayors or chairs have taken advantage of this situation to buy the allegiance of councillors, thereby maximizing attendance at council meetings, for which councillors are paid a sitting allowance. The councillors therefore tend to owe their allegiance more to the councils than to the electorate. Under such circumstances, issues like waste management do not get the attention they deserve.

Corruption — Corruption is a feature of African governments. It is said to permeate to the highest echelons of government in most African countries (Harsch 1993). In Tanzania, corruption has been decried at both national- and local-government levels in recent years. According to Mwapachu (1995), corruption has taken root in Tanzania and manifests itself across the social fabric, involving the leaders and people of all walks of life.

One oft-cited definition characterizes corruption as "behaviour which deviates from the formal duties of a public role because of private-regarding ... pecuniary or status gains; or violates rules against the exercise of certain types of private-regarding influence" (Nye 1967, p. 419). Corruption encompasses outright theft, embezzlement of funds, other appropriation of state property, nepotism, favours to personal acquaintances, and abuse of public authority and position to exact payment and privileges (United Nations 1990). The extent of corruption in urban government in Tanzania is not well documented, but corruption is often cited and decried. Manifestations of corruption include embezzlement of funds, over-invoicing, dubious land-management and tender-awarding practices, exaction of payment for services rendered or for granting licences, and exaction of payment to condone malpractices.

Citizen apathy — Although urban governments perform badly and they could be accused of corruption and inefficiency, it is rather surprising that citizens are generally apathetic about urban-government issues. Few citizens take any interest in council affairs, for example, by attending council meetings, reading council minutes, or taking the councils to task. Mbago (1985) noted that the urban population has generally shown little interest in local elections. In his study of the 1983 elections in Dar es Salaam, he found that out of the 634 123 people expected to register, only 179 434 (28 %) actually did so, and only 76 319 (12 %) turned out to vote.

Similar apathy was shown during local-government elections of October 1994, despite the restoration of multipartyism. In Dar es Salaam, for example, 700 000 people (a definite underestimate) were expected to register for local elections. Only 175 638 (25.1 %) (an absolute figure, lower than that registered in 1983) did so (Maliyamkono 1995). In the majority of cases (54 %), people did not register because they did not believe that the elections would bring about any change. This point was also highlighted by Mbago (1985). The second major group (15 %) thought that elections were a waste of time (Maliyamkono 1995). It appears therefore that people have little confidence in local-government elections. Lack of interest in local elections may have greatly contributed to the election of councillors who feel that they owe their allegiance more to the councils than to the electorate and who therefore pay little attention to issues that citizens may consider pressing.

THE EMERGING CIVIL SOCIETY

Civic organizations have been an important feature of the social and economic life in Tanzanian urban areas since colonial times. Many of these organizations were based on ideas of tribal or home-town identity and of helping new urbanites to cope. These organizations were suppressed during the first decade of independence. The economic problems of the 1980s led to the resurgence of

118

home-area development associations, but an increasing number of these civil organizations are entirely urban and neighbourhood oriented. Because people identify more and more with urban areas, organizations are cropping up with the aim of addressing local issues and filling in the lacunae created by nonperforming urban authorities.

In terms of infrastructure investment and maintenance, groups have sprung up in Dar es Salaam that invest in and maintain roads and other services, for example. Civic bodies have emerged to promote and protect the interests of private bus operators and informal business owners. Other such bodies have developed to look after the environment of their areas. Some of these have benefited from association with donors and foreign NGOs (Kyessi and Sheuya 1993; Mbyopyo 1993; Byekwaso 1994).

119

The relation between councils and these emerging civil associations is lukewarm. In most instances, the DCC does not cooperate with these operators. Many of the self-help efforts lack the legal framework and technical know-how to achieve their goals, and support from the councils would be most helpful. This issue will be revisited in relation to the governance of waste management in the next section.

ANALYSIS OF THE INSTITUTIONAL ARRANGEMENTS FOR URBAN WASTE MANAGEMENT IN TANZANIA IN GENERAL AND IN DAR ES SALAAM IN PARTICULAR

THE ROLE OF THE CENTRAL GOVERNMENT AND NATIONAL INSTITUTIONS

Although waste management could be considered a local issue, the central government and national institutions play a big role and carry considerable responsibility in the whole system of urban waste management:

- The Prime Minister's Office (PMO) is the overseer of all local authorities through the Ministry of State for Local Government. The PMO approves the budgets of local governments and sees them through Parliament. The PMO approves the allocation of funds from the Treasury to local governments and handles any negotiations for external assistance. Moreover, all bylaws made by local governments must be approved by the PMO, such as bylaws to keep the environment clean or to charge various levies. The efficiency of the relationship between the PMO and urban authorities has a major effect on the governance of waste management.

- The MLHUD is responsible for urban development, housing, land policy, land-use planning, and land administration. The MLHUD is responsible for preparing or approving land-use schemes, including those concerning land required for waste management. The MLHUD handles such matters as compulsory land acquisition and grants of land rights.

- The National Planning Commission is responsible for preparing national development plans and for seeing them through Parliament. This Commission has an urban development section and formulates plans that may involve major investments, such as in infrastructure.

- The Ministry of Communications and Works has considerable powers and responsibilities for road construction and maintenance in many urban areas, including construction and maintenance of drains.

- The MWEM is responsible for both the supply of water and the overall design and construction of sewers in urban areas. It is also responsible for operating low-cost sanitation units. The Dar es Salaam Sewage and Sanitation Department (DSSD) operates in part under the MWEM.

- The Ministry of Health has overall responsibility for public health and special responsibility, though the government chemist, for analyzing hazardous waste, especially that produced by industries.

- The Ministry of Natural Resources, Tourism and Environment oversees issues related to the environment, including the prevention of pollution resulting from the indiscriminate disposal of waste.

- The Ministry of Trade and Industries (MTI) licences businesses and industries and can sue polluters.

- The Ministry of Agriculture and Livestock is responsible for and can control pesticide pollution of ground- and surface-water systems and provides technical assistance on pollution control.

- The National Environmental Management Council (NEMC), whose main role is to sensitize society on environmental issues, exerts regulation and control where necessary, advises government, and coordinates environmental issues. NEMC deals with all aspects of the environment, including control of pollution with hazardous waste.

It will be clear that the central government has a major role in urban-waste management, chiefly at the level of policy formulation, but also at the operational level. Besides, in view of the unsatisfactory situation of waste management in Dar es Salaam, the central government has had sometimes to intervene directly to clean the city. The recent major intervention was the emergency cleanup of the city carried out in 1993/94, when the central government provided contingent resources to move tonnes of accumulated waste.

THE ROLE OF THE URBAN AUTHORITIES IN WASTE MANAGEMENT

Urban councils are charged with most day-to-day duties and responsibilities in dealing with urban waste. These duties and responsibilities are spelled out in a number of pieces of legislation.

The legal framework

Solid waste — The *Local Government (Urban Authorities) Act* of 1982 gives considerable responsibility to urban authorities for waste collection and disposal. It requires urban authorities to, among other things, "remove refuse and filth from any public or private place" (s. 55(*g*)). Also, urban authorities are required to provide and maintain public dustbins and other receptacles for the temporary deposit and collection of rubbish. Section 55(*i*) provides for the prevention and abatement of public nuisances that may be injurious to public health or to good order. Urban authorities are also empowered to ensure that residents keep their premises and surroundings clean. This responsibility derives from the Township

Rules, made under the *Township Ordinance* of 1920. These rules have been retained over time and are operative under the *Local Government (Urban Authorities) Act.* To meet these responsibilities, the DCC drafted a number of bylaws relating to waste management. The most important of these are the *Dar es Salaam (Collection and Disposal of Refuse) Bye Laws* of 1993. Other related bylaws include the *Dar es Salaam City Council (Hawking and Street Trading) Amendment Bye Laws* of 1991 and the *Dar es Salaam City Council (Animals, City Area) Bye Laws* of 1990.

The Township Rules impose the following requirements:

- Rule 23 requires the occupier of any building to provide a receptacle to store refuse. Receptacles must be maintained to the satisfaction of the city inspectors. Garbage bins should be placed alongside roads for collection.

- Rule 24 empowers the DCC to require a person to remove the accumulated refuse he or she deposits anywhere.

- Rule 25 prohibits the throwing of refuse on any street or in any public area. Sanctions are a fine of up to 400 TZS or 4 months' imprisonment.

- Rule 27 requires the occupier of any plot or building to keep the surroundings free from accumulated refuse.

The *Dar es Salaam (Collection and Disposal of Refuse) Bye Laws* were passed to enable the privatization of waste disposal. They require occupiers of premises to maintain receptacles to keep waste and bind the DCC to collect and dispose of waste. Among other things, these bylaws prohibit people from causing a nuisance and throwing or depositing waste on streets or in open spaces not designated as collection points. The DCC may require an offender to remedy the situation.

However, the DCC cannot enforce these rules and bylaws and is itself unable to fulfil its own duties. Moreover, it could be argued that these rules are outdated, having been enacted during the colonial period. They do not reflect the circumstances prevailing today in urban areas.

Liquid-waste — With regard to liquid waste, the *Local Government (Urban Authorities) Act* sets the following requirements:

- Section 54(2)(*g*) requires urban councils to provide for "the disposal of all sewage from all premises and houses in its area so as to prevent injury to health";

- Section 54(2)(*i*) requires urban councils to provide for the prevention of any nuisance that may be injurious to public health;

- Section 54(2)(*k*) requires the urban councils "to make, keep, and maintain clean and in good order, all streets and sewers"; and

- The schedule made under s. 55(2) requires urban councils to prevent the pollution of water in any river, stream, watercourse, etc.

123

In Dar es Salaam, responsibilities for liquid-waste management are delegated in accordance with the DCC's *Sanitation and Service Bye Laws* to the DSSD, which is responsible for constructing, maintaining, operating, and managing collector sewers and local oxidization ponds. These bylaws define charges for individual services, like pit emptying and sewer connections. The DSSD deals with, among other things, sewerage and low-cost sanitation.

The *Public Health (Sewerage and Drainage) Ordinance* of 1955 gives local authorities powers in dealing with public sewers, drainage, and latrines in new and existing buildings.

The *Water Utilisation Act* of 1974, as amended in 1981, gives the Central Water Board and the regional water boards, created under its provisions, powers to control the pollution of water bodies through emission of effluents. In Dar es Salaam, these powers are vested in the NUWA.

Industrial waste — Most of the legislation cited above also applies to industrial waste. Other relevant legislation is as follows:

- Under the *National Industries Licensing and Registration Act* of 1967, licencing authorities have some powers to prevent environmental pollution by industries; and

- The *National Environmental Management Act* of 1983 created the NEMC and provides it with powers to monitor and regulate environmental pollution.

It will thus be clear that there is a reasonable legislative base to deal with urban-waste management. Nevertheless, much of this legislation goes unenforced, and some of it is completely out of date, especially in terms of sanctions provided to deal with offenders. Also, implementation is adversely affected by power overlaps.

Institutional setup

Solid waste — Three DCC departments have responsibility for solid-waste management: Health, Engineering, and Urban Planning (Figure 1). Immediate responsibility for solid- and liquid-waste management lies with the Health Department. This is divided into three subdepartments: Curative Services, Preventive Services, and Social Welfare Services. The Preventive Services subdepartment is further divided into five sections: Malaria Control, Cleansing, Buildings, Food and Water, and Inspectorate. The Cleansing Section is the executing body for waste (including liquid waste) collection and disposal, street sweeping, and, with the assistance of the city engineer, unblocking drains. This section is also responsible for formulating policy on solid-waste management. Nevertheless, it will be clear from the above that waste disposal is given relatively little weight in the organizational setup of the DCC, being tucked down into a section of a subdepartment of the Health and Social Welfare Department.

Each of Dar es Salaam's three districts (Kinondoni, Temeke, and Ilala) has its own day-to-day setup for solid-waste management, headed by the health officer, after whom come the foreperson, the heads, and the cleaners. All daily operations are based at site offices in the three districts. The activities of city cleansing are supervised by the Health Standing Committee, which plans, evaluates, and advises on all matters concerning health, including waste removal and disposal. To see waste removal as a health issue is perhaps to take a narrow focus, as it subsumes other aspects of waste generation and management. The concentration on cleansing does not bring into the forefront important aspects, such as waste generation and recycling. It is noteworthy that the private sector, CBOs, and the public are not included in the waste-management setup of the DCC.

The Engineering Department is responsible for matters related to vehicles, plants, and equipment, as well as purely engineering issues, such as roads leading to disposal sites. The Urban Planning Department is responsible for setting aside land for waste collection and disposal, and in these matters it must liaise with the MLHUD (Figure 2).

Any proposal from the Cleansing Section passes through various stages before it can be approved. Starting from the section itself, the proposal goes to the Health Department, then to the Health Standing Committee, the Administration and Finance

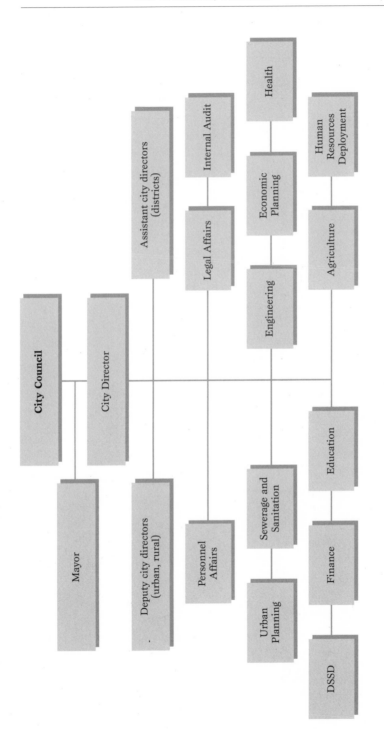

Figure 1. The structure of the Dar es Salaam City Council. Source: Dar es Salaam City Council. Note: DSSD, Dar es Salaam Sewage and Sanitation Department.

125

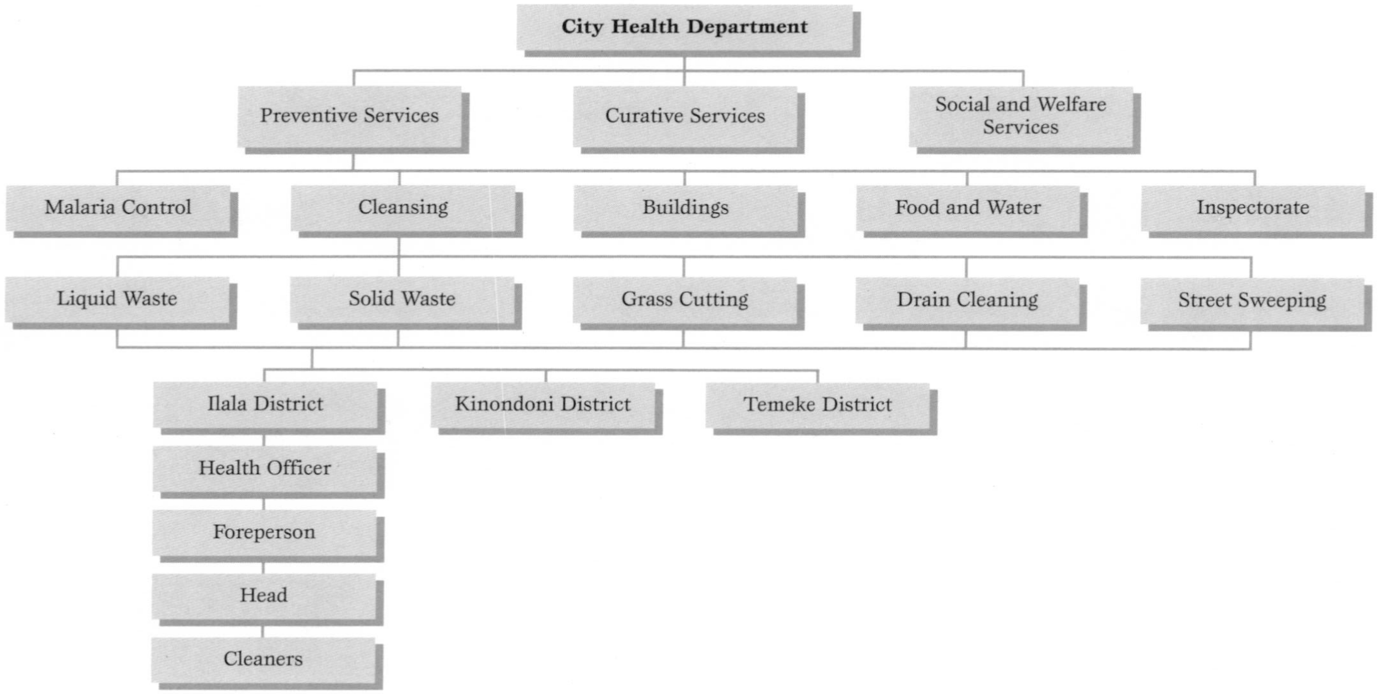

Figure 2. The waste-management structure of the Dar es Salaam Health Department. Source: Dar es Salaam City Council.

Committee, the full DCC, the Regional Development Committee, the Minister for Local Government, and then finally to Parliament. This procedure can take a year or more to complete. As well, the Cleansing Section completely lacks autonomy, even in crucial matters such as the purchase of fuel or spare parts. It does not have a separate budget, and any money that it collects goes to the DCC's general revenue.

Since mid-1994 the DCC has privatized waste collection in the city centre. This is discussed in detail later in this section.

127

Liquid waste — Two DCC departments deal with liquid waste: the semi-independent DSSD and the Health Department. The Health Department was discussed above. Because of the dearth of resources, the DSSD now accomplishes the actual day-to-day management of liquid waste.

The DSSD was established with the help of the World Bank and was, at first, located in the MLHUD. It was later transferred to the MWEM, and now it is a semiautonomous department under the DCC. The DSSD has five divisions (Figure 3):

- Sewerage, which deals with sewers and pollution control;

- Finance, which is responsible for tariff administration and cost recovery;

- Low Cost Sanitation, which deals with VIP latrine construction, cesspit-truck emptying, and health education and promotion;

- Mechanical and Electrical, which is responsible for maintenance and the mechanical and electrical parts of the sewer system; and

- Administration, which deals with general matters of administration.

As with solid waste, liquid waste is under the Cleansing Section of the Preventive Services subdepartment of the Health Department. For each of Dar es Salaam's three districts, liquid-waste management is headed by the health officer, under whose authority are the foreperson or head, the drivers, and the labourers. Powers and functions overlap considerably between the Health Department and the DSSD, particularly as the DSSD is related to the MWEM.

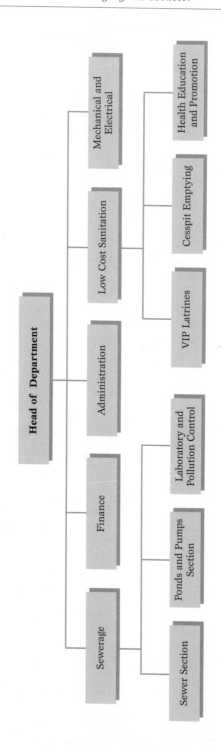

Figure 3. The structure of the Dar es Salaam Sewerage and Sanitation Department. Source: Dar es Salaam City Council.

Industrial waste — The setup described above for solid and liquid wastes applies to industrial waste as well. Nevertheless, many industries have their own private arrangements for dealing with wastes, including local treatment, discharge into water bodies, and transportation to the city landfill.

THE ROLE OF THE PRIVATE FORMAL SECTOR IN WASTE MANAGEMENT

129

Although, as pointed out above, the private sector is considered part of civil society, it is dealt with here as a separate entity.

Various firms, industries, and institutions have their own in-house arrangements for dealing with waste, including the Kariakoo Market Corporation, which handles waste from the largest market in Dar es Salaam, at Kariakoo; the University of Dar es Salaam; the Tanzania Telephone Company; the National Housing Corporation; and the National Bank of Commerce. Some private companies also offer services for solid- or liquid-waste removal to individuals, firms, and institutions, but their overall impact is still limited.

The privatization of solid-waste collection in the city centre of Dar es Salaam

Of major interest, however, is the decision by the DCC to privatize solid-waste collection in the 10 wards of the central area of the city in 1994. The privatization of solid-waste collection in Dar es Salaam is closely related to the activities of the Sustainable Dar es Salaam Project (SDP).

The SDP started its operations in Dar es Salaam under the auspices of the Habitat Sustainable Cities Programme. Its main aim is to bring together the various actors on the urban scene, including central and local governments, the private sector, various donor organizations, and the CBOs, to agree on strategies to address the environmental problems of cities.

In August 1992, the SDP organized the Dar es Salaam City Consultation on Environmental Issues. The City Consultation identified waste management as a priority environmental issue to be addressed immediately, recommending that cross-sectoral, multiinstitutional working groups be established to implement a five-point strategy of intervention. This initiative included launching an emergency cleanup of the city; privatizing the collection system;

managing disposal sites; establishing community-based collection systems; and encouraging waste recycling. To achieve this strategy, five working groups were set up: emergency cleanup; privatization; management of disposal sites; recycling; and community collection. This strategy was revised, and currently the focus is on three working groups: strengthening privatization, strengthening disposal sites, and recycling.

With this framework, the SDP was instrumental in bringing about the emergency cleanup of Dar es Salaam in 1993/94 (for which the central government and the donor community provided considerable resources) and the privatization of waste collection in the city centre in 1994. Currently, the SDP is overseeing and formulating policies related to waste management in Dar es Salaam. The SDP is an example of how important an impact a foreign institution can have on the governance of Dar es Salaam.

Privatization was made possible after passage of the *Dar es Salaam (Collection and Disposal of Refuse) Bye Laws,* in 1993, which enabled the DCC to impose refuse-collection charges (RCCs) on the occupants of premises where refuse is collected. Failure to pay RCCs may lead to a court suit. The bylaws also stipulate that no business licence is to be issued unless RCCs have been paid. A private contractor, Multinet, is responsible for street sweeping and also for the collection and transfer of solid waste from the privatized area to the landfill site.

The relationship between the private contractor and the DCC

Privatization of solid-waste management in Dar es Salaam's central area has been in operation now for more than a year, and it is possible to make some observations. It is important to remark that relations between the DCC and the private contractor have been far from cordial as envisaged when the privatization began.

In fact, the DCC appeared to be not very keen on the privatization but to accept it because external agencies proposed it and perhaps also because the donor community could be expected to support privatization with resources. The following observations would tend to support the view that the DCC was reluctant to embark on privatization:

- The DCC dillydallied in taking action to ensure that the RCCs were linked to business licences, as envisaged under the privatization proposals, and that, in this respect, there was cooperation with the MTI, and it failed to establish another system that would operate.

- The DCC failed to set up a public education campaign on the whole privatization exercise and its benefits.

- The DCC failed to take action against RCC defaulters.

- The DCC failed to act on most of the proposals put forward by the consultants to smooth the privatization exercise.

- Under the terms of the privatization contract, the DCC was supposed to vacate its depot at Temeke, which would then be occupied by Multinet, and Multinet was supposed to construct an alternative building for staff and activities displaced from Temeke. But neither the DCC nor Multinet fulfilled its part of the agreement. Their signing of the lease agreement was also delayed considerably.

- It took a long time for the DCC to sign the various agreements required under the privatization contract.

- In the privatization contract, Multinet was supposed to rent the DCC's vehicles, but it has not been paying. As of January 1994, the DCC was owed 21.8 million TZS in rent for the period from 1 July to 31 December. As well, the DCC has owed Multinet 29.7 million TZS for collecting refuse from city markets, schools, dispensaries, and the city hall itself and for other services rendered between 1 July and January 1995. Both of these claims have since more that doubled, and neither has settled. Recently, the DCC withdrew its vehicles from Multinet, leaving the contractor stranded.

- In early 1995, Multinet was facing the wrath of the income-tax people, who were threatening to seize Multinet's assets to cover its liability for sales tax, stamp duty, and withheld tax. By June, the DCC had done nothing to obtain a tax exemption or at least an amicable understanding with the tax people with respect to Multinet, although in actuality, Multinet was collecting the RCCs on behalf of the DCC.

The whole privatization contract was the subject of scrutiny by the new councillors elected in October 1994. The councillors felt that the contract had something fishy about it and that the DCC had made a bad deal. This feeling was increased by the fact that the contractor had not paid a penny to the DCC, despite the terms of the contract (*Uhuru*, 13 May 1995). This led to the suspension of various key DCC officials, including the city's solicitor, health officer, town planner, and acting city director.

132

It was envisaged that the privatization of waste management in the city centre would be a profitable venture and be extended to cover the rest of the city. However, the experience with privatization has not been very encouraging, chiefly as a result of the poor relationship between the DCC and the private contractor.

THE ROLE OF THE REST OF THE EMERGING CIVIL SOCIETY

All said and done, the DCC, together with the private contractor and the formal private sector and institutions, collects only about 10% of all the solid waste generated in the city. This section looks at the various ways society deals with its waste. It is worth mentioning that there has been no major popular protest from the people of Dar es Salaam about the authorities' failure to collect waste. Nevertheless, a study of the newspapers reveals that the press has expressed considerable concern over uncollected waste. In one local daily, the issue of accumulating waste in Dar es Salaam was highlighted at least four times in the month of July 1995 alone (see *Majira*, 3, 6, 17, and 24 Jul 1995). A visit by the new mayor of Dar es Salaam to various markets revealed that markets, although used by the public, were among the dirtiest places in the city, with accumulated waste and filthy toilets (*Nipashe*, 28 Jul 1995).

However, notable protests took place to force the DCC to move from its old dumping place in the area of the Tabata community and to abandon those earmarked for it in Kunduchi and Mbagala, as highlighted below. Otherwise, society has learned to live with the inadequacies of the formal system for collecting waste and has put in place a number of ways of dealing with the problem. Some of these are described below.

Partnerships with the DCC

The DCC and waste generators have formed a number of partnerships for waste collection and disposal. The following are examples:

- A number of business people, especially hoteliers, are known to pay the DCC some fees or to give incentives to its workers to collect their waste, as and when required.

- Traders at some markets collect money to hire waste-collecting vehicles. For example, traders at the Buguruni market formed a cooperative (Wauza Mazao Buguruni Cooperative Society). These people operate a fund they collect from themselves, which they use to hire vehicles, including those of the DCC, to collect market waste. The charge paid per trip is 6 000 TZS.

- In some parts of the city, as in the drive-in area, the DCC has set aside a place where waste can be dumped. Waste is collected from the generators by various means, including hand carts. At the dump, the DCC has stationed a skip and two employees, who put together the waste and then burn it. Occasionally, the DCC collects the skip and the waste that may have accumulated around it.

The roles of NGOs and CBOs

The role of the NGOs in waste management in Dar es Salaam is still limited, but it is growing. A number of CBOs have been established or are in the process of formation in the communities of Dar es Salaam, Buguruni, Kigogo, Kijitonyama, Tabata, Hanna Nassif, Sinza, and Changanyikeni. These CBOs mobilize local and foreign resources to address environmental problems in their areas. Areas of concern have included road and drain construction, drainage, tree planting, and waste management (Gossi 1994). The SDP is also instrumental in encouraging the formation of NGOs and CBOs. Already in the area of Hannah Nassif such civic bodies have been formed to deal with waste management.

The Tabata Development Fund CBO deserves special mention. It was formed after the successful efforts of the people of Tabata to move the city dumping site from their area and was registered as a CBO in March 1993. It has so far managed to mobilize peoples' efforts, raise resources, and encourage partnerships to

133

construct a bridge, rehabilitate local roads, plant trees, and construct storm drains. Recently, it won an award of 504 million TZS from the World Bank to help in the construction of infrastructure in the area.

It must be pointed out that a number of CBOs have clearly been formed with the aim of benefiting from external funds. Indeed, some of the better known CBOs are highly dependent on external agencies for funding and motivation, and this may not be a good thing, as such CBOs may lack sustainability if the external funding dries up. However, an increasing number of CBOs are inward looking, and their major objective is not to obtain external funds but to mobilize local resources.

The more common modes of dealing with solid waste in Dar es Salaam

A survey carried out for this study showed that the majority of urban residents have devised ways to deal with their own waste. Table 1 shows the ways in which interviewees reported dealing with their solid waste.

From Table 1 it will be clear that people do not throw solid waste haphazardly into their plots. It is either put in a pit within the plot or put somewhere outside the plot. Use of waste bins and waste bags is prevalent only in the privatized areas (Upanga and the city centre). The prevalence of waste bags in the low-income area of Buguruni is possibly a result of the activity of an environmental NGO (Plan International) in the area. With the exception of the city centre (where collection is relatively efficient), waste is overwhelmingly seen as a major irritating problem, and the services of the DCC are either bad or nonexistent. It is also clear from the data that the people of Dar es Salaam have hardly ever been involved by the DCC in issues of solid-waste management.

In many areas, solid waste is dumped on public or unused private land, including road kerbs and cemeteries, and in valleys and drains. In some areas an informal system of collection has developed; usually the collectors use handcarts to remove waste from houses or trade premises. The charge per load collected varies from 50 to 200 TZS. These collectors dispose of the solid waste in a common dumping area. Waste deposited at these informal dumping areas is commonly burned, usually by waste collectors or those living nearby. Sorting is rarely done at the households.

Table 1. Results of a field survey on aspects of urban residents' solid-waste management in selected neighbourhoods of Dar es Salaam's three districts, Dar es Salaam, 1995.

	% of respondents							
	Kinondoni			Ilala			Temeke	
Topic and response options	Manzese (n = 41)	Mnyamala (n = 40)	Upanga (n = 10)	City centre (n = 29)	Buguruni (n = 41)	Shauri Moyo (n = 39)	Mtoni (n = 42)	Tandika (n = 35)
Means of solid-waste disposal								
Thrown in plot	—	—	—	—	5	—	—	—
Thrown in pit in plot	34	33	—	—	17	26	98	23
Thrown outside plot	10	8	—	3.4	—	—	—	20
Thrown in pit outside plot	15	8	80	2.4	33	28	54	—
Put in waste bin	7	13	10	37.9	17	8	2.4	—
Put in waste bag	17	13	10	—	44	10	—	—
Other means (e.g., thrown in a distant open space)	22	35	10	58.5	10	10	—	—
Whether solid waste is a major irritating problem								
Yes	100	100	90	55	100	97	100	88.6
No	—	—	10	45	—	3	—	11.4
Rating of the DCC's solid-waste collection services								
Good	—	—	40	38	—	2	—	—
Bad	—	—	60	24	42	85	57	9
Nonexistent	100	100	—	38	59	13	43	91.4
Whether the respondent has ever been involved by the DCC in issues of solid-waste management								
Never	100	100	90	93	100	100	100	97
Ever	—	—	10	7	—	—	—	3
Willingness to pay for solid-waste collection								
Not willing to pay	37.6	17.5	10	20.7	25	15	24	34
≤99[a]	14.6	2.5	—	3.4	12	8	19	6
100–299[a]	26.8	50	20	13.8	22	36	31	40
300–999[a]	17	20	70	24.1	24	31	26	17
1 000–9 999[a]	4	10	—	10.3	17	10	—	3
≥10 000[a]	—	—	—	6.9	—	—	—	—
Sum not stated	—	—	—	20.7	—	—	—	—

Source: Field survey, July 1995.
Note: TZS, Tanzanian shilling (in 1998, 665.8 TZS = 1 United States dollar [USD]).
[a] Fee (TZS/month) that would be acceptable.

135

Informal sorting and scavenging take place. This reduces the waste and scatters it so that it more readily decomposes. Kaseva (1995) pointed out that 600 people scavenge in Dar es Salaam, but this is definitely a gross underestimation. These recyclers have no organized forum, nor do they have any relationship with the DCC. They use recyclable materials themselves or sell them to others.

Dealing with liquid waste

136   Much liquid waste is left to overflow onto common land, like roads, open spaces, and unused plots. However, a class of people, known locally as *Chura*, specializes in draining full pit latrines, usually by emptying the contents into a nearby pit, which is subsequently covered with earth. This process is known as *Kutapisha*. These people have no relationship with the DCC and operate on informal rules agreed on between themselves and their clients.

Dealing with industrial waste

Solid industrial waste is usually burned or buried on site, although some is transported to the city's dumping site. Some recycling is practiced. Liquid industrial waste is discharged through connections with the city's limited network into local oxidization ponds (many of which do not work) or, completely untreated, into local streams and drains.

Some general observations

The biggest problem with waste management in Dar es Salaam would appear to be that, although the generators remove waste from their immediate surroundings, a lot of it accumulates at dumping sites or on common grounds, with little coordinated remedial action.

The most common methods of dealing with waste have their own major problems:

- In high-density areas, no land is available to dig pits for solid waste, and no open spaces are available for draining liquid waste;

- Disposal of waste in open spaces, on common lands, or in valleys and drains is a major cause of pollution (smell, for example) and health hazards and can block natural or artificial drains, erode civic morals, and have other aesthetically offensive results;

■ People who dispose of waste indiscriminately do so in defiance of council bylaws, which prohibit the uncontrolled disposal of waste, and defying one law leads people to defy others; and

■ Indiscriminate waste disposal has occasionally led to social conflict.

137

THE POLITICS OF WASTE-MANAGEMENT ARRANGEMENTS

Historical perspective

During the colonial era, waste management, like other aspects of urban life, was conceived on the basis of racial bias. Urban infrastructure and services were concentrated in areas designated for the non-African races. These areas tended to be central-city and low-density residential areas, like Oyterbay in Dar es Salaam.

During the 1940s and 1950s, however, Tanzanian Africans agitated for better living conditions. Coupled with rapid urban growth and the prospect of independence, their protests forced the colonial government to address the question of servicing areas occupied by Africans in Dar es Salaam. The new, minimal services were concentrated in the areas planned for at that time, leaving out the growing unplanned areas.

During early independence, there was the need to modernize cities and to consolidate political power. Considerable emphasis was placed on urban infrastructure and servicing. However, the 1970s saw the centralization of political power, and Tanzania encountered economic problems. This distanced the government from the people, and the former began to lay less emphasis on urban services.

The 1980s have been years of economic crises, coupled with rapid urbanization. Dar es Salaam, for example, has grown at more than 7% per annum since the 1940s. Likewise, the urban proportion of the national population grew from 13.8% in 1978 to 27.6% in 1988. Between 1991 and 1995, the overall average growth rate was only 3.4%, but for the urban population it was 20.2%.

At least two political factors have shaped waste-management arrangements:

- Centralization of political power meant there was less sensitivity to local problems, although the central government and key politicians intervened now and then, on an ad hoc basis, to clean up the city. A major example of this was the emergency cleanup of Dar es Salaam in 1993/94. Some other interventions involved key personalities, such as the country's president and top ministers. They, however, did not go full throttle to ensure that urban authorities became serious in meeting their responsibilities.

- The tradition of cheap or free services and a lack of transparency and accountability made it politically difficult to introduce service charges, and this, together with a lack of resources, led to delivery constraints.

Waste management in Dar es Salaam is shaped less by popular political pressure than by international and national interventions and the need to avoid confrontation with the local populace. It is also shaped by the need to concentrate, at least symbolically, on politically important areas to the near total exclusion of the interests of people living in low-income areas, a level of neglect amounting sometimes to outright oppression.

International aspects of the governance of waste management

Several international interventions have occurred in various aspects of the management of Dar es Salaam. The Japanese government intervened in waste management in 1987 by financing studies on waste generation and management in Dar es Salaam and by following this up with a donation of several pieces of waste-management equipment, including tipper lorries and emptying trucks. The Italian government also intervened in 1991, with a grant of six compactor trucks. Possibly more significant is a generous international intervention with respect to the emergency cleanup of Dar es Salaam in 1993/94. This may have been because Dar es Salaam was the capital city, and many foreign diplomats stayed there. The SDP, which is trying to bring a new outlook to the governance of the city, including the privatization of waste management and the involvement of the community, is a foreign-conceived and -funded project.

In addition, as pointed out above, many CBOs are foreign motivated and funded.

The preponderance of international interventions has repercussions. It convinces the DCC that it always has a good prospect of getting the international community to intervene and that it therefore does not need to seek local solutions to the problems of urban governance. This creates a dependency syndrome, and it transforms the DCC's outlook from one of policy-making to one of policy-receiving. Also, most proposals from international agencies are usually considered uncritically, even when they could be considered inappropriate, as the following examples show.

- Even without the benefit of hindsight, hinging the success of privatization on business people paying 80 % of the RCCs a year in advance (see below) was definitely misguided, but the idea was accepted, possibly because it came from outside. Also, possibly as a result of the dependency syndrome, the DCC offers little input on the choice of technology. Whatever is offered by the donors is accepted. For example, a consultant for the SDP found (in February 1995) (MCAL 1995) that the small DCM Toyota trucks (3–7 t), procured by Multinet, were more efficient than the Isuzu or Calabresse trucks offered by the donors. They had lower loading and running costs. In fact, the Calabresse trucks donated by the Italian government were out of commission within 6 months for lack of spare parts. Even after they had been revived during the emergency cleanup of Dar es Salaam, the consultant noted that these Calabresse trucks had very high operating costs and recommended that they not be ordered again. Yet, the DCC had uncritically accepted the suggestion to buy these trucks.

- During the preparations to privatize solid-waste collection, the DCC's original acceptance of waste-collection points (where households would take their refuse for the contractor to pick up) was perhaps a result of foreign-consultant intervention, as these collection points had major disadvantages that would have been obvious to local people.

139

National political aspects of the governance of waste management

Being the seat of the central government, Dar es Salaam has generally been more favoured by government grants and subsidies than other urban areas. Although the total amount granted has only been a fraction of what the DCC wanted, it has been sufficient to insulate the DCC from any need to effectively tax its residents. Also, the central government has been less assertive in forcing the DCC to efficiently collect local revenue. This has resulted, again, in a dependency syndrome and insufficient revenue. Indeed, at critical moments, the central government has come to the rescue of Dar es Salaam with resources or even the personal intervention of key officials and politicians. For example, during the emergency cleanup, millions of shillings were poured into Dar es Salaam as a nonrecoverable grant. It is possible, moreover, that the emergency cleanup was funded with the 1994 local-government elections in mind. The ruling party originally won all the seats in the DCC. During the election campaign, public buses also ran to distant locations in Dar es Salaam as never before, and this stopped as soon as the election was over.

With such dependency, the DCC finds it much more expedient to rely on the central government for funding and to blame the same central government for not allocating sufficient resources to ensure, among other things, efficient waste management.

Local political aspects of the governance of waste management

City centre versus the rest of Dar es Salaam — Over the years, the efforts of the DCC in waste collection have been observably concentrated in the central area on the argument that this area had no alternative mode of disposing of waste. This is not entirely true. In the high-density unplanned areas, hardly any space is available to dispose of waste, yet the efforts of the DCC have never been concentrated in such areas. Ilala, where the city centre is located, is the most favoured of the three districts. Next is Kinondoni, which has the most well-off residential areas in Dar es Salaam. Temeke, considered the poorest of Dar es Salaam's three districts, usually gets the lowest preference. The central area is favoured because accumulated solid waste or uncollected liquid waste is visible there and creates a major political problem that concerns the national and foreign governments, top business enterprises, and high-income households.

Social oppression at the landfill site — Solid waste in Dar es Salaam is collected from various parts of the city and deposited at a sanitary landfill at Vingunguti, which is a low-income area. The keen concern shown for removing waste from the central area is not shown for Vingunguti, where the waste is dumped. The people of Vingunguti now suffer from fumes, smell, noise, and vibrations as garbage collected from all over the city is simply dumped in their area, rather than entering the envisaged sanitary landfill. Although it is clear that the people of Vingunguti are suffering, consultants recently proposed that the road to the dumping site (which is breaking down because of the heavy lorries using it) be strengthened to enable it to take more vehicles and that lighting be provided at the dumping site to allow dumping to be done day and night. Little consideration is shown for the people of Vingunguti. Even the income collected at the landfill site is not necessarily used to improve conditions at the site. The people of Vingunguti can thus be ignored and oppressed by the DCC because it is a low-income area and the residents lack political muscle, such as that of the people of Tabata, who stopped the DCC from depositing waste in their area.

141

Poor relationship between councillors and officials — The governance of Dar es Salaam has suffered adversely from the poor relationship between the councillors and the officials. Issues of ethnicity, corruption, and education have directly or indirectly contributed to their sour relationship. It is now a political problem. In practice, the roles of the councillors and those of the officials have been improperly defined. Councillors look on the officials' plans, suggestions, or actions with suspicion, and in some instances it is clear that the councillors have had a vendetta against the officials. The result has been a high turnover of officials. Also, in February 1995, it was noted (Kironde 1995) that all key DCC officials were acting in the counterparts of their actual positions. On the other hand, the councillors promote their personal interests in council. Key interests have hinged on land allocation and acquisition, trade, and councillors' incomes. Waste management has not been among the key issues on the minds of the councillors, and the poor relationship between councillors and officials has prevented formulation and implementation of a clear waste-management policy.

Poor relationship between the councillors and the public — It has been observed that the councillors of Dar es Salaam have very little interaction with their electorate, and many consider themselves more as employees of the council, from which they benefit from hefty allowances, than as representatives of the people (Kironde 1994). Thus, issues that may be burning in the minds of the electorate — such as lack of roads, drains, and water or overflowing waste water and uncollected solid waste — do not get the attention they deserve. With multiparty democracy, the situation may perhaps change, but in the past councillors bothered little about the needs of their electorate.

142

It may be appropriate to conclude from general observation that the DCC is afraid of its people. This results in low taxation or none at all, which in turn means low revenue and less accountability to the people.

The politics of privatization — The privatization of solid-waste management in the central area of Dar es Salaam shows all signs of the part played by politics in determining the RCCs and the areas to be privatized. The central area was privatized first, not only because of its political importance, but also because it is occupied chiefly by Aboriginals and business people. Here, the RCCs were much more likely to be accepted than in other areas. Charges were also determined so that business people paid 80 % of the expected charges, and residents in predominantly non-African areas paid as much as seven times the fees paid by residents in African areas.

The relationship between councillors and NGOs — The councillors do not seem to be any more keen on the emerging NGOs than they are on the officials. Many NGOs operate without the involvement or cooperation of the councillors. It has been suggested that the councillors see NGOs as eroding their own political position and status.

Political apathy — The electorate appear to be apathetic about what happens at the DCC. This is demonstrated in the poor voter turnout during local elections and by the electorate's failure to take action to force the councillors to respond to their needs and be transparent and accountable. Observers have wondered why non-performing councillors are elected year in and year out. Some have concluded that either the people of Dar es Salaam do not know their rights as citizens or voters are easily bribed by corrupt politicians. Legislation requires urban governments to do a number of things, including removing waste, providing public toilets, and naming streets. Nonimplementation means breaking the law, yet no action is taken by the public against nonperforming authorities. Few members of the public attend council meetings or read the DCC's minutes, although these activities are allowed by the law. It may well be that this apathy is a hangover from the time of single-party rule. It is observable, moreover, that local politics in Tanzania has generally been shunned by the more educated in society, although this may now be changing. A lot of the management of Dar es Salaam's development could greatly improve if the councillors consulted the people and tried to find ways to solve their problems.

143

Surely, undisposed waste is a major political issue, but some of the councillors we talked with were content to say that their people had their own ways of disposing of waste and that the greatest part of the blame should go to the central government, which does not allocate sufficient resources to the DCC for this.

THE ECONOMICS OF WASTE MANAGEMENT

Historical perspective

General urban management in Tanzania has not historically been based on economic considerations. The colonial government in Dar es Salaam lavished considerable services and infrastructure on low-density (that is, high-income) areas, with little consideration of cost. It paid little attention to servicing the high-density areas, which because of their high densities are cheap to service. Most services were provided either free or at subsidized rates or were not provided at all. Possible sources of revenue, such as land rent, were usually kept artificially low.

Economic considerations in waste management

An efficient waste-management service requires considerable capital and recurrent financing to, for example, purchase or maintain vehicles, lay and maintain the necessary infrastructure, pay labour, and enforce regulations (policing). In the past, public authorities attempted to institute user charges for certain aspects of waste management. For example, the DCC provides solid-waste collection free of charge to most domestic residents; a fee of 1 000 TZS per trip is charged for collection of waste from commercial, indus-trial, and business premises. Likewise, the DSSD charges a fee for connection to a sewer or for emptying pit latrines or septic tanks. Nevertheless, these charges do not usually cover the necessary costs. The DDC spent an estimated 31 million TZS on solid-waste collection in 1987/88. It collected only 222 000 TZS for this service.

In 1993, the DDC's total budget for solid-waste management amounted to around 194 million TZS, and around 150 million TZS of this was provided through a special intervention from the PMO as part of the emergency cleanup of Dar es Salaam. This did not include labour costs, budgeted separately by the DCC. It meant, however, that the DCC approved only 44 million TZS toward the fuel and maintenance costs of trucks and the landfill. These funds were insufficient to both operate the Vingunguti landfill and fuel the DCC's fleet of trucks. Thus, the DCC was only able to operate 8–10 of its fleet of 20 tipper vehicles and, at most, 1 of its compactor trucks during a single work shift. This was just one-sixth of the DCC's potential and met only a tiny fraction of the requirements.

In March 1994, it was calculated (MCAL 1994) that the DCC needed 517 million TZS/year to ensure waste collection in the cen-tral area alone and several times that to ensure collection through-out Dar es Salaam. Under existing circumstances, the DCC cannot possibly raise such an amount, as it may spend no more than 60 million TZS/year on waste management (including labour costs). As a result, the waste-management processes are unsustainable, as will be shown below in the case of vehicles.

Economic considerations also affect the choice of dumping area. Distant locations may be cheaper to run, but transportation costs will be high. Dumping in nearby locations needs to be effec-tively managed. Experience from Dar es Salaam indicates that managing a landfill to the required standards is almost impossible, chiefly as a result of lack of resources, and the DCC has used the sites earmarked for solid-waste disposal as crude dumping sites, rather than sanitary landfills. At the moment, the DCC has a major problem raising sufficient resources to manage its current landfill, let alone develop new ones.

Even with a more effective system for collecting local rev-enue, the DCC is highly unlikely to be able to raise or commit suf-ficient resources to ensure conventional waste management, that is, using the public sector to collect, transport, and dispose of all the waste. Cost recovery, user charges, or a more efficient exploitation of current revenue sources is needed because this can allow the DCC to establish a number of partnerships. Privatization, support for alternative modes of waste management, especially by small-scale operators, and public participation would appear to be other avenues for effectively managing waste in the future.

Many times, issues related to cost recovery and user charges ignite an imbroglio of controversy about whether the people, particularly those in low-income households, can afford to pay the charges. Equity is another issue. Without more reliability of data on income and expenditure, however, the issue of affordability is difficult to resolve. Various studies (Gossi 1994) have established that many households and firms pay for the collection of their waste. Many people interviewed in this study showed a willingness to pay for waste collection (see Table 1), and many said that they already paid small-scale handcart operators to remove waste from their premises. In a study of the low-income area of Hannah Nassif, Rubindamayugi and Kivaisi (1994) found that 28% of the interviewees paid waste collectors: 100 TZS was paid per trip or 50 TZS for a 15-kg load. This means that on a monthly basis, low-income people in Hannah Nassif pay more for the collection of their refuse than people pay in the better-off central parts of the city (like Kariakoo) in areas 2 and 3 (Table 2), served by the private contractor, Multinet. They pay only 150 TZS/month. The possibility of generating more money from waste management is very high.

Privatization of solid-waste management in Dar es Salaam as a feasible economic venture

In the light of the DCC's persistent failure to manage waste, the SDP came up with the idea of privatization (SDP 1995). This undertaking in Dar es Salaam illustrates the potential of the privatization of solid waste. No major plan has been developed to privatize liquid-waste management, although private operators empty septic tanks.

In the early 1990s, external consultants were hired to advise the DCC on the process of privatizing solid-waste management. The consultants calculated (MCAL 1992) that waste collection could be turned into a profitable business that could earn the DCC

145

Table 2. Monthly RCCs under the *Dar es Saalam (Collection and Disposal of Refuse) Bye Laws* of 1993, Dar es Salaam, 1993.

Type of waste and type of premises	Area 1 (10³ TZS)	Area 2 (10³ TZS)	Area 3 (10³ TZS)	All areas (10³ TZS)
Domestic refuse[a]	0.9	0.15	0.15	
Trade refuse[b]				
Every trade licence holder				
Normal trade licence	3.5	1	1	
Nguvu Kazi licence	0.3	0.2	0.15	
Hotels and guest houses (rooms)				
1–10	20	3	2.5	
11–15	30	20	10	
16–25				55
26–50				75
51–75				100
76–100				150
> 100				200
Restaurants and bars	30	15	2.5	
Shops and offices (employees)				
1–5				5
6–10				7.5
11–15				15
16–20				20
21–25				30
26–50				55
51–75				75
76–100				100
> 100				150
Construction				
Skips (7-m³ container)				10
Markets				
15-m³ container				19
7-m³ container				10

Source: *Dar es Saalam (Collection and Disposal of Refuse) Bye Laws* of 1993, Dar es Salaam City Council.

Note: Area 1, Upanga east and west, Kivukoni, Kisutu, Mchafukoge; area 2, Gerezani, Kariakoo, Jangwani; area 3, Mchikichini, Ilala. RCC, refuse-collection charge; TZS, Tanzanian shilling (in 1998, 665.8 TZS = 1 United States dollar [USD]).

[a] Payable quarterly in advance.
[b] Payable annually in advance.

considerable income and strengthen the public waste-collection service. The consultants proposed that privatization begin with the 10 central-area wards. After they were cleaned up, the service could be extended to other parts of the city. Multinet was then contracted to carry out waste collection in the city centre.

In October 1992, a draft Refuse Collection and Disposal Contract was drawn up. However, having a direct contract between the private waste collector and the DCC was seen as unworkable, owing to the financial unreliability of the DCC. The DCC envisaged cross-subsidization between high- and low-income areas. The DCC prepared draft bylaws and originally intended having the RCCs for commercial premises paid annually in advance and linked to the issuance of the business licences. For residential premises, payment was to be quarterly in advance. The DCC envisaged that, later on, the RCCs would be based on property values and linked to the payment of property rates.

147

Because the DCC was unable to run its whole fleet of vehicles, it agreed to lease eight tipper trucks and six compactor trucks to the private contractor to supplement the council's budget. The contractor also agreed to lease part of the DCC's premises for its operations, pay refuse-disposal charges (RDCs) for the use of the Vingunguti landfill site, and install a weighbridge at Vingunguti to monitor the amount of waste discharged. The DCC envisaged that as it extended privatization, it would be able to restrict its role to one of monitoring the performance of the contractors and move out of any direct involvement in solid-waste management.

It was estimated (MCAL 1994), in March 1994, that the annual costs and revenue from the privatization exercise would be as is shown in Table 3 and that these activities would realize a profit of nearly 37 million TZS.

Envisaged financing of private solid-waste collection — The bylaws that enabled privatization, the *Dar es Salaam (Collection and Disposal of Refuse) Bye Laws* of 1993 set out a schedule of RCCs for different types of waste generators (for example, domestic) and different categories of trade refuse. The charges also differed according to wards. The privatized part of the city was divided into three areas, roughly according to the perceived income levels of the inhabitants. Area 1 included the city centre and the Upanga area, chiefly occupied by Aboriginals and top business people. Areas 2 and 3 are supposed to be low-income areas occupied mainly by Africans and secondary business people. The DCC set charges for area 1 higher than those of areas 2 and 3. The RCC levels appeared to be politically motivated. It must have been conceived that households and firms in area 1 would more readily accept RCCs than those in the other two areas. In addition, the mayor of Dar es Salaam

Table 3. Expected annual costs and revenue from the privatization of solid-waste collection in Dar es Salaam city centre, March 1994.

	Amount (10^6 TZS)
Annual costs	
Collection and disposal	
Operational costs	188.4
Salaries	98.0
Capital costs	73.5
Lease of trucks	76.0
Disposal costs	56.9
Road sweeping	
200 workers at 36 000 TZS/month	129.6
Supervision, 15 %	19.4
Total costs	**641.8**
Annual revenue	
RCCs	576.0
Market wastes (18 container loads/day at 19 000 TZS)	102.6
Total revenue	**678.6**
Profit	**36.8**

Source: MCAL (1994).
Note: RCC, refuse-collection charge; TZS, Tanzanian shilling (in 1998, 665.8 TZS = 1 United States dollar [USD]).

Table 4. Rates of domestic solid-waste generation, Dar es Salaam, 1988.

	Area			
	Mtoni	Manzese	Kariakoo	Mchafukoge
Number of people per household	8.4	6.7	5.7	5.1
Monthly income per household (TZS)	2 600	3 770	2 260	6 080
Waste-generation rate (kg/day per person)	0.37	0.35	0.32	0.30[a]

Source: Haskoning and M-Konsult (1988).
Note: TZS, Tanzanian shilling (in 1998, 665.8 TZS = 1 United States dollar [USD]).
[a] Average waste-generation rate was 0.34 kg/day per person.

was also the councillor for Kariakoo ward in area 2, which may account for the very low RCCs for areas 2 and 3.

The schedule of RCCs is shown in Table 4. Because waste generators were supposed to pay the RCCs in advance, the DCC thought that this arrangement would raise sufficient revenue to enable the contractor to carry out solid-waste management without problems. The DCC was supposed to enforce the payment of the RCCs by taking any defaulters to court. In effect, however, the DCC has not met its responsibility.

Details of how the DCC determined the RCCs are unclear. But it did not base them on the cost of collecting the waste from the producers or on the amount of waste they generated. In any case, in the original proposals, waste producers were supposed to dump their waste at preestablished collection points; thus, the private contractor would not be in direct contact with the producers of the waste. Instead, the DCC based the RCCs on the type of waste producer (domestic, trade) and the location. In one sense, the DCC's determination of the RCCs was supposed to bring about a cross-subsidy between trade and domestic waste producers and between high- and low-income areas. This approach was apparently politically motivated, to get the majority of payers, that is, households, to accept the RCCs. Ease of collection, particularly from business people, was apparently another criterion.

149

Although the privatization undertaking is economically feasible, as detailed above under "The relationship between the private contractor and the DCC," it is operating under difficult conditions, emanating from the poor relationship between the contractor and the DCC. This is a clear example of bad governance.

The sociology of waste management

Observers of urban development in African cities sometimes argue that many Africans carry their rural habits to the urban areas. Some people, it is argued, may not be conscious of the need to keep their environment clean. This is a doubtful point of view. Almost all of our respondents (see Table 1) said that waste was a major nuisance. The survey therefore indicated no culture of waste.

Conclus.

Nevertheless, people seem to have become indifferent to the issue of waste. They have come to accept having to live with this waste in their environment. It only suffices for one to remove the waste from one's own backyard. Little consideration is shown for waste dumped in common areas, although the people interviewed agreed that this pollutes the environment. Many people, too, let their waste water flow onto common land, like roads, which, in many residential areas, double as playgrounds for children. This is perhaps a result of people's despairing of the DCC ever making things better.

Our study found that most people still rely on the city to solve the waste-collection problem. Most expressed the view that the DCC simply needs to have more vehicles, collect the waste more frequently, and make waste bins and bags available, as in the past. This attitude needs to be changed, and people must start to evaluate their own roles in the governance of waste management. However, in both Kariakoo and the Buguruni market, where private waste-collection systems are in place, people expressed the view that private arrangements for waste collection were the more promising solution.

Waste management involves some gender considerations. A survey carried out for this study found that moving waste from the household premises was overwhelmingly considered a female responsibility, whereas men chiefly collect waste and sort it for recycling. Such considerations may be important when it comes to formulating feasible waste-management policies.

When considering alternative waste-management methods, one must take cultural considerations into account. Rubindamayugi and Kivaisi (1994) found that there were some cultural barriers to waste sorting within households in their study area, Hannah Nassif. However, people sorted the waste at the dumping areas, and 98% of the interviewees showed a willingness to be employed in waste management.

WASTE GENERATION AND HANDLING IN DAR ES SALAAM

Solid-waste generation

Various studies have been carried out in recent years on waste generation, storage, collection, transportation, and disposal in Dar es Salaam (Haskoning and M-Konsult 1987, 1988; MCAL 1992). The *Dar es Salaam Masterplan* of 1979 (Tanzania 1979) addressed the question of waste generation and concluded that average domestic waste generation was 0.17 kg/day per person in squatter areas and 0.33 kg/day per person in planned areas. Although results differ, recent studies have tended to conclude that average domestic waste generation in Dar es Salaam ranges between 0.34 and 0.39 kg/day per person.

A survey carried out in 1993 (Ame 1993) concluded that waste generation in Dar es Salaam differed according to income groups, as follows: high-income households, 0.45 kg/day per person; medium-income households, 0.38 kg/day per person; and low-income households, 0.34 kg/day per person, with an average generation of 0.39 kg/day per person. On the other hand, Haskoning and M-Konsult (1988) found that waste generation was lowest in the high-income ward of Mchafukoge (see Table 4). This is contrary to conventional observations that poor people yield less waste than the rich. Rubindamayugi and Kivaisi (1994) found that the low-income Hannah Nassif area also had a rather high waste-generation rate of 0.605 kg/day per person. This must definitely be on the high side, accounted for by the high sand content in the waste studied. Another study carried out in the same area in the same year during the wet season found that the waste-generation rate was 0.30 kg/day per person, and this was also considered to be on the high side (Gossi 1994). What this suggests is that one should consider the data on waste generation with care.

The total daily waste generation in Dar es Salaam has been calculated variously over the years, as shown in Table 5.

One study carried out in 1992 by Manus Coffey Associates Ltd (MCAL 1992) showed that nearly 60 % of the waste generated in Dar es Salaam was, as shown in Table 6, in the category food and vegetation. Although other studies differ in detail from this, it is generally concluded that food and vegetation is the major category of waste generated, and this has been the case over a number

Table 5. Calculation of daily waste generation from various sources, Dar es Salaam, 1988–95.

	Waste (t/day)		
Waste category	Haskoning and M-Konsult (1988)	MCAL (1992)	DCC (1995)
Domestic	650	860	935
Commercial	45	50	80
Institutional	60	80	185
Market	200	200	375
Industrial			225
Street cleaning			60
Car wrecks	185	230	40
Hazardous waste			50
Construction waste			15
Hospital waste			35

Source: DCC (1995a).

of years. The DCC currently accepts the figure of 2 000 t/day as representing the total waste generated in Dar es Salaam. However, figures seem to conflict for the central area, which over the years has been the major area of concern for the authorities. In a report (DCC 1995b) to the Health and Social Welfare Committee, written in January 1995, the acting city director pointed out that the central area generated 600–800 t of waste daily. On the other hand, Mpinga (1993), assuming a population of 183 859, calculated that the domestic waste generated daily in the central area was 236 t. But a consultant, called on in March 1995 to advise on the privatization of waste management, calculated that actually 140 t/day of waste was generated in the central area (MCAL 1995), as shown in Table 7.

152

This figure appears to more realistic, but it is clear that the figures for waste generated are unreliable, and policy decisions are therefore made on the basis of uncertain data.

The record of waste management by the authorities in Dar es Salaam is very poor. Within the central area, which has been privatized, waste collection has improved considerably. Some 100 t is collected daily, but this leaves another 35–40 t uncollected. The DCC itself is supposed to collect waste from the rest of the city,

Table 6. Typical waste components,
Dar es Salaam, 1993.

Waste component	% by wet weight
Food and vegetation	59.8
Paper	8.7
Metals	2.8
Plastics	1.9
Glass	0.4
Textile	0.9
Others	25.5

Source: MCAL (1993).

Table 7. Type and quantity of waste,
Dar es Salaam's central area, 1995.

Type of waste	Quantity (t/day)
Commercial waste	46.7
Market waste	35.3
Residential waste	57.8

Source: MCAL (1995).

including markets and hospitals, but its total collection is only between 30 and 100 t/day. Other institutional and private collection services deal with about 32 t/day. This means that only about 10 % of the waste generated in Dar es Salaam is collected.

In practice, no special arrangements are made for waste storage, although in the past the city gave out dustbins. People store waste using any possible means, including paper and plastic bags, bamboo baskets, and so on. The DCC used to have specified collection points in the city, but these have become dumping grounds, and the DCC has in fact discouraged their use. Skips are provided in some places, especially markets, but these are not regularly cleared, so they are sometimes completely buried under waste. Tipper lorries transfer the waste. The DCC has arrangements to provide and manage landfills for waste disposal, but they are not as sanitary as they should be. The DCC has no policy on recycling, although the SDP is trying to encourage recycling, and there are plans to establish a biogas plant (Takagas). Informal recycling, however, is done by scavengers at the dumping and landfill sites.

Resources available to the DCC for solid-waste management

Human resources — The DCC employs 800 people to clean the city, 500 of whom are sanitary labourers. Table 8 shows the structure of human resources in the Cleansing Section. Shortage of equipment and low morale among the staff are two major problems

Table 8. Structure of human resources in the Cleansing Section of the DCC, Dar es Salaam, 1992.

Category	n
Cleansing superintendent	1
Health officer	1
Assistant health officers	5
Forepersons	23
Heads	65
Loaders and drivers	232
Street cleaners	337
Drain cleaners	86
Clerks	8
Casual employees	42

Source: DCC Health Department records.
Note: DCC, Dar es Salaam City Council.

153

facing the waste-disposal operations of the DCC. Loaders have no protective gear, for example. It was reported in mid-July 1995 that the DCC Cleansing Section workers had gone on a 1-day strike to protest against poor working conditions (*Majira*, 13 Jul 1995).

Technical resources — The Cleansing Section has 30 tipper trucks, each with a capacity of 7 t and a loading volume of 12 m³. Only 20 of the trucks are working. The allocation of trucks over the three districts is as follows: 19 in Ilala; 6 in Kinondoni; and 5 in Temeke. The trucks in Ilala work on two shifts; those elsewhere work on a single shift. Each truck makes one or two trips per shift each day. Trucks are loaded manually, using rakes and bamboo baskets. One should note the concentration of resources in Ilala, the district with the city centre, and the high-income, mainly Aboriginal-occupied area of Upanga. Since 1987 the DCC has procured 30 tipper, 3 container, and 6 compactor trucks and 3 bulldozers, but the number in operation has been dwindling, as shown in Table 9.

The DCC has had grossly inadequate equipment and money to purchase fuel and spare parts and to pay incentives to workers. Some of the vehicles have been unsuitable and have been plagued with spare-parts problems. Thus, although it could be argued that the vehicles, for example, are inadequate, the DCC is unable to operationalize even those few that it has. The DCC does not have enough resources to keep its fleet of trucks working. The fleet is working at less than 20 % of its 1995 potential capacity, as a result of the shortage of funds for fuel, maintenance, and labour. Consequently, the DCC leased some of these vehicles to the private waste-collection contractor.

Financial resources — The DCC pays for its waste-management operations out of its general financial resources, which it derives directly from central-government grants or subsidies or from its own sources of revenue. The efficiency of waste management depends on how much money the city has and how much it can allocate to waste management. As pointed out above, the DCC has had financial problems as a result of inadequate allocations from the central government and inadequate collection of local revenue. Waste management suffers further from inadequate allocation from the DCC itself, as the DCC does not regard waste management as priority.

Calculations for 1994 and 1995 suggest that the DCC spends no more than 60 million TZS/year on waste management,

Table 9. Acquisition of trucks and other equipment for waste management, Dar es Salaam, 1987–95.

Year	Equipment procured	Equipment in operation
1987	30 tipper trucks 3 container trucks	30 tipper trucks 3 container trucks
1988	—	30 tipper trucks 2 container trucks
1991	6 compactor trucks	28 tipper trucks 2 container trucks 6 compactor trucks
1992	—	28 tipper trucks 1 container truck 2 compactor trucks
1993	—	26 tipper trucks 4 compactor trucks 1 container truck
1994	3 bulldozers	24 tipper trucks 1 compactor truck 1 container truck 3 bulldozers
1995	—	20 tipper trucks 1 compactor truck 1 container truck 1 bulldozer

Source: Dar es Salaam City Council Health Department and Engineering Department records.

including running the vehicles and other equipment, operating the landfill, and paying labour costs. Yet, in March 1994, it was calculated (MCAL 1994) that the DCC needed 517 million TZS/year to ensure waste collection in the central area alone.

As noted above, from mid-1994, waste collection in the 10 central-area wards of Dar es Salaam has been privatized, and residents and business operators pay RCCs to the private contractor. The DCC expected to benefit from this financially, as the contractor was bound to pay hire charges for DCC's vehicles and a depot was leased to the contractor. As discussed above, this has not worked out. On the other hand, some revenue is generated from RDCs, paid for dumping waste at the Vingunguti landfill site. These were originally set at 800 TZS/t. This was based on the assumption that there would be a weighbridge and possibly that all waste would be delivered by motor vehicles. But the weighbridge never materialized and the waste can be delivered by a variety of means. Consequently, RDCs are based on estimates, as follows: carts of less than 1 t, 400 TZS; pickups of 1–3 t, 1 600 TZS; lorries of 4–6 t, 2 400 TZS; lorries of 7–10 t, 4 000 TZS; and lorries of more than 10 t, 8 000 TZS.

Some evidence collected for this report indicates that the RDCs are not levied. Some people dump refuse early in the morning before the DCC workers report for duty; others use it after working hours. Considerable revenue is lost because of this.

It was reported that between January and May 1995, RDCs of 8.83 million TZS were collected at the landfill, a lower figure per month than in the previous year, when 7 million TZS was reportedly collected in 2.5 months from October 1994. But no separate account was opened for this income, apart from the normal DCC accounts, and the money was not necessarily used for landfill management.

Physical resources — Most of the waste that the DCC and the formal private sector collect is currently dumped at the landfill site in Vingunguti. This was supposed to be run as a sanitary landfill, but the site is used simply as a dumping area, and this is a major nuisance for the local residents.

Before the DCC started dumping waste at Vingunguti, it had a major problem finding a place to dump the waste. From the early 1960s to 1991, it dumped waste at a site in Tabata, which was destroyed by fire. As far back as 1979, the *Dar es Salaam Masterplan* (Tanzania 1979) suggested opening sanitary landfills along the urban periphery — at Kimara, Mbezi, Pugu, Mbagala, and Kivukoni — to replace the Tabata dump, which was then described as follows:

> *The Tabata site has been filled well beyond capacity for sometime, and refuse tipping is presently encroaching on the Luhanga river, causing excessive downstream pollution. Besides, covering is not being practised and because of machine failure, proper spreading and compacting is not done.*
> (Tanzania 1979, p. 31).

A report prepared for the DCC in 1968 (cited in Tanzania 1979) had recommended the use of sanitary landfills for waste disposal. In 1976, the Dar es Salaam region decided to develop one of these sites at Kimara. The area was compulsorily acquired by the government and was surveyed, but strong objections from residents led the DCC to postpone using the site, which was apparently subsequently abandoned. Thus, Tabata continued to be used as the dump (Tanzania 1979).

As urban growth overtook this site, dumping waste there became a major nuisance. Eventually, residents in the neighbourhood organized to have it removed. After a protracted struggle, residents won the battle, and the courts ordered the DCC to abandon the site. A new site was identified at Kunduchi, but here again, residents took the issue to the courts and the DCC was forced to abandon this site as well. Another site, identified at Mbagala, was similarly abandoned. This struggle demonstrated that people power can be effective but left unsolved the issue of where to dump Dar es Salaam's waste. Nobody, including councillors, wants a waste-dumping site in their area.

157

In early 1992, the DCC struck an agreement with the population of Vingunguti to use a large valley in the area as a sanitary landfill to control soil erosion. The negotiations were spearheaded by the local ruling-party chair and his supporters, who, it later transpired, had personal interests in the dump. Their goals were to stem soil erosion, which threatened some houses; to use waste to feed local livestock; and to engage in recycling, particularly of metals.

But after some 3.5 years, residents are no longer happy and have on occasion organized to block the continued use of Vingunguti as a landfill because of the nuisance it causes and because the DCC did not keep up its end of the bargain by improving the environment for the residents and by operating the site as a sanitary landfill (*Nipashe*, 13 May 1995). Indeed, the landfill was recently been described as "a cloud of flies and stench" (*Daily News* [Tanzania], 15 Apr 1995). A considerable concern is that the people of Vingunguti will at any time strike and block the continued use of the area as a waste-dumping site. In any case, the former ruling-party chair who was instrumental in bringing the dump to Vingunguti has lost his position. At the moment, therefore, the DCC has no reliable dumping site.

If the Vingunguti landfill was well managed, it could last for many more years, although according to some experts, Vingunguti is not at all suited for a landfill (Mgana 1993). Plans for a new landfill site at Kinzudi are not going well. It was reported in June 1995 that plans to fence the area to ward off encroachers were not carried out because of lack of funds (SWMWG n.d.). The site does not seem to be favoured by foreign experts, although local experts say it is ideal. Another neighbourhood in the Mtoni area has invited the DCC to dump waste there, as a way of controlling erosion. Some waste is dumped there, but it is not treated in any way, and so it has again become a major nuisance for local residents. Nevertheless, it is a fact that Dar es Salaam has no reliable dumping site and has to depend on the charity of some neighbourhoods. The DCC does not seem to be worried, and it does not appear to take seriously any plans to get a permanent solution. The continued use of Vingunguti as a landfill site would appear to be hinged on the fact that "the whole area of Vingunguti is a low income area and is poorly served with roads or other infrastructure" (*Daily News* [Tanzania], 26 Apr 1995), and the efforts of the people to stop dumping in the area are easily ignored by the DCC. Also, scavenging may offer some benefits for the local residents.

The DCC has failed to run the Vingunguti site as a sanitary landfill. In November 1994, the residents closed the access road to the site, as the DCC had not maintained the road. Because the bulldozer lacked fuel and the tipping area was also blocked, waste could not therefore be properly managed. Multinet had to provide fuel for 2 months to keep the landfill site in operation, and the DCC clearly failed to take action or appreciate the urgency of the situation.

The landfill site is suffering from major technical and financial problems. A bulldozer and a road grader, purchased with Belgian and Canadian help, are now in operation, but getting them fuelled is sometimes a problem. Soon they will present problems of spare parts. In addition, the landfill site lacks cover material. A minimum of 500 t of fill material was required in March 1994 (MCAL 1994) to cover the existing waste. Only one truck was available to do this while the wheel loader was awaiting repairs. The loader had earlier been set on fire by street traders (locally known as *machingas*), as they were being evicted from the city centre.

Typically, the required fill material is equivalent to about 15 % of the waste. As the Vingunguti landfill is currently taking around 350 t/day, about 50 t of clay is required daily. Sites must be identified to provide this landfill material. The nearby hills proposed for this use are occupied by people, and the authorities' record of paying compensation in cases of expropriation is so poor that these hills cannot possibly be used for this purpose. Apart from these sites, at least two heavy trucks and a wheel loader are required. Without this equipment, it is impossible to operate a landfill in a sanitary manner.

The Vingunguti landfill site is now used haphazardly. Surface water behind the landfill is also finding its way into the waste, thus increasing pollution. The consultants (MCAL 1994, section 5, p. 1) have called for immediate action to remedy the situation:

> *Unless tight control is kept over this landfill, it is inevitable that the past history of the DCC being evicted from one landfill after another must repeat itself, and Dar es Salaam will have another waste disposal crisis on their hands within a short period. The control of leachate from the landfill will now be difficult to manage as the wastes are spread over such a wide area and problems with pollution of the river and the ground water can be expected.*

159

Table 10 shows some data related to the use of the landfill in 1994. This information provides some insight into the operation of the emergency cleanup of the central area, as well as the operation of the various actors in waste management in Dar es Salaam. From Table 10, it is clear that the delivery of soil cover almost ceased at the end of the emergency cleanup in August.

Table 10. Waste deposited at the landfill site in Vingunguti, Dar es Salaam, 1994.

	Quantity (t)			
	Waste brought by Multinet	Waste brought privately	Waste brought by DCC trucks	Soil cover delivered to the landfill site
Jan	—	897	3 540	430
Feb	—	1 107	3 123	930
Mar	—	786	3 006	900
Apr[a]	—	1 122	3 333	770
May	—	720	2 142	640
Jun	—	1 395	4 857	320
Jul	—	1 209	5 832	550
Aug[b]	—	1 392	2 685	20
Sep[c]	1 307	1 086	1 677	10
Oct	1 670	2 940	1 419	—
Nov	1 893	1 008	1 167	—
Dec	1 393	11 970	1 527	—

Source: *Annual Report on Sanitary Landfill.*
[a] Privatization started.
[b] Multinet started collecting waste in the city centre at the end of emergency clean up.
[c] Bulldozer arrived from Belgium.

The landfill site provided 7 732 240 TZS in revenue in 1994. This, however, must represent a gross undercollection. With 55 430.8 t deposited, at 800 TZS/t, more than 44 million TZS should have been collected. If the waste brought by the DCC is set aside, still close to 17 million TZS should have been collected. From the above, it can be seen that the balance of the private sector deposited around 41 t/day at the landfill site.

Resources available to the private contractor for solid-waste management

The financial resources expected to be available to the private contractor were described above. The following highlights its human, technical, and physical resources.

Human resources — As of July 1995, Multinet employed 313 people, as shown in Table 11. However, these employees work under very difficult conditions. Multinet pays 1 000 TZS/day to the drivers and supervisors and 600 TZS/day for loaders for an 11-hour workday, without holidays. Consultants (MCAL 1995) evaluating Multinet's performance noted that rates of pay were very low, and the hours worked were excessively long. Indeed, in mid July 1995, the workers complained through the press that their employment terms were very poor. They were all casual employees, even after a

Table 11. Multinet's labour force, Dar es Salaam, July 1995.

Category	n
Operational manager	1
Assistant operational manager	1
Office staff	7
Sweepers	90[a]
Casual sweepers	20
Loaders	121[a,b]
Casual loaders	30
Workshop workers	15
Collectors	12
Cash collectors	4
Transport officers	2
Checkpoint controllers	3
Watchpeople	5
Scouts	2

Source: Multinet records.
[a]16 in this group are supervisors.
[b]120 in January 1995.

year of being employed with Multinet. Thus, they received daily payment but had no other benefits; they had no specific working hours, many working from 7:30 AM to 8:00 PM without any overtime pay; and they could not protest, because whenever they complained, they were always threatened with the sack (*Majira*, 13 Jul 1995). Like the DCC workers, they lacked protective gear, and trucks were loaded manually, using bamboo baskets and rakes. The contractor argued that given the poor collection of RCCs (discussed above), it had no choice but to pay low wages.

However, the productivity of this labour is apparently much higher than that of the DCC, as these 313 men collect around 100 t/day, whereas the 800 DCC workers collect only between 30 and 60 t/day.

Technological resources — As of January 1995, capital equipment available to Multinet was as shown in Table 12. It will be recalled that some of this equipment was on hire from the DCC. For reasons discussed above, pertaining to the uncertainty of the collection of RCCs, Multinet has invested in only four 3-t tipper trucks (Toyota DCMs). At present, only 13 of the trucks are operational, but not on a daily basis. The collection fleet sometimes diminishes to seven trucks per day, as a result of breakdowns and lack of spare parts. Multinet complains that the vehicles leased to them under the terms of the contract were the worst in the DCC's operating fleet. The company has subsequently spent huge amounts of money on repairs.

Physical resources — During the emergency cleanup, six collection points were designated in Dar es Salaam, at Kidongo Chekundu, Kivukoni, Mkunguni, Shule ya Uhuru, the Buguruni market, and

161

Table 12. Capital equipment required by and available to Multinet, Dar es Salaam, 1995.

Equipment	Number required	Number available
Tipper trucks (7 t)	⌐ 8 ⌐	9
Tipper trucks (4 t)		4
Compactor trucks	6	1
Skip trucks	2	—
Containers	Several	—

Source: Multinet records.

the Ilala market. Soon, however, people recognized the disadvantages of these collection points (Mpinga 1993):

- They were few and far between, with the result that unauthorized dumping points developed;

- Only part of the waste deposited got transported from these collection points, with the result that these points became permanently occupied by waste;

- The environment around these points was polluted and degraded from smells, flies, and litter, as a result of waste not being collected or of its being scattered by wind and scavenging;

- Dumping at collection points reduced the responsibility of the waste generators vis-à-vis waste management, and, because much waste remained uncollected, this convinced the public that nothing was done to collect the waste, which encouraged indifference to uncleanliness;

- Collection points proved politically inexpedient, especially as 1994 was a local-election year; and

- Direct cost recovery was also made difficult after waste generators moved the waste from their premises.

However, the privatization contract required the contractor to rely on these collection points. The advantages were supposed to be ease of collection and lower costs. It is also possible that collection points were favoured because they involve less direct contact with the waste generators, which means less transparency and accountability.

As a result of these disadvantages, particularly the political problems, the DCC argued that it had been unable to find locations for collection points without creating a nuisance and therefore backed out of the collection-point option. The contractor now conducts a door-to-door collection.

As pointed out above, the contractor uses the city landfill site at Vingunguti and was supposed to pay RDCs. Owing to the problems with the collection of RCCs, the contractor is in arrears in its payment of RDCs.

Waste collection by the private contractor — Between 1 July and 31 December 1994, a total of 12 312 t of solid waste, or an average 90–100 t/day, was collected. Between January and June 1995, an average of 121 t/day was collected. It is important, however, to consider these figures with care, as in actuality Dar es Salaam has no waste weighbridges and estimates are based on the tonnage of vehicles and the number of trips they make to discharge waste at the landfill site. Multinet and the evaluating consultants claim that 73–78% (MCAL 1995) of the refuse in the privatized area is collected daily. Although this is impressive, it leaves behind some 35 t of waste uncollected daily, and the dumping of waste in open spaces is still going on in the privatized area.

Under the contract, Multinet was supposed to provide a collection service 6 days a week from designated collection points within the central area and 3 times a week from designated collection points in the residential areas. Households and business people were supposed to deliver their waste to these collection points, at which point Multinet was to take charge of the waste. As pointed out above, this was not to be the case, and the contractor collects door to door, using a loudspeaker to call on people to bring their waste to the vehicles. Nevertheless, people are apparently ill-informed about the Multinet services. Also, collection is only possible during work hours, and working in shifts is impossible.

The collection service is relatively good in the prime commercial and residential wards of Mchafukoge and Kisutu, in the prime residential wards of Upanga East and West, and in the government-area ward of Kivukoni. The service is relatively inadequate in the other, lower status wards. However, a considerable number of people complain that the contractor fails to properly discharge its duties.

Liquid-waste generation and handling

Less than 5% of the population of Dar es Salaam (of 2.3 million people) is connected to the sewer system, which is 130 km long, grouped into 11 systems and supported by 17 pumping stations. This system covers the central areas, some industrial areas, and a few outlying residential areas. Effluent is discharged into oxidation ponds and local watercourses and directly into the ocean. The central areas discharge directly into a sea outfall, where the end of the 1 040 m long pipe lies in less than 2 m of water; numerous fractures discharge raw sewage onto the mud flats exposed at low tide. Many of the oxidation ponds no longer operate, as a result of a lack of maintenance, and raw sewage therefore discharges into the surface drainage system.

About 80 % of the 2.2 million people living outside the central areas have access to on-site facilities — 70 % of these use pit latrines; 30 %, septic tanks — and the remaining 20 %, or about 440 000 people, lack even elementary sanitary facilities. Even in areas served by water facilities, some residents have erected additional pit latrines for emergencies resulting from unreliable water supply (DCC 1992). In 1988, Dar es Salaam had a population of 1.7 million. The people, industries, and institutions generated each day some 126 t of biochemical oxygen demand, 133 t of chemical oxygen demand, 212 t of suspended solids, 372 t of dissolved solids, 18.7 t of nitrogen, and 3.77 t of phosphorus. An estimated 2.46 million inhabiter equivalents were being produced each day.

The DSSD and the Health Department operate tanker lorries to empty septic tanks and pits, usually at the request of people living in the area. Also, a number of parastatal organizations and private business people have their own emptiers. Nevertheless, few of the publicly owned vehicles are operational at any given time. The tendency is for people to remove the liquid but leave the base-load sludge. Water tables are high in most parts of Dar es Salaam, particularly during the rains, which exacerbates problems with poor sanitary conditions, as many septic tanks and pit latrines overflow into the surrounding public lands and drainage systems.

Groups of entrepreneurs offer manual pit-emptying services, but the waste is discharged into on-site trenches, rather than being transported to oxidization ponds. This considerably pollutes the surface drainage systems, the groundwater, and the ocean.

Industrial-waste generation and handling

During the first two decades of independence, Dar es Salaam introduced many industries to enhance economic development. These industries in Dar es Salaam include those for metal-working, steel, and iron; cotton textiles, leather, and sisal; chemical; food processing and beverages; paper and wood products; and nonmetal products, including cement and asbestos. Although most of these industries have had major problems since the 1980s and many are working at below 50 % capacity, they generate considerable waste. Indeed, their economic problems make this situation worse, as the machinery gets worn out and cannot be replaced, and they therefore have no resources to operate an efficient waste-disposal system.

The amount of waste generated was discussed above. Rough calculations suggest that about 94 % of the industries in Dar es Salaam are connected to a piped-water sewerage system. About 6 % are connected to septic tanks and soakaways. The major mode of treatment is through oxidization and stabilization ponds, and the treated waste is then usually discharged into rivers and thus ultimately into the ocean. Various studies suggest (Haskoning and M-Konsult 1989) that industrial waste is not pretreated before it is discharged into oxidization ponds. The level of water pollution is high, as is evident from findings on one of Dar es Salaam's major rivers, the Msimbazi, known for its clean water during the colonial times and currently the recipient of many industrial effluents.

The coliform count in the Msimbazi at entry into Dar es Salaam (at Kiserawe) is 75–100 per 100 mL of water, a relatively low count, indicating good-quality water. When the Msimbazi leaves Dar es Salaam (at Salander bridge), the coliform count is between 250 000 and 400 000 per 100 mL of water, indicating heavy contamination. This is more than 1 000 times the coliform count considered safe to just swim in. The lower stretch of the Msimbazi is, therefore, an open sewer. Causes of this pollution are varied, but they include the city's excessive reliance on on-site modes of sanitation and its tendency to discharge raw domestic and industrial effluents into rivers and natural channels (Yhdegho 1991). Even toxic waste, including pathogenic waste from hospitals, is crudely dumped, without any pretreatment.

Although 58 pieces of legislation deal in one way or another with the environment, most of these laws are unknown, unenforceable, or outdated. The NEMC, created in 1986, lacks regulatory powers and can therefore only advise. Much industrial pollution is in practice uncontrolled.

EVALUATION

WASTE MANAGEMENT AS PROVIDED BY THE DCC

The DCC collects only a small fraction of the solid waste generated in Dar es Salaam, and its efforts are equally marginal in the collection of liquid and industrial waste. The city lacks an effective policy on waste storage and collection, with the result that many former collection points have become dumping places.

The waste is transferred from collection points to vehicles by hand-loading, and many workers lack protective gear. The productivity of the workers and the vehicles operated by the DCC is very low. A lack of a standardized system for waste storage makes transfer difficult. Currently, a lot of waste is left at the collection points. As noted, transportation is beset by a plethora of problems, hinging on the unsuitability of the vehicles and lack of funds to purchase fuel and spare parts and properly maintain the vehicles. Currently, Dar es Salaam lacks a waste disposal area, and the current landfill site at Vingunguti is not used as a sanitary landfill, but just as a dumping area, causing nuisance, pollution, and environmental degradation. It can therefore be correctly concluded that Dar es Salaam's waste-management system is grossly inadequate and very liable to break down, as it is operated haphazardly and unsustainably.

WASTE MANAGEMENT AS PROVIDED BY THE PRIVATE SECTOR

The private sector has been given a major role in solid-waste collection in the central area of Dar es Salaam. This has no doubt considerably improved the collection of waste in the privatized area. But the contractor has only been able to collect 10% of the expected RCCs, even though it collects 70% of the waste. It has not, therefore, made the expected investments in vehicles, buildings, and other equipment, and this keeps the collection service from being what it was intended to be.

On the other hand, with 13 vehicles on the road and just more than 300 workers, the contractor collects about 100 t/day of waste, whereas the DCC, with a fleet of 22 vehicles and 800 workers, collects around 50 t/day. This is definitely a positive measure of efficiency. However, it is important to emphasize that the contractor pays very low wages and the workers work long hours without benefits. There is also concern that privatization may suffer adversely if no improvement is made in the relationship between the DCC and the contractor. Waste generators who use the services of private collectors and emptiers, including small-scale operators, seem to be happy with the services, but these operators have not solved the problem of the final disposal of this waste.

Evaluating waste-management arrangements in Dar es Salaam in terms of certain aspects of governance

Public participation

Official waste-management arrangements in Dar es Salaam are generally implemented with little or no participation of the key actors. Except in Upanga and the city centre, where around 10% of the interviewees said that they had ever been consulted by the council, the residents are not consulted. Even the privatization was undertaken without public consultation. In particular, the business people, who were supposed to pay 80% of the RCCs, were not involved in determining the amount or mode of payment. Local leaders, who could have helped in mobilizing the public to adopt specific methods for waste management or pay RCCs, were not involved in the exercise. Although this shortfall was made up later, and the consultants recommended remedial action, the DCC has yet to involve the local leaders in the whole issue of waste management.

167

The institutional setup of the DCC makes no provision for participation of the public or of local leaders. Everything hinges on the operation of the Health Department. It is noteworthy, too, that within the SDP, the Community Participation Working Group is the least active. The private contractor, the SDP, and a good proportion of the general public have decried the lack of public participation. The blame is generally laid on the DCC, which should, but does not, ensure that participation takes place.

Citizens' rights

As seen above, the citizens of Dar es Salaam are apathetic about what happens in the DCC. The council seems to take advantage of this to operate with little concern for citizens' rights. It does not seem to conceive of the right of the citizens to live in an environment without waste, and the citizens do not seem to be interested in fighting for this right. The DCC operates therefore in a system where citizens' rights are not pressed for, or cared about.

Accountability and transparency

The DCC generally operates with little accountability or transparency. Some suspect that the DCC's desire to avoid accountability was the reason it required the business people to pay 80% of the RCCs for Multinet's service, although they generate only

33.4% of the central-area waste. Domestic households, which produce 41.3% of the waste, were supposed to pay only 20% of the RCCs. This meant fewer problems collecting the RCCs but also less transparency and accountability. A desire to avoid accountability and transparency was also the motive for the DCC's choice of collection points (with their many disadvantages) in the original privatization contract, rather than choosing house-to-house collection. The DCC chose collection points, despite the evidence of the Opinion Poll Concerning Waste and Environment of Residential Areas of Dar es Salaam, carried out in October 1993 (MCAL 1994), which showed that in Ilala district, 63.7% of the population was prepared to buy garbage bags and 83.3% of the households would use garbage bags if they had them. This suggests that house-to-house collection was both an acceptable and a more feasible system than the system of collection points originally adopted. In fact, the whole privatization exercise appears to have been conceived and effected with little transparency, and the new Dar es Salaam city director has admitted this.

Local neighbourhood and ward leaders also complained that they did not know how council budgets were arrived at or what allocation (for example, for solid-waste removal) the various neighbourhoods had. The DCC, rarely, if at all, comes back to its citizens to inform them about issues of finance or service delivery.

Financial efficiency

It was pointed out above that the DCC is inefficient in collecting its revenue and that the money that it has collected has not been spent on citizens' priorities. The waste-management system has high levels of inefficiency and low productivity. Moreover, the private contractor is apparently more efficient than the DCC, collecting more than the DCC but with less than half the human resources.

Sustainability

As shown, from the 1970s the Dar es Salaam waste-management system has been largely unsustainable. Capital equipment (vehicles, for example) may all be inoperative in a few years' time. Funds are usually not set aside to cover maintenance or depreciation. When things look like they are coming to a standstill, the DCC has recourse usually to the central government or to the donors. It is interesting to note that in 1994–95, despite privatization, the DCC requested 89 million TZS from the central government to repair existing vehicles and equipment and buy new ones. Vehicles aside, the DCC usually lacks money to buy fuel. This study found that in each of the months of July and August 1994, work at the landfill site came to a standstill for 6 days for lack of fuel for the bulldozer.

This study found that most of the landfill sites earmarked in the 1979 masterplan (Tanzania 1979) have largely been occupied by builders, as the DCC failed to take them up or protect them. A similar process is now taking place at the earmarked landfill site at Kinzudi. The DCC does not seem to have any long-term plans for waste-disposal sites.

169

The SDP is geared to creating sustainability in Dar es Salaam. Yet, it was observed that the relationship between the DCC and the SDP may need to improve. At the moment, it appears that the SDP has set up its own system, parallel to that of the DCC, and that the SDP may be unsustainable without foreign assistance.

In principle, privatization of waste management would be sustainable if various impediments are removed, including the lukewarm attitude of the DCC, its ill-conceived policies, and the lack of public participation.

POLICY OPTIONS AND RECOMMENDATIONS

Waste management cannot be considered in isolation. Therefore, recommendations must cover wider issues related to general aspects of urban governance, as well as issues specific to waste management. For example, much of the planned part of Dar es Salaam lacks passable roads. Lack of surface-water drainage means that many existing roads are easily eroded or flooded during the rainy seasons. Moreover, by far the majority of Dar es Salaam's residents live in unplanned areas, with very limited space for roads. Any plans to improve Dar es Salaam's roads or any plans to upgrade Dar es Salaam's unplanned areas have a bearing on the ease with which waste can be collected and transported.

INSTITUTIONAL COORDINATION AND RATIONALIZATION

Many institutions — local, national, and international — have a considerable role in urban management. These need to come together and streamline their powers and roles, with a view to improving the position of local governments. This is what the SDP is trying to do in Dar es Salaam, although success is still elusive, as many institutions still prefer to work in isolation.

CENTRAL–LOCAL GOVERNMENT RELATIONSHIPS

The ambiguity of the central government's treatment of local government needs to be addressed. In particular, it must start to show a drive to have strong local governments. A key aspect of this drive must be to enhance the collection of adequate local revenue and to manage local finances more beneficially. To some extent, the central government is aware of the financial and managerial problems of the DCC. The central government has made a number of statements in the past and appointed a number of probe committees. However, it has rarely acted on the recommendations of these committees. Such recommendations have included splitting Dar es Salaam into a number of smaller municipalities and strengthening the neighbourhood level of local government. Many such proposals remain unimplemented. The steps that are taken must not alienate the councillors but enhance the relationship between councillors and officials.

The complaint in Tanzania is that councillors generally have a low level of education, and the central government has a duty to rectify this. This includes popularizing knowledge of the role of councillors in local government. This needs to be remedied, and in particular, the civic spirit among the councillors must be revived.

A central government should encourage the effective decentralization of power from itself to the local governments, as well as encouraging decentralization of power within local governments. The idea of dividing Dar es Salaam into smaller municipalities appears plausible. Whether or not this division is accepted, powers need to be devolved to the ward and neighbourhood levels.

Together with decentralization, the central government needs to enhance public participation in local politics and activities. This includes sensitizing people so that they take part in local elections and take an interest in council plans, deliberations, decisions, and finances. It also entails encouraging people to establish local community organizations. Some have suggested that mayors and chairs be elected by popular vote, rather than being elected by the councillors, as one way of bringing more life and accountability into local politics.

170

The central government must show a drive to make local governments operate more transparently and with more accountability, both to itself and to the citizens. Both the central and local governments also need to see each other as partners in development, not as foes.

INTRA-LOCAL-GOVERNMENT RELATIONSHIPS

The relationships between councillors and officials in local government must be improved. Their roles and powers are ill defined and muddled up. Also, the DCC must enhance its relationship with its citizens. This is necessary if the DCC wants to collect more revenue from them and have them take up more of the burden of the provision of services.

171

As well, the DCC needs to work closely with local organizations, including the NGOs and CBOs that are emerging and trying to address local problems. Much of the local effort to deal with pressing local issues (including waste management) is frustrated by technical and legal problems and lack of coordination among various actors and between these actors and the DCC.

TECHNICAL ISSUES

The experience in Dar es Salaam indicates that privatization can be a feasible option, provided it has political support and the public is involved. It is possible to slowly privatize waste collection and disposal throughout Dar es Salaam, involving various kinds of actors and using various forms of partnerships. The DCC might begin to identify and plan for disposal sites, supervise the collectors, and enforce cleanliness regulations.

The kinds of partnerships envisaged might entail adopting processes and enacting waste regulations that include NGOs, CBOs, and small-scale collectors and sorters and that address issues like local dumping sites, waste-disposal pits, and ways to deal with waste locally, such as burning, burying, composting, recycling, manual and other forms of pit-emptying, and local treatment of waste. The regulations must be relevant to local problems and solutions and enforceable at the local level, depending on the type of waste. Waste should be discussed at a local level; a consensus should be reached; and regulations should be passed.

Such partnerships must also investigate appropriate technology. The current system is based on capital-intensive imported equipment. The role of hand-drawn carts and manual emptiers, for example, must be investigated. Harnessing of local resources for waste management is important. This must involve local leaders, including 10-cell leaders (neighbourhood leaders, originally each *loongi* after 10 houses), local elders, neighbourhood chairs, and religious leaders. As there is possibly no need to collect all the waste, the role of sections of households and other actors engaged in waste management should be investigated. This includes women, as they are the ones concerned with removing waste from the household premises. And it includes informal sorters, who are mostly men. Waste management definitely can generate income, particularly though recycling but, to a lesser extent, through composting and energy production.

Finally, a public-education campaign is needed to encourage people to participate in maintaining cleanliness, not just on their own premises, where current efforts are producing a satisfactory environment, but also in open or public areas.

CONCLUSION

The collection and disposal of liquid, solid, and industrial waste are major problems in Dar es Salaam. Although undealt with waste is a visible testament to failure in local governance, this is not a unique problem. Problems are experienced in other areas of urban governance, including the provision, management, and maintenance of infrastructure and other public services. These problems are rooted in the whole management arena of Dar es Salaam. Overlapping institutional arrangements, poor local revenue collection, poor relationships between councillors and officials, poor relations among the DCC, the citizens, the private sector, and the NGOs and CBOs, and lack of accountability and transparency have all contributed to poor urban governance that manifests itself in poor waste management. Waste management in Dar es Salaam is poor, despite the move toward privatization. Proposals have been advanced that may improve this situation, but they all hinge on overall improvement in the governance of Dar es Salaam.

Chapter 5

Johannesburg, South Africa

Mark Swilling and David Hutt

Introduction

The transition to a nonracial democracy in South Africa has had profound implications for this country's cities and the urban-governance system. In particular, because this transition is taking place in a global context in which previous conceptions of governance are rejected or severely criticized, South Africans must find new solutions to old problems specific to South Africa's socioeconomic and politicocultural conditions. No ready models are available to provide quick-fix recipes. This trend toward innovation and creative experimentation provides a research opportunity to track processes that may have continental or even global implications.

This paper addresses the changing nature of local governance in Johannesburg, South Africa, first, by generally exploring the concept of governance to arrive at an understanding of how this

173

concept can be operationalized most usefully. This is followed by a general survey of the process of local-government transition in South Africa. This general overview is needed to establish the context for the specific institutional arrangements that are the focus of this paper. The second section provides a detailed case study of the solid-waste system in Greater Johannesburg. Because the range of issues to be covered is wide and space is limited, liquid and industrial wastes are not dealt with. The original terms of reference of the study stipulated an emphasis on solid waste, and this has also helped to focus the study. The third section assesses the institutional options for managing solid waste in light of the changes occurring in local governance. The fourth section provides a set of policy options and recommendations.

CHANGING MODES OF LOCAL GOVERNANCE IN SOUTH AFRICA

There are a number of ways of approaching the subject of local urban governance. Halfani et al. tackle the issue by "integrating the notion of governance itself into urban development" (Halfani et al. 1998, p. 2). To do this, they address the conceptual debates about governance in general and then, after arriving at their own conception, apply this to the urban-development debate, with the aim of redefining the terms of this debate. They explicitly state that they are "not defining 'local governance'" (Halfani et al. 1998, p. 2). By this they presumably mean that they are not interested in the local manifestations of governance in general, but only in the implications of the governance paradigm for the management of urban development at all levels. The problem with this approach is that the urban-development processes cannot be assumed in Africa to be localized by definition because, for example, what are deemed to be rural economies are often subsidized by urban wage earners, which effectively means that many so-called rural areas depend in large part on the nationally structured urban economy. Also, many aspects of urban-development policy are not set at the local level. The spatial dimension of urban governance, therefore, needs to be conceptualized in a way that is not given in the concept of urban governance on its own.

Another approach is that adopted by Picard et al. (1999), who focus on the changing role of local-government institutions in southern African politics. They surveyed these changes over the decades via two frameworks, namely, the rhetoric and reality of decentralization policies and the ideals and failure of the notion of development administration. In other words, their entry points into local urban governance are the decentralization and development-administration debates, rather than the governance literature. They concluded that for "good government to occur, participatory processes need to evolve at the level where public institutions and policies impact upon society. The local state is that part of the state structure which impacts upon and is influenced by individuals and groups" (Picard et al. 1999, p. 3). Although more state-centric in their approach than Halfani et al., Picard et al. arrived at what the former researchers called a governance approach, but unlike these researchers, Picard et al. stopped short of actually defining the concept of governance, despite the fact that they use this concept throughout their argument. This conceptual inadequacy is compensated for, however, by a very strong definition of their spatial point of reference, namely, the local level. They do not, however, have any special concern for urban issues, and therefore they do not address the specificity of the problems of governance in urban areas.

The growing literature on governance constitutes an attempt to capture the shift in thinking that is taking place across the globe about the nature of the state and its relationship to society. The shift from *government* to *governance*, from structure to relations, from independence to interdependence, from linearity to feedback loops, from rational structuration to chaos as process, is influenced by the combined universal disillusionment with the nature of the state and the impact of the postmodern imagination, which has abandoned the myth of human self-unification and the vision of a utopian end-state. But it was the World Bank's 1989 report on sub-Saharan Africa (World Bank 1989) that forced the word *governance* into the mainstream debate. Although World Bank institutions resisted dealing with Africa's governance problems for many years, as a result of the dominant influence of quantitative economics in the World Bank's post-Cold War view, the problems of Africa were, at root, issues about poor governance, that is, personalization of power, denial of human rights, corruption, undemocratic government, low levels of participation, etc. The solution, it followed, lay in programs aimed at promoting good governance, particularly stronger public management, increased accountability

175

of politicians and officials, an effective and independent judiciary, autonomy of the press, independence of civil-society formation, and transparency in financial reporting (Landell-Mills and Serageldin 1991) — in short, a liberal democratic prescription.

In general terms, governance refers to the founding values and constitutional "metapolicies" (Hyden 1992) that constitute the nature of governing institutions, guide their actions, and shape the complex relations between them and society. Governance is defined, however, in a number of different ways in the literature and in southern African political discourse. Four basic positions exist. The first is the crude prescriptive position of many international development agencies, which equate good governance with the classic liberal-democratic model (separation of powers, bill of rights, federal intergovernmental arrangements, an independent judiciary, limited roles for the state, neutral and effective public service, political pluralism, etc.). The second approach is unconcerned with the nature of the state and government but focuses on state–society relations. In line with a rich and growing literature on state–society relations (Chazan et al. 1988), this approach argues that the governance paradigm refers to the relationship between civil society and the state (Halfani et al. 1998). Once the focus shifts to this relationship, then the issue of democratic governance is about empowering civil-society formations to enable them to participate in decision-making and policy formulation.

The third approach views governance as an ideological device that post-Cold War Western governments have chosen to use to mask the imposition of capitalist market policies (via structural adjustment) on highly unequal societies, with the consent of increasingly disempowered state systems that no longer represent the real interests of the poor majority. As it is argued, this is a formula that leads to increased political conflict and a return to authoritarianism, rather than promoting democratic governance (Leftwich 1993). Leftwich's main contribution to the debate has been to note how the governance paradigm has turned the development debate on its head in the context of the new world order. Whereas in the 1960s conventional wisdom rested on the assumption (provided by modernization theory) that socioeconomic modernization was a precondition for political democracy, in the 1990s political democracy is seen as a precondition for successful development. This somersault is intimately bound up with the end of the Cold War, which has allowed Western governments to impose their own constitutional prescriptions with impunity. The rise of prodemocracy movements has also played a role.

The fourth approach goes beyond these normative and critical approaches by attempting to theorize what Hyden called the "governance realm" (Hyden 1992). Hyden's primary concern has been the dynamic of what he calls the "civic public realm" in Africa, that is, the sphere of public and political life that is not reducible to the state–public sector, as it cannot be maintained that the state is the only player in formulating and setting of public policy. His assumption has been that the nature, health, and texture of the civic–public realm depend on the substantive content of governance relations.

177

Hyden argued that governance "is the conscious management of regime structures with a view to enhancing the legitimacy of the public realm" (Hyden 1992, p. 7). In other words, governance is about the way the power structures of the day (what Hyden calls the "regime") and the frameworks within which civil society operates are managed. Together these interdependent elements can make up a robust and healthy civic–public realm. Hyden suggests four essential elements of governance. The first is the degree of trust that exists among classes, clans, and political elites in the nature, purpose, and rules of sociopolitical interactions and practices. Without trust, individuals and organized interests will see no reason to actively engage in public life (or development) because they will have no faith in the possibility that social action will yield tangible results. Where trust exists, the actors tend to form multistakeholder strategic alliances across the public, private, and community sectors and voluntary multiclass and multiethnic associations within civil society.

The second element of governance is the extent to which effective relations of reciprocity are established in the public realm. Reciprocity exists if associations and parties are allowed to form and defend and promote stakeholder interests within the public realm via political competition, pressure, negotiations, and conflict resolution. Reciprocity is unlikely if trust does not exist, but trust without reciprocity soon dissolves into cynicism.

The third element is the degree of accountability, that is, whether the governors can be held responsible by the governed via institutionalized procedures and processes (for example, elections, public oversight, and referenda). Trust and reciprocity within civil society cannot be sustained over time without the eventual implementation of structures of accountability, nor can formal accountability mechanisms attain real meaning without trust and reciprocity across society.

The fourth element is the nature of authority, that is, how political leaders make policies and implement them to resolve the problems of ordinary citizens and promote the legitimacy of the public realm — what many in southern Africa refer to as the capacity to govern. With these taken together, Hyden's approach allows us to ask concrete questions about relations of trust, reciprocity, accountability, and authority, and this is more fruitful than prescriptive liberal-democratic models or simply the critique of these models as masks for the logic of international capital accumulation. Hyden's approach also allows us to go beyond a descriptive equation of governance with state–society relations.

However, Hyden's framework has two problems. First, it is still state centric, despite his introduction of the concept of the regime to escape the structuralist bias of the state concept. The concept of the regime still places the formal political system at the centre of governance. As Halfani (1995) has pointed out, state-centric conceptions of governance often ignore the efficacy and power of nonstate modes of governance, which can, at times, have an even greater influence on the distribution of urban resources than the state itself. This certainly happens more often at the local urban level of government than at any other. The way out of state centrism may lie in the conception of governance developed by a group of European writers in a recent volume edited by Kooiman (1993). They argued that as societal and economic relations have become increasingly complex, diverse, and dynamic (that is, postmodern) in a context of mounting fiscal constraints, tension has opened up between governing capacities that were previously located exclusively within the state and governing needs that the old state forms can no longer respond to. The result is a shift from state-centric assumptions about the locus of the right to govern to the creation of new governing partnerships, entered into by state agencies, private-sector businesses, and nongovernmental organizations (NGOs) or community-based organizations (CBOs) in response to the new governing needs of postindustrial societies. This approach is what the European writers refer to as the new, responsive mode of governance that has replaced three increasingly outdated modes of governance, namely, the traditional hierarchically organized Weberian–Westminster state; the large,

178

institutionalized corporatist state; and the autonomous welfarist state, in which services are delivered uniformly to all as a basic right (Jorgenson 1993). This is a search for governance in the space created by unmet governing needs in a context where the state is incapable of developing the necessary capacity to respond to the complexity, diversity, and dynamism of rapidly changing conditions. This framework provides a very useful framework for understanding what is happening in southern Africa's towns and cities. It shares the assumptions of the critique of the postapartheid public administration in South Africa, developed by Cranko and Wooldridge, who argued that the traditional modes of governance are premised on rationalist assumptions that are out of kilt with the rapidity of change in late-20th century societies, especially South African society (Cranko and Wooldridge 1995). Although southern Africa's governing problems arise from the role of the state in the struggle for modernity, rather than from the crisis of postmodernity, the search for governance in the space created by the incapacity of the state is common to both contexts. Put another way, the futile attempts of Africans to develop a deracialized modernist state from forms left by colonialism can now be recognized as such and replaced with conceptions of governance more appropriate to societies to which the rationalist, reductionist assumptions of capitalist modernization have never been applicable. Hyden (1983, p. 78) holds that "entrepeneurialism through the public service is an impossibility." However, his desperate plea to reverse this is more Quixotic than realistic. At least now there is a chance that the rest of the world may begin to hear African discourse as it really is — creative, multinodal, and "circular" (with feedback loops) — a discourse that has for decades been suppressed by the rationalistic reductionism of the kind of development modernism imposed on Africa by Western development theorists for decades.

179

The second problem with Hyden's framework is that his conception of governance is only useful for analyzing the relationships between organizations, and he fails to ask what governance means for the internal management of African organizations. This is not to suggest that we should go back to the sterile literature on institutional development or urban management that has been so roundly criticized. Instead, we could turn to an interesting and emerging literature on the management of African organizations (Blunt and Jones 1992; Christie et al. 1993; McClagan and Nel

1995; McClennan et al. 1995). One of these contributions is a recent path-breaking book by two South African-based management experts who have used the governance concept to provide a fundamental critique of what they call the "authoritarian mode of governance" (McClagan and Nel 1995) that characterizes the managerial practices of South African business organizations. They posit, instead, the notion that organizations can be managed in accordance with the precepts of democratic governance. The most important precept that McClagan and Nel argued for is that of having thoroughgoing participation of all the stakeholders in an organization in the course of setting and implementing its vision, strategy, and policies. This point of departure represents very different concerns from the conventional public-administration concerns of the institutional-development school and those expressed in the development-administration literature.

In short, if we bring the various arguments together, it is possible to suggest that an analysis of governance must start by identifying the locus of governance across a spectrum running from the central state, through to the decentralized parts of the state, and then beyond the state to nonstate formations in civil society. Along with this, we need an analysis of the degree of trust and reciprocity within civil society (as per Hyden). One must also analyze the extent of accountability and the capacities of organizations in both the state system and civil society to meet the governing needs of the society in general. In other words, whereas the issues of trust and reciprocity are about the values that underpin organizational relationships, those of accountability and governing capacity are about the ways these organizational relationships are constituted and organized throughout society. Cutting across all of this is the question of the internal organizational management of institutions, associations, and organizations in all sectors.

It is possible to conclude this section by summarizing four basic approaches to governance in Africa, that is, the four ways the concept is used in reference to institutional, political, and development arrangements:

- *Good governance is good administration* — This approach tends to be used by multilateral aid and development agencies that are limited to nonpolitical interventions. These agencies tend to focus on building the administrative,

regulatory, planning, and problem-solving capaci
African public administrations.

- *Good governance is about political democratization* — This approach equates good governance with the creation of liberal-democratic institutions and therefore limits governance to traditional modes of political participation (via the electoral process). Not surprisingly, Western governments are the protagonists of this approach, which is often supported by social movements and opposition parties in societies in which the government resists democratization.

- *Governance is about state–civil-society relations* — This approach essentially sees participation as more than mere political participation via the electoral process, and this approach advocates organized participation in policy-making and implementation by civil-society organizations. The development NGOs in their rising numbers are clearly the main champions of this position, but it has widespread support across other sectors as well (especially the professions).

- *Governance is about civil society taking over responsibility for development* — This position is mainly advocated by anti-state social movements and CBOs (with some support from libertarians on the other side of the political spectrum) that have concluded that the state structures are irretrievably lost to corrupt power mongers or international capital. These organizations therefore conclude that the only hope for development is if the state has as little as possible to do with it and direct responsibility for it is placed in the hands of the grass roots.

All four approaches are evident in the South African context. The third approach is in the official ideology of the Mandela government's Reconstruction and Development Programme (RDP), whereas the day-to-day work of the public service is premised on the assumptions of the first approach. The fourth approach underlies the statements and programs of an increasing number of movements representing constituencies that do not stand to benefit from the RDP. Our approach, however, is more holistic than these other four approaches, as it is premised on a systems view of the world, in which the whole is more than the mere sum of its parts.

Looking at the relations of trust, reciprocity, accountability, and capacity, our focus is less on the parts of the system and more on relationships between the elements of the system. If governance is about relationships, then the intention must be to focus on the way the relationship between the parts defines both the essential nature of each part and the dynamics of the whole.

OVERVIEW OF THE LOCAL-GOVERNMENT TRANSITION IN JOHANNESBURG

The negotiated settlement at the national level in South Africa, finalized in 1993, created an interim Constitution that completely reconstituted the governmental system at national, provincial, and local levels. A final Constitution will soon be negotiated by the Constitutional Assembly. This assembly was created by the interim Constitution. Although media and public attention have focused, since the first general election in April 1994, on the setup and workings of national government and the nine provincial governments, very little attention has been paid to the transition at the local level or the implications of this transition for the reconstruction and development process. Between 1993 and 1996, more than 800 new local governments were established, and in most of them democratic local elections have already taken place.

Chapter 10 of the Constitution provides for a framework for managing the transition at the local-government level. Not only does this chapter entrench the local-government transition, but it also lays down certain constitutional principles to effectively protect the autonomy of local governments within the framework of a quasi-federal three-tier governmental system. Whereas South Africa has now joined literally dozens of countries in Latin America, southern Europe, eastern Europe, Asia, and Africa that have gone through a nonrevolutionary regime transition to democracy over the last 25 years (O'Donnel et al. 1986), no other case has been found of a national-level constitutional transition that parallels this complex, locally determined process of local-level transition.

The graphic images of the apartheid city are now world famous. On the one hand, the opulent white suburbs have commercial services and municipal-service standards on a par with those in societies with gross domestic products (GDPs) several times higher than that of South Africa. On the other hand, the sprawling black townships on the peripheries of the towns and cities have their uniform housing units, poor services, and ever-widening bands of informal housing erected by an increasing number of homeless people. The local-government transition will have major implications for the future quality and durability of South Africa's newborn democracy and for the ecological sustainability of the envisaged development process. It also defines the institutional context of this local study of Johannesburg's waste-management system.

183

South Africa's population of 38 million in 1990 is expected to double over the next three decades. The Urban Foundation estimated South Africa will have a population of 46.5 million by 2000 and 59.7 million by 2010. The black population alone is expected to increase by 130% between 1980 and 2010, from 21.1 million to 48.5 million (Coetzee and de Coning 1992). It has been calculated that 65% of the population was functionally urbanized by 1989. The 3.4% growth rate in the urban population between 1980 and 1985 is expected to level off at 3.09%. The main contributing factor will be rural–urban migration and the natural increase in the size of the urban population, with the latter now the dominant factor in, rather than being a secondary cause of, urban-population growth rates (Coetzee and de Coning 1992). It is expected that 69% of the black population will be living in urban areas by 2000.

South Africa has five major metropolitan agglomerations: the Pretoria–Witwatersrand–Vaal (Gauteng) region (which includes Greater Johannesburg and is now one of the nine provinces), Greater Cape Town, the Durban Functional Region (DFR), Port Elizabeth–Uitenhage, and East London–Mdantsane. By 2010, 75% of the population is expected to live in these five metropoles, which, in turn, will be responsible for 75% of GDP. The Gauteng is the primary metropole and is expected to have a population of 12 million and be responsible for the production of up to 50% of GDP by 2010. However, the indications are that the Gauteng's economic performance is weakening relative to other centres, such as the DFR.

Although apartheid did little to affect the process of urbanization, it created a settlement pattern that Coetzee and de Coning (1992) summed up as follows:

- People are concentrated in five metropolitan areas, which are in turn dispersed and sprawling conurbations characterized by extremely inefficient land use, long travel times, much better access to services between richer areas than in poorer areas, and distribution of urban poor on the peripheries both in formal townships and, increasingly, in sprawling squatter settlements providing shelter for at least 7 million people;

- The nonmetropolitan population is distributed in some 300 settlements outside the homelands;

- Urban populations are growing in 293 towns inside the former homelands, many of which had economic bases supported by the government's industrial decentralization policies;

- Semi- and peri-urban informal settlements are proliferating inside homeland boundaries, but on the peripheries of metropolitan economies from which they derive some of their income; and

- The rural population is expected to increase from 11.4 million to 15.3 million between 1985 and 2010.

The entire structure of the apartheid city was governed by the racial regulation of urban space via the *Group Areas Act*, passed in the 1950s. This Act empowered urban administrators to slice up the cities into four racial segments, exclusively reserved for whites, Africans, coloureds, and Indians. Each segment was then governed and administered separately, and over the decades a different body of planning, municipal, and administrative law developed for each segment. By the beginning of the transition to democracy in 1990, each area had its unique local-government, urban-planning, housing-delivery, and ownership systems, etc.

Underlying the apparent division of the cities along racial grounds, however, was an integrative urban-economic and ecological logic that worked in favour of the white urban classes. In other words, whereas the ideology of racial division was justified in terms of the need to separately develop the different racial groups, in reality the economic relationship between the white and the black (that is, African, coloured, and Indian) halves of the city was similar to a colonial relationship of exploitation and unequal exchange. This was most evident in the way local-government finances were structured.

Because of apartheid zoning, all the major commercial and industrial areas were located in the white areas and fell under the jurisdiction of the White Local Authorities. Economic activities were concentrated in the central business districts (CBDs), around which most South African cities developed. However, the metropolitan urban areas have been undergoing suburbanization and deconcentration since the 1970s. Calculations have shown (Planact 1990) that between 50 and 70% of all the revenue of the White Local Authorities came from property rates and service charges in the commercial and industrial areas. This was the revenue used to cross-subsidize the development of high-level services in the white suburbs. None of the revenue that accrued to the White Local Authorities was spent in the black areas (Swilling et al. 1991).

185

As far as the black townships were concerned, they had virtually no commercial or industrial base. They were residential areas populated by people who worked in the white areas. Revenue for their services came from service charges and rents charged for the largely state-owned housing that they lived in. Grants from the national government subsidized up to 30% of the cost of running the townships. This meant that the economic base of the white areas was built up by labour from the townships working in the white areas, as well as by consumer spending in white areas (which was necessary, as black areas had no commercial services). This economic base, in turn, created a sustainable tax base for the White Local Authorities, which enabled the cross-subsidization of white suburbia. As a result of the net financial drain of resources from the poor black to richer white areas, the black townships were systematically underdeveloped. This was the system of exploitation that held the apartheid city together as a single interdependent urban system.

The transition to democracy that began in 1990 was largely the product of locally and nationally constituted social movements, driven by organized workers, students, youth, women, and urban residents. Although the 1973 general strikes and the 1976 student uprisings triggered a collective organizational consciousness, it was not until the 1980s that large-scale organized social movements made a decisive impact on the structures, policies, and strategies of both the state and mainstream economic institutions. By the mid-1980s, however, it was generally acknowledged that a stalemate had set in. The state did not have the combined coercive, strategic, and legitimate power required to force through a top-down Brazilian-style reform by imposition. Nor did the extra-parliamentary opposition social movements and the exiled liberation movements have the combined military, organizational, and logistical resources to mount a successful revolution. With neither reform from above nor revolution from below, both sides began to make attempts, from the mid-1980s, to find a negotiated resolution to this conflict. These efforts were made at the national level as regime incumbents and regime opponents began to hold exploratory meetings. This process culminated in formal negotiations in 1990, after Nelson Mandela was released (Swilling and Van Zyl Slabbert 1989). However, even before the commencement of national negotiations, similar processes took place at the local level, and these continued well beyond the date of national settlement.

In numerous ways, people resisted and challenged the form and function of the apartheid city during the 1980s. Although one-off demonstrations, stayaways, strikes, and collective, violent crowd actions against specific targets were commonplace, sustained mass action tended to have the most decisive effect. Communities across the country mounted consumer and rent boycotts. Although these actions were successful to the extent of the strength of their grass-roots organization and the capabilities of their leadership, they created localized stalemates that neither targets of these actions (white shopkeepers, Black Local Authorities) nor the social movements behind them could tolerate for very long. The targets were deprived of money, and constituencies of the social movements were deprived of services. The result was frequently the so-called local-level negotiations. By the early 1990s, hundreds of these local-level negotiations had broken out across the length and breadth of the country. Inevitably, the parties involved were representatives of various local-government structures, businesses, municipal-service providers, civic associations, residents' organizations, political parties, trade unions, and numerous other community organizations. Their activities resulted in the formation of the local negotiating forums.

Local forums became the schools of the new South African democracy. They were where networks and relationships were built, mutual learning took place, and a new culture of governance and consensus-building developed. Imperfect and fraught with tensions and instabilities, these local forums nevertheless became the model for similar structures that emerged at the regional and, eventually, at the national level. There it took the form of the Negotiating Council that finally negotiated the national constitutional settlement during 1993–94. The first and most well known of these local forums was the Central Witwatersrand Metropolitan Chamber, which covered Greater Johannesburg.

Although the local forums began to be organized in 1989, they were unable to change substantively the fundamental aspects of the local-government system or, indeed, the urban system as a whole. Instead, they became superordinate policy-making bodies that set policies to be implemented in the old structures. However, during 1992–93, the national negotiators realized that a national framework was needed to guide the local-government transition via the local forums. As a result, the National Local Government Negotiating Forum (NLGNF) was established in early 1993. The main players in this forum were the national government, organized associations of local governments, political parties, and the political alliance led by the African National Congress, including trade unions and the South African National Civic Organization, which represented local civic associations.

187

The NLGNF very rapidly negotiated a framework for guiding the local-government transition. This was embodied in draft legislation eventually enacted as the *Local Government Transition Act* in late 1993. This Act transformed the local forums into statutory forums, with prescribed structures and procedures. The local forums were then mandated to negotiate locally appropriate solutions consistent with the principles of nonracialism, democracy, one tax base, accountability, and so on. Their first task was to create new local-government structures. In smaller towns, these new structures were single, integrated local governments called Transitional Local Councils (TLCs). In metropolitan areas, a two-level system was established, namely, the Transitional Metropolitan Council (TMC), for the whole metropolitan area, underpinned by Metropolitan Sub-Structures (MSSs). The job of the local forums was to define the boundaries, structures, and financial systems of the TLCs and TMCs and then appoint councillors to sit as a new kind of political leadership, drawn from both the former white political establishment and the political parties that had hitherto boycotted participation in local-government structures. These appointments were to last for the duration of the preinterim period between the appointment of the new political leadership by the negotiation forums and the municipal elections. The Act then made provision for democratic municipal elections that were held in 1995. The elections were to usher in elected transitional structures planned to last as long as the interim phase from the time of the elections to the time the elected Constitutional Assembly agreed on a final Constitution, incorporating local government into a new, three-tier system. In other words, the *Local Government Transition Act* provided a framework for a negotiated transition to local governance that parallels the finalization of the Constitution by the Constitutional Assembly. Both processes will converge on this final Constitution, which is to be the basis for the next general election in 1999.

Finally, it should be noted that the *Local Government Transition Act* and its implications were written into chapter 10 of the Constitution. This meant that locally driven negotiated transformation of local governance across the country was protected by both the Constitution and by other legislation. In other words, new local-government structures cannot be imposed from above by either the provincial governments or the national government elected on 27 April 1994.

Greater Johannesburg is built around the Johannesburg–Soweto urban core and is an integrated metropolitan area. It is also the hub of the newly created Gauteng province and the economic heartland of South Africa. The Gauteng province constitutes only 2% of the land area of South Africa but accounts for 43% of the gross national product, 50% of mining and manufacturing, and the bulk of financial services. Also, Gauteng is generally accepted as being the economic heartland not only of South Africa but also of the southern African subcontinent as a whole.

Gauteng contains five fairly distinct metropolitan subregions, namely, Greater Pretoria in the north; East Rand, stretching from Kempton Park–Germiston eastward; Vaal (Vereeniging–Van Der Byl Park and environs); West Rand, from Krugersdorp westward; and Greater Johannesburg. Greater Johannesburg is by far the most diversified subregion, and it contributed 35% of Gauteng's GDP in 1988. It is an urban economy that has been declining for a number of years. For example, although formal employment in the Gauteng grew by 3.9% for the 11 years to 1991, for the same period a 3.5% loss in formal jobs occurred in Greater Johannesburg (Brenner 1992).

As formal-sector employment has contracted, informal-sector employment has rocketed in the services and distribution sectors. For example, surveys conducted during 1979–80 of hawkers operating in Johannesburg's CBD estimated that only 200–250 hawkers were operating in the area. By 1993, however, surveys revealed that no less than 13 000 hawkers traded in the streets and transport termini of the CBD. The contribution of the informal sector to GDP was estimated at 18 % nationally. However, the same estimates suggested that about half the economically active population earned their living from the informal sector. Estimates for Gauteng suggested that the informal sector contributed up to 25 % of the GDP of the province (Brenner 1992).

189

Gauteng has been the residence of about 24 % of the country's total population of about 40 million people and has had the highest population growth rate, with an annual growth rate of 3.1 % for the 5 years ending in 1990. This compares with 2.5 % for the country as a whole. Although reliable figures are not yet available, Greater Johannesburg appears to be the residence of nearly half the total Gauteng population, or about 4 million people, of which only a quarter at most is white. The figures for Soweto varied in 1989 from 1.2 million to 2.5 million. Most significant of all, however, is the fact that 90 % of Gauteng's population is functionally urbanized.

The Housing Task Team of the Metropolitan Chamber estimated that 200 000 new dwellings would be required in Greater Johannesburg over a 10-year period, beginning in 1992, if both existing needs and those resulting from future growth were to be met. This has major implications for solid-waste management because it means that those who do not have access to formal dwelling live in serviced and unserviced shack settlements, where solid-waste removal is notoriously complex to manage. In addition, the Water and Sanitation Task Team of the Metropolitan Chamber estimated that as many as 2 million people, or nearly half of the total population, were without adequate water and sanitation services. Given that this figure refers mainly to people living in shack settlements, the solid-waste problem in these areas must be exacerbated by poor sanitation services. The health risks of illegal dumping, combined with the runoff of raw sewage, are well known and need no repetition here.

During apartheid, local-government institutions in Greater Johannesburg were, of course, divided according to race. The largest white part of Johannesburg was its municipal area, with more than 1 million people. Before the transition, it was governed by the Johannesburg City Council (JCC), which employed about

20 000 people in 1994. The JCC has traditionally been the largest local authority in the country. The other white local governments were the Roodepoort City Council, Randburg Town Council, and the Sandton Town Council. All these structures were constituted in terms of the *Transvaal Local Government Ordinance* of 1939 — a piece of provincial-level legislation.

The Black Local Authorities, constituted in terms of the national-level *Black Local Authorities Act* of 1982, were the Soweto City Council, Diepmeadow City Council, Dobsonville Town Council, and Alexandra Town Council. Most of the coloured and Indian areas were governed by management committees as adjuncts of the White Local Authorities, with limited executive and fiscal powers. National- and provincial-level structures, products of the 1983 Constitution, governed Ennerdale and Lenasia South directly. Informal settlements outside proclaimed municipal areas were governed directly by the former Transvaal Provincial Administration (which the 1993 Constitution subsequently replaced with the Gauteng provincial government).

In line with reformist initiatives of the period before the transition in 1990, the former National Party government introduced metropolitan-wide structures called regional services councils. They were premised on "consociational" principles (structured, horizontal coordination between vertically autonomous political entities), and they imposed new levies on businesses to fund infrastructure upgrades in black areas. The Central Witwatersrand Regional Services Council (CWRSC) was established in 1986, and it brought together all the local governments. Together the local authorities of the region plus the CWRSC were responsible for an annual budget of 4 billion ZAR by the early 1990s (in 1998, 4.4 rand [ZAR] = 1 United States dollar [USD]).

The classic structure of South African local governments and that of Greater Johannesburg in particular (excluding the management committees for the coloured and Indian areas) were replicas of the British model in most respects. In other words, each local government had a council that was directly elected on a ward basis, a small executive elected by the council, and a committee-based policy-making system. The chief executive officer was the town clerk, and the administration was structured according to departments, with executive directors as departmental heads.

The organizational culture came with the British notion of having hierarchical, vertically integrated departments led by professionals and controlled from the top through a system of paper-based directives and upward reporting. Frontline workers were disempowered, and services were rendered to mass markets with little differentiation and negligible consumer feedback. During the late 1980s, attempts were made to replace this extremely inefficient management model with scientific management approaches borrowed from US and UK private-sector models. Departments became cost centres, departmental heads were supposed to be managers first and professionals second, and paper-based directives, rules, and reports were replaced with financial accounting, zero-based budgeting, and outputs. This management approach was never properly implemented, leaving a mishmash of both the old professional and the new corporate management models. The implementation was half-baked because management consultants who drove the process took an externally imposed expert-based approach that empowered the management to redesign things from the top, with little active involvement or understanding from middle management and frontline workers. Resistance and the costs of retrenchments also helped to confound the best plans of the human-resource directors and their consultants.

191

After many months of very intensive negotiations involving numerous deadlocks and breakthroughs, the Metropolitan Chamber finally adopted a constitutional–institutional–financial model that provided in essence for a strong TMC and four MSSs, with an arbitration procedure to determine precisely how many and what the boundaries of the latter should be. After public hearings, the arbitrators announced the final result by declaring that there would be seven MSSs. This position, however, was overturned in August 1995 when the Gauteng provincial government succeeded in obtaining a court ruling that supported having only four MSSs.

The basic elements of the system of metropolitan government in Greater Johannesburg, as negotiated by the Metropolitan Chamber, can be summed up as follows:

- All preexisting local governments were dissolved, and all policy control over their administrative structures, staff, assets, and liabilities were transferred to the TMC.

- The TMC was given a 120-member council, appointed by the Metropolitan Chamber, and an executive committee, with an executive chairperson elected by the TMC.

- The TMC appointed a chief executive officer, who in turn established a core metropolitan administration.

- Although it was agreed that powers and functions should be distributed between the metropolitan and submetropolitan levels, metropolitan-wide powers and functions — such as bulk infrastructure, planning, financial policy, economic development, environmental management, and transportation — were reserved for the TMC.

- An important innovation was the provision for further decentralization to the MSS level. This was possible by way of a mechanism that required MSSs to develop a strategic management framework as the basis for requesting the transfer of TMC-level powers and functions to the MSSs. This framework must be motivated in terms of predetermined criteria, built into the agreement, and the TMC can only deny the request by giving adequate reasons in terms of these criteria.

- A sophisticated change-management approach was built into the agreement that defined the process and principles for transforming the former administrative structures and systems to fit the newly established constitutional structures and to be more oriented to development (more on this below).

These points relate mainly to the pre-interim phase. It was envisaged that sometime in 1995, the political representatives appointed by the Metropolitan Chamber to the new structures would be replaced by elected representatives. In accordance with the *Local Government Transition Act*, these elections were to ensure that 40 % of all TMC representatives were elected on the basis of proportional representation against party lists for the metropolitan area as a whole and that the other 60 % were to be elected on a ward basis, with a built-in weighted vote in the former white areas. These elections took place in November 1995.

Given that the governance of Greater Johannesburg was transformed via multistakeholder negotiations, the agreement is testimony to the advantages of a process-driven transformation of governance with management knitting together new patterns of knowledge, relationships, and institutional arrangements to support the formal process of change. The change-management approach was probably the most innovative aspect of the agreement because it demonstrated an understanding of the critical connection between newly established constitutional structures and the need to create results-oriented citizen-friendly development administrations. The change-management approach was premised on the assumption that organizational change should be a process managed in accordance with the following principles:

- Organizational change should be strategy led, that is, structures and systems should flow from an agreed strategy;

- Strategic vision must be collectively generated by groups of senior and middle management, as well as including frontline workers, rather than determined from the top via a conventional strategic-planning approach;

- The knowledge base for organizational change should be derived from expertise located within the organization at all levels, rather than being derived from outside management consultants operating in accordance with predetermined expert models; and

- The quality and sustainability of organizational change depend on the degree to which leadership at all levels is developed and empowered to understand and guide the change process.

It has been agreed that the change-management process will be jointly driven by management (which is still largely white) and the municipal trade unions (which are largely black). These approaches to the type of change-management process outlined above will fundamentally challenge the rigid, hierarchical, bureaucratic, and user-unfriendly administrations that have developed over the decades to serve mainly the white citizens. Instead, as evidence from implementation of the process has already begun to reveal, the process generates a vision of governance that is results rather rule driven, citizen led rather than citizen oppressive, outward rather than inward oriented, empowering rather than domineering, flexible rather than rigid, market responsive rather than monopolistic, and, above all, development oriented rather than exploitative. This approach to change management was clearly influenced by a governance approach aimed at building trust, reciprocity, accountability, and capacity, particularly given the context of transition, from a race-based regime to a nonracial, democratic mode of governance.

By the time of writing, in early 1996, it was, however, clear that there was still one major outstanding problem with the new two-tier metropolitan government for Greater Johannesburg. In brief, this was the failure to reach consensus on what the distribution of powers and functions should be between the metropolitan and substructural (primary) levels. The Greater Johannesburg Transitional Metropolitan Council (GJTMC) was adamant that it should be given the powers and functions of a genuine metropolitan government, with the capacity to govern the metropolis as a whole — the Toronto model was often cited as a sound example of this. The MSSs and the Gauteng provincial government, however, believed that it would be preferable to transfer substantial powers to the MSSs. These two levels of government shared this view for different reasons: the MSSs were aware that the GJTMC's excessive control could undermine their autonomy and accountability, and the Gauteng provincial government was clearly worried that an overly powerful metropolitan government would have the capacity to challenge its authority and political leadership. These competing interests led to interminable battles over what powers and functions should be located at which level. This has major implications for service delivery because the change-management strategy depends on reaching an agreement on powers and functions. For a sector like solid-waste management, it meant that no concrete forward planning was possible because the GJTMC and the MSSs were unable to establish a satisfactory division of responsibilities between the two levels. This institutional and political impasse is a fundamental aspect of waste-management issues in Johannesburg.

SOLID-WASTE MANAGEMENT IN TRANSITION

INSTITUTIONAL ARRANGEMENTS

The GJTMC is responsible for providing a refuse-collection and disposal service for the areas now integrated into this metropolitan entity. Before the GJTMC was established, each racially structured local authority in the Greater Johannesburg area had its own system for solid-waste management in line with national policy under apartheid. Metropolitan functions, such as selecting waste-disposal sites, were managed by the former JCC. This meant there were four solid-waste systems:

- A fully contracted service, with provision of labour and vehicles;
- A partially contracted service, with the provision of vehicles with driver and assistant, the labour and supervision being provided by the administration;
- A full service provided by the administration; and
- A community-driven collection service, as no service was provided.

The breakdown of the staffing and budget for the administrations in the GJTMC is as follows:

- *JCC* — Number of people employed in the department, 1 800; budget, 107 million ZAR; number of people serviced, 867 000; ratio of staff to serviced population, 1 : 482; budget per number of people serviced, 123.41 ZAR/person per annum; frequency of service, minimum of once a week, with the provision of a refuse bin and the separate issue of two refuse bags per bin each week. A regular street-cleaning service is also provided. The full spectrum of other refuse-collection and -disposal services is provided.

- *Sandton City Council* — Number of people employed in the department, 265; budget, 16 million ZAR; number of people serviced, 171 000; ratio of staff serviced to population, 1 : 645; budget per number of people serviced, 93.57 ZAR/person per annum; frequency of service, minimum of once a week, with the provision of a refuse bin but with refuse bags not supplied. A limited street-cleaning service is provided.

- *Roodepoort City Council* — Number of people employed in the department, 152; budget, 10.5 million ZAR; number of people serviced, 176 000; ratio of staff serviced to population, 1 : 1 158; budget per number of people serviced, 59.66 ZAR/person per annum; frequency of service, minimum of once a week, with refuse bags not supplied. A limited street-cleaning service is provided under contract, and the staffing and costs are not included.

195

- *Randburg Town Council* — Number of people employed in the department, 125; budget, 5.8 million ZAR; number of people serviced, 130 000; ratio of staff serviced to population, 1 : 1 040; budget per number of people serviced, 44.62 ZAR/person per annum; frequency of service, minimum of once a week, with refuse bags not supplied. A limited street-cleaning service is provided.

- *Soweto City Council* — Number of people employed in the department, 468 (including contracted staff); budget, 29.7 million ZAR; number of people serviced, 1 129 000; ratio of staff serviced to population, 1 : 2 412; budget per number of people serviced, 26.31 ZAR/person per annum; frequency of service, minimum of twice a week, with refuse bin supplied. A limited street-cleaning service is provided; however, problems with large dumps on street corners are never properly addressed.

- *Alexandra City Council* — Number of people employed in the department, 142 (including contracted staff); budget, 7.27 million ZAR; number of people serviced, 327 000; ratio of staff serviced to population, 1 : 2 303; budget per number of people serviced, 22.23 ZAR/person per annum; frequency of service, twice a week, with refuse bin supplied. An infrequent street-cleaning service is provided by contractors. The contract does not include increased densification or service in certain squatter camps. Problems with large dumps of refuse are not adequately addressed.

- *Ennerdale Town Council* — Number of people employed in the department, 29; budget, 1.5 million ZAR; number of people serviced, 43 000; ratio of staff serviced to population, 1 : 1 483; budget per number of people serviced, 34.88 ZAR/person per annum; frequency of service, minimum of once a week. Almost no street cleaning is provided.

- *Lenasia South* — Number of people employed in the department, 54; budget, 2.2 million ZAR; number of people serviced, 45 600; ratio of staff serviced to population, 1 : 884; budget per number of people serviced, 51.16 ZAR/person per annum; frequency of service, minimum of once a week. Almost no street cleaning is provided.

- *Dobsonville Town Council* — Number of people employed in the department, 67; budget, 1.1 million ZAR; number of people serviced, 170 000; ratio of staff serviced to population, 1 : 2 537; budget per number of people serviced, 6.47 ZAR/person per annum; frequency of service, minimum of twice a week. Almost no street-cleaning service is provided.

- *Settlements administrated by the Transvaal Provincial Administration* — Number of people employed in the department, 3; budget, 0.63 million ZAR; number of people serviced, 85 000; ratio of staff serviced to population, 1 : 28 333; budget per number of people serviced, 0.74 ZAR/person per annum. Service almost never occurs in areas occupied by squatters or informal housing units in the peri-urban areas to the south of Johannesburg.

It should be clear that the legacy of apartheid policies in Johannesburg was a highly uneven distribution of resources for the delivery of solid-waste services. This reflected the general inequality of service provision under the apartheid system as a whole. Given the overall political context, this was reflected in massive differences in the quality of service between white and black areas, which in turn, were a cause of the sustained rent and service-charge boycotts that social movements mounted. By the time the GJTMC took over solid-waste management, payment for service had still not been made, despite calls by local community and political leaders to resume payment.

In line with the *Local Government Transition Act* and the agreement negotiated in the Central Witwatersrand Metropolitan Chamber, responsibility for all the solid-waste departments was transferred from the disbanded local authorities to the GJTMC. A joint administrative structure was established in January 1995, comprising department heads, who were charged with responsibility for keeping service provision going until the entire sector could be transformed. This effectively meant that the preexisting solid-waste departments were politically accountable to the GJTMC but remained structured according to the previous racial division. The challenge for the GJTMC was to transform the 11 departments in each of the administrations into 1 metropolitan solid-waste department responsible for the bulk of solid-waste management and 4 primary-level solid-waste departments to be, in future, politically accountable to the MSSs. This, however, could only be worked out once the Gauteng provincial government (which is legally responsible for the regulatory framework of local government in Gauteng province) clearly defined the distribution of powers and functions between the GJTMC and its four MSSs. At the time of writing (first quarter of 1996), this had not yet been clarified.

198

The reason for the delay has been the Gauteng provincial government's inability to agree, at a political level, on a conception of metropolitan government it is willing to promote. A weak metropolitan government would have meant promulgating ordinances that transferred as many powers and functions down to the MSSs as possible, including virtually every aspect of solid-waste management other than regional waste dumps. A strong metropolitan government model would imply weak MSSs and the creation of a strong centralized metropolitan solid-waste department, with the MSSs playing an agency role. A middle position would imply the division of solid-waste functions between a metropolitan solid-waste department and the MSS solid-waste departments. However, it was unclear at the time of writing where the dividing line was to be drawn.

The only clear policy guideline that the GJTMC had set during the course of its first year of existence was that the resources for effective and efficient service delivery across Greater Johannesburg should be redistributed to overcome the inequities of the past. This, however, was easier said than done, for reasons of the unevenly developed infrastructure, financing, and staffing capacities of the administrations in different parts of the city. This can be highlighted by breaking down the 11 preexisting administrative structures into the newly constituted MSSs in the following way:

	Southern MSSs (%)	Northern MSSs (%)	Western MSSs (%)	Eastern MSSs (%)
JCC	59	19	—	22
Soweto				
Lenasia South				
Ennerdale				
TPA	72	7	21	—
Sandton				
Alexandra	—	—	—	100
Randburg	—	96	—	4
Diepmeadow	—	54	46	—
Roodepoort	—	—	100	—

Note: JCC, Johannesburg City Council; MSS, Metropolitan Sub-Structure; TPA, Transvaal Provincial Administration.

The reorganization of the metropolitan solid-waste system will need to take into account the nature and quality of the existing services. The existing solid-waste departments currently use a mix of solid-waste methods, ranging from advanced postindustrial systems to simple site-and-service systems.

FINANCING OF WASTE MANAGEMENT

The current budgets are calculated on the basis of historic inadequacies, with the result that the estimates for the current financial year will be overexpended. The methodology is to provide for the overexpenditure in previously black areas. The operating budget for the entire metropolitan region is estimated at 348 million ZAR, which is to provide for the full cost of a uniform service throughout the region. The allocated budget is currently sufficient to remove the accumulations of refuse and to provide a sustainable service to all areas, thus reducing the deficit in the previously disadvantaged areas. The capital requirements have been estimated at 13.5 million ZAR, including the costs for establishing an incinerator and a landfill site. Payment for the service is determined via a tariff approved by the Metropolitan Council, using the agreed-on principle of cross-subsidization. The charges are allocated according to stand size and affordability; a large stand pays considerably more than a small stand or squatter shack. The nonpayment for refuse collection is continuing in the disadvantaged areas, although the service is provided. The current outstanding debt is 30 million ZAR for the metropolitan region. The funding of the shortfall will be carried by the rates account and will be transferred as a deficit to the 1996/97 estimate. The solid-waste operating budget is 8.7% of the total operating estimate for 1995/96. Neither the provincial nor the central government pays a subsidy for the cost of solid-waste removal. The cost of refuse removal is about 5% of the total cost to each ratepayer. A special effort is envisaged to ensure recovery of the cost of the refuse-collection service.

199

SERVICE MAGNITUDE

The area serviced by the GJTMC covers nine administrative areas, with about 500 000 refuse-collection points. The bulk of these collection points are found in relatively well-developed urban areas, mainly the former white suburbs. On average, 6 200 t is disposed of in this region each day, at seven sanitary landfill sites. In accordance with the solid-waste bylaws for this region, refuse bins are supplied, together with refuse bags, for each service user. These bags and, where applicable, refuse bins are collected and removed at least once a week, on average, from each property. This average, however, masks the disparities between some former white suburbs where collections are made regularly once a week and some informal settlements where refuse is irregularly collected from central points once in 3 weeks. Streets are cleaned according to litter-generation patterns, and the frequency of cleaning varies from irregular cleaning in the former black townships and low-density suburbs to intense cleaning in the CBDs. Street cleaning is done by the staff of the solid-waste departments. Community-based approaches have sometimes been used. In this approach, the community leaders, in conjunction with the officials, select people from the community to collect and remove refuse from the informal settlements or squatter camps to a designated collection point. These people are paid to do this work, either through an employment contract or through donations from institutions, such as the Keep South Africa Beautiful Association. The services within the sites are contracted to an acceptable standard; however, the removal from the collection points is problematic. The refuse bags provided to the community are often dumped at the collection point, adding to the general litter problem. The cost of the service is not being recovered, as the communities expect to be paid for keeping their own areas clean. The areas where this type of service is provided are Orange Farm in the Southern area and Swetla in Alexandra. In some areas, as a result of poor refuse-collection service, as well as inadequate awareness of the correct use of the service, illegal dumping of refuse still occurs, which reduces environmental quality. The consequences of illegal dumping of refuse are well documented. It adds an operating cost that no community can afford. Refuse dumped on open land or in the street increases the populations of rodents, vermin, and flies. The high summer temperature makes the heaps putrefy, and they are therefore prone to emitting strong odours. The illegal dumping of refuse is a consequence of inadequate service, combined with tariff avoidance. The type of refuse dumped in areas such as Dobsonville and Soweto is basically domestic with high levels of ash. Animal carcasses are also dumped on street corners, as no service is provided for removing them as in the previous black townships. The illegal dumping of commercial and industrial refuse complicates its removal and adds to the risk of environmental damage.

The cost of removing contained refuse is 110 ZAR/t, and that of removing uncontained, illegally dumped refuse is more than 750 ZAR/t. The control of illegal dumping is problematic, as most people consider illegal dumping socially unacceptable, and it therefore usually occurs at night to avoid the neighbours' observing it. Efforts to curb refuse dumping have, to date, been sporadic and had little planning, thus little success. A large problem in the CBD of Johannesburg is that of tariff avoidance by shopkeepers who dump their refuse on the pavement. The increase in street hawkers congesting the pavements has aggravated this problem. The conflict between established businesses in the formal sector and the emerging contingent of street hawkers has had the result that numerous complaints are made about street litter and the blame goes to the street hawkers.

Waste collection, transportation, and disposal are done primarily by the staff of the solid-waste departments, using capital equipment paid for by the local authorities. However, in certain former black areas, where staffing has been a serious problem over the last 10 years, certain aspects of the system are contracted out. In Soweto, the service was contracted out in 1987, as a result of the workers' going on strike to disrupt local government. The contractor provides door-to-door service and charges a fixed rate per tonne. The contractor is from the white-minority group and employs people living outside Soweto. This results in a high level of anger among the people living in Soweto. Cooperation between the community and the contractor is not very satisfactory, and this is one of the major factors contributing to the poor service in Soweto.

In areas such as Johannesburg, contractors are engaged to supply 21-m^3 refuse-compaction vehicles, along with the driver and operator. This is largely due to the poor performance of the repair service of fleet managers of the JCC. The backup ratio for vehicles in this fleet was 1 : 1, thus doubling the cost. The fleet supplied by the contractors has a backup ratio of 1 : 6. This method for supplying vehicles has been successful and has reduced the cost of the service to users.

The landfill sites provide a service for municipal solid waste. Greater Johannesburg has seven landfill sites, with a capacity to meet the needs of the area. Each site has its own life span, with the

201

shortest (Kya Sands) ending in 1999 and the longest (Goudkoppies) ending in 2056. The GJTMC is considering two new sites, with a possibility that future solid-waste disposal arrangements will take into account the need to recycle. To date, however, approaches to solid-waste disposal have been focused more on efficiency than on sustainable resource management. This is why very limited recycling takes place.

202

The most serious problem with existing systems for solid-waste disposal is that the landfill approach is inappropriate for disposal of hazardous industrial waste. A number of private-sector waste-management companies have become increasingly involved in attempts to remedy this, but their environmental practices have led to numerous conflicts with the residents of nearby suburbs. It is now generally recognized in the waste sector nationally that the available hazardous-waste landfill sites are inadequate to meet the needs of industrial development in South Africa and, indeed, that the approach to hazardous waste in general is inappropriate.

CURRENT REFUSE-COLLECTION METHODS

Every service point in the formal housing areas in the former black townships and white suburbs is issued a standardized bin, and generally each week every property is issued two refuse bags per bin when the full bags are collected. Although in some areas collection is less frequent because of capacity problems, this system is generally used throughout the metropolitan region, and each area is serviced on a particular day on a regular basis.

A task team made up of representatives from each of the administrations coordinates the schedules for the whole of Greater Johannesburg. The task team now focuses on areas in each of the MSSs, as refuse collection is the responsibility of the MSSs. The type of vehicle used for this is fitted with a compactor unit with loading capacity of 21 m^3, or about 10 t refuse per load. The vehicles should be expected to transport, on average, 30 t of refuse to the landfills on a daily basis, 5 days a week. This, however, is not achievable in all areas in the region, for a number of reasons. The primary reason for low productivity is a poor balance of rounds and a poor work ethic in some areas, which is due to the low level of supervision and almost no management of the service in the black townships. The other factor is the frequency of breakdowns of council-owned vehicles and the lack of adequate backup.

In each refuse-collection round in this region, nine workers and a supervisor are allocated to a refuse truck on a daily basis. Four of these workers are used to load the refuse into the truck, and the remaining five go ahead of the vehicle and issue two refuse bags to each service user. The filled refuse bags are collected by the refuse worker and stacked at a point where the refuse truck stops and the workers collect the accumulated bags. With this method, the controls on the refuse-collection process are simplified, as the entire process is ergonomically designed for optimum use of both the workers and the vehicle.

The solid-waste department of the former JCC is responsible for taking care of 50% of all solid waste in Greater Johannesburg. Because of the magnitude of this undertaking, this department has been able to build up a core of expertise and an infrastructure that is a key strategic resource for the city as a whole. Owing to the cross-subsidization of JCC from the township resource base, the JCC has been able to direct considerable budgetary resources into the solid-waste department, effectively providing a First World service to an island of privileged whites in a racially secluded enclave in the middle of a Third World metropolis. As this department was never required to service poor township areas, where people would have found it difficult to pay the service charges, it was possible to retain First World standards. This, however, is all going to change, as the task of meeting a much wider set of needs will begin to eat into this core of capacity and resources.

Solid-waste services in greater Soweto, Randburg, Sandton, Ennerdale, and Alexandra are similar to those provided in the former white areas of Johannesburg. In Soweto, Diepmeadow, Randburg, Sandton, and Ennerdale, the supply of refuse bags to the service user is problematic, as these areas do not have the staff infrastructure to deliver the refuse bags on a weekly basis. The refuse rounds, although planned for collection, are based on a system of loading from the service point directly to the refuse-collection vehicle. The worker allocation varies from area to area but is generally 10 workers per refuse round, with 6 people loading the vehicle and 4 people bringing the bins or bags to the side of the road for collection. This system does not increase the cost per bag; however, it increases spillage of refuse in the loading process, thus adding to the street-cleaning cost.

203

WHEELED BINS

In Roodepoort, Lenasia Southeast, and the CBD of Johannesburg, a mobile wheeled bin system is in place. It is a 240 L bin, which is emptied into the back of a refuse-compactor vehicle by means of a lifting mechanism. The labour allocation is similar to that of the previous system and requires that the bins be moved from the collection point to the back of the vehicle and replaced after they are emptied. These bins are supplied to the affluent areas and give the occupant additional refuse storage space in suburban areas. In the CBD, this system was introduced to accommodate the limited storage area in buildings, as well as to reduce refuse spillage during the loading process.

The disadvantage of this system is that the lifting mechanism reduces the payload of the vehicle, increasing the cost per kilometre–tonne. As well, refuse-bag loading is faster than with the lifting mechanism. The advantages, however, in many ways outweigh the disadvantages, as the system reduces litter and spillage. The system gives the user increased storage, and the hinged lid reduces the attraction of flies and other vermin. The cost of the system is high and inhibitive in a developing community. The cost of the wheeled bin is triple that of a standard bin, and the slower loading times means that 25 % more vehicle– and person–hours are required. Because it is necessary to provide a service to the whole community, the additional resources required discount this option.

INFORMAL SETTLEMENTS

The service to the informal settlements (squatter camps) has been rendered on an emergency basis. A 5.5-m^3 bulk-refuse container is allocated to every 200 shacks. In theory, shack dwellers deposit their refuse in these containers. The containers are emptied on a regular basis, normally at least once a week. This type of service has the problem that the refuse is dumped around the container, and the refuse in the container is set on fire (as a way of getting rid of it when too much collects around the bin) and smoulders for days, polluting the atmosphere. These containers are placed at points in the settlements after negotiations with the settlement leaders, and constant community liaison is required to ensure the success of this service. As not all solid-waste departments employ personnel dedicated to this activity, the system frequently breaks down, giving the impression in the settlements that local government's waste-removal service is inadequate.

Instead of trying to improve the container system in the informal settlements, the new administrations instructed the solid-waste departments to change over to the refuse-bag system. Although this could increase the cost per unit by as much as 2.10 ZAR in areas that can least afford this level of service, it is politically imperative to demonstrate the normalization of service provision to a uniform standard throughout the metropolitan region. About 20 recognized self-standing informal-settlement areas can be found in the region, with about 50 000 shacks, housing an estimated 250 000 people. It will cost local governments 13.50 ZAR/household to extend the conventional bin-bag system to all these households, which will be recovered via the policy of cross-subsidization. Alternative community-based approaches have unfortunately not been fully considered, despite their having proven successful in some areas. The vision of refuse-collection methods will have to accommodate the needs of the overall community, and all the methods will have to be tested to ensure an appropriate level of service and cost.

205

STREET CLEANING

The point-to-point refuse-collection system moves the refuse from the house or business to the landfill site but does not take into account the litter generated or the illegal dumping of refuse in open public spaces. To maintain an acceptable standard of street cleaning in open public spaces, the city needs to provide a street-cleaning service. The litter-generation patterns are monitored, and workers are deployed to sweep and collect the litter for proper disposal. About 780 km of streets are swept within commercial areas, and 464 km are swept within residential areas (including portions of the motorways) on a daily basis, removing an average of 150 t/day of litter throughout the metropolitan region. In some areas, the amounts of litter and illegally dumped refuse equal that removed via the point-to-point refuse-collection service. Certain streets of the CBD are regularly flushed with water and disinfected in places where these streets are fouled by pedestrians who defecate on the pavement because there are no public toilet facilities. Although an inadequate point-to-point refuse-collection system in certain areas may explain the need for some people to dump their refuse illegally in public spaces, education programs are also clearly very much needed to improve people's awareness and understanding of appropriate practices. The city also clearly has an opportunity to use informal labour for street-cleaning purposes. This, however, would run afoul of formal labour-relations practices and would be unacceptable to the trade unions.

PRIVATE-SECTOR INVOLVEMENT

The private sector is getting involved in waste management in a number of ways. The private sector comprises large service users, who demand a high level of service, and this sector is influential in determining policy. Owing to the attraction of the metropolitan region for investment, the needs of the private sector in service standards cannot be ignored. The private sector has started a number of initiatives in service delivery that are largely independent of metropolitan government. The provision of funding to local communities to keep their own areas clean is part of the private-sector involvement. The use of additional private resources to clean the streets adjacent to their properties is welcome because these activities reduce the need for municipal cleaning. The use of the private sector in the provision of service has been both successful and unsuccessful. In this regard, the experiences in Soweto will have a direct bearing on future policies.

COMMUNITY PARTICIPATION

The community can have many levels of involvement in service delivery. Four forms of participation, however, will be of concern here, namely, formal political representation in policy formation, organized community involvement in policy formation, citizen participation in daily operation and maintenance, and involvement of contractors and labour in the execution of service delivery, or what can be referred to as economic participation.

Up until the dissolution of the apartheid form of local government and the establishment of the GJTMC and its MSSs, formal political representation and organized community involvement via ratepayers' associations were limited to the white community. These forms of representation of community interests constitute a recent phenomenon for the black communities. It is, therefore, premature to comment on the efficacy of political representation via the newly elected councillors. However, if for all communities the new system replicates the patterns that prevailed in the white community before deracialization, then political representation will have absolutely no impact on the solid-waste system, beyond the approval of budgets and minor adjustments to service standards. Service levels, long-term planning, and day-to-day management have traditionally been insulated from direct political intervention by elected representatives. White ratepayers' organized community involvement in policy may have affected service standards and operating deficiencies but has rarely had input into service levels, technology, or management systems. The civic associations that formerly represented black-community interests have been severely weakened because their best people have been creamed off for local government. These associations have to be rebuilt before the organized community involvement of black communities will be possible again.

207

This leaves citizen participation and economic participation. If solid-waste removal is to be efficient, citizens need to be aware of their daily responsibilities, which means not simply the abstract idea of citizen commitment to the system but knowledge of daily routines, collection timetables, standard procedures (such as what kind of bags are acceptable), and location (where bags should be deposited), etc. Whereas this has been well developed in the white suburbs, with decades of awareness campaigns and habits combining to ensure the effective participation of the users, this has not been the case in the former black townships. Instead, irregular and inadequate services, constantly changing collection systems, poor relations between citizens and officials, corruption, and lack of investment in awareness have combined to ensure low levels of commitment to the service and widespread ignorance (and even apathy) about timetables, procedures, and routines. This is reflected graphically in the continued failure of rent and service-payment schemes after April 1994. Political legitimation is not the only factor in the relationship between users and the service provider. Another is the long-term process of building a cooperative culture of mutual trust between users and the service provider.

The most promising area in which to expand community participation is doubtless going to be that of the economic participation by certain community interests in service delivery.

This began long before the end of apartheid. During the 1980s, the National Party government made numerous attempts to co-opt supportive elements in black communities and incorporate them into the service-delivery system as subcontractors. With the onset of change in 1990, these practices were expanded because black business people began to lobby for a policy of contracting out government services. By the mid-1990s, with the ascendance to leadership of politicians who were connected to these emerging black business interests, the need to formalize economic participation in service delivery had become generally accepted at both the political and managerial levels. Although for-profit contractors are the primary actors in this emerging arena, nonprofit organizations in housing and environmental conservation have also expressed interest in participating in some aspect of waste management, particularly community-based waste collection in squatter settlements. Organizations representing the interests of the unemployed have also added their voice, calling for labour-based or labour-intensive waste-management policies, or both.

Economic participation is clearly an important stimulus to other forms of participation. Bringing in networks of contractors led and staffed by people from the communities creates an economic interest in the success of the solid-waste system, which can act as a catalyst for organized community involvement in policy formation, especially if aspirant contractors also occupy leading positions in community associations, such as in Orange Farm. Because of the economic status of contractors, they are also generally well placed to influence popular perception and cultural norms in their communities. This can lead to improved user participation in the service-delivery system.

In conclusion, it needs to be pointed out that since late 1995 all four modes of community participation have been evident, taking different forms, but with economic participation being the most effective. Fortunately, during the 1990s, considerable space exists for this kind of reciprocity, which has been reinforced by the introduction of democratic accountability. However, building trust between users and service providers and between the solid-waste departments and contractors will depend to a greater extent on whether governing capacities can be significantly improved.

INSTITUTIONAL OPTIONS FOR THE
GOVERNANCE OF SOLID WASTE

The future governance of solid waste in Johannesburg must address three issues:

- Administrative reorganization into a two-tier metropolitan system, with clear responsibilities at both levels, including the appropriate financing mechanisms;

209

- Redistribution of financial, staffing, and infrastructural resources to overcome the historic inequalities in the levels and standards of service provision; and

- Establishment of partnerships between the public, private, and community sectors to maximize the mobilization of public, private, and community resources.

The Solid Waste Directorate of the GJTMC is clearly the leading stakeholder when it comes to finding ways of facing these challenges. The Solid Waste Directorate has as its mission "to improve the quality of our environment by effectively managing the waste stream of our community" (SWD n.d.)

The refuse-collection and -disposal systems have been established over many years, and the policies determining these aspects may be found in applicable legislation. In terms of both national and provincial legislation, it is required of a local authority to create a refuse-collection system; however, no guidelines are available on the method or frequency of service. This directorate has formally accepted, at the policy level, that three factors will affect future selection of waste systems:

- The affordability of extending the high-standard system developed in the white areas to the whole metropolitan area, as the tax base is likely to be incapable of supporting this (thus both cross-subsidization and a change of standard would be required);

- Pressures for increased community involvement in waste management, especially smaller contractors; and

- The need for thorough awareness of, and education on, waste issues.

The Solid Waste Directorate began in early 1994 to rethink the governance of waste. To date, the mode of governance in the white areas has been the traditional local-authority model. This implies centralized management following strict guidelines and procedures, with political leadership playing the role of the watch-dog over policy and the budget. Administration–community relations have been distant and, at best, mediated by the political leadership. In the black areas, service was irregular and poorly financed, and the administration had very poor relations with the community. Where innovative inclusion of small contractors has been attempted, the success levels have not been very high, for reasons primarily of poor contract management.

To tackle these issues, the Solid Waste Directorate, working in conjunction with the other solid-waste departments, initiated a policy-development process. The Cleansing Task Team drafted the policy document to be discussed with the community and the newly democratically elected councillors. At the time of writing, this process was incomplete. However, the policy was noted and agreed to in principle by the Metropolitan Council.

The policy process was premised on the need to provide a sustainable refuse-collection and -disposal service. To achieve this, the Solid Waste Directorate adopted the following strategic objectives:

■ To identify clear areas of immediate need;

■ To provide an efficient and effective service to all refuse generators, according to set quality and productivity standards;

■ To establish systems for incorporating the communities' needs into the decision-making process; and

■ To establish structures and systems of management and control to ensure the implementation of policy.

Policy guidelines have been accepted as the basis for the institutional reorganization and management of the system to ensure delivery of the following services:

■ *Refuse collection* — The Solid Waste Directorate has accepted that all refuse generated on all residential and nonresidential properties requiring regular removal for health reasons should be stored, handled, and removed as efficiently and effectively as possible, on a metropolitan-wide basis. The acceptance of this guideline marks a decisive shift away from the discriminatory approach to service delivery during apartheid.

- *Street cleaning (street sweeping and litter collection)* — The purpose of the street-cleaning service is to prevent environmental pollution by maintaining the cleanliness of streets and publicly owned places.

- *Removal of garden refuse, building materials, and bulky and special domestic refuse* — The purpose of this service is to remove bulky excess and other wastes generated on an irregular basis and wastes that cannot be removed through the normal refuse-collection system so as to minimize fire and health hazards and to maintain the environment. This service includes provision of sites for people in the community to dispose of their garden refuse, thus discouraging illegal dumping of discarded building material.

- *Refuse disposal* — All refuse generated must be disposed of in accordance with all relevant legislation and applicable standards. All refuse-disposal sites are to be operated in accordance with the relevant legislation.

- *Maintenance of service standards* — Service standards have been developed to measure the quality of service and the performance of the service provider.

The *Solid Waste Bylaws* of South Africa have been amended to establish the regulatory framework for a two-tier metropolitan solid-waste system. In essence, the metropolitan government will be responsible for landfills and incineration, and the MSSs will be responsible for refuse collection, street cleaning, and garden-refuse collection and sites. The principles contained in these bylaws are the following:

- All service users have a right to a refuse-collection service;

- All refuse collected will be disposed of in an environmentally acceptable manner;

- All polluters will be prosecuted; and

- All persons have a duty to keep their environment free from refuse.

The *Solid Waste Bylaws* incorporate these principles and set out the core policies governing the management of solid waste in the metropolitan region.

211

These policies and principles strongly reflect a desire to redistribute resources to ensure the delivery of an efficient and effective solid-waste service to all communities on a uniform basis. To this extent, the new mode of democratic accountability in general has resulted in a change in the governance of solid waste.

However, from a governance point of view, these policies and principles can be criticized in three ways. First, none of the policies or principles refer explicitly to the need for or structure of public–private–community sector partnerships. This is particularly surprising, given the acknowledged financial constraints and limited infrastructure of the solid-waste departments. The policies and principles, in short, effectively narrow the space for reciprocity, and this could, in turn, make it difficult to build new relations of mutual trust. Second, none of the policies and principles refer to the need to change from a distant, technocratically competent mass-delivery culture to a more service-oriented development administrative culture that understands governance. A third criticism might be that the intention is to preserve the aesthetic and health standards of the social environment. Very little is done to make alternative use of waste, which the sustainable approach to resource use tends to advocate. This third criticism is directly related to the second and first because, as experience in the city of Curitiba in Brazil demonstrates, a sustainable approach to resource use depends on the kinds of partnerships and interdependencies that good governance implies.

Taking into account the resource constraints and the wide range of socioeconomic conditions across Greater Johannesburg, the Solid Waste Directorate has accepted, at the policy level, that a number of methods will be required to collect refuse from the various types of communities and to transport it to an appropriate disposal facility. It has also accepted that each of these methods will have a different impact on the levels of service provided. The Solid Waste Directorate has considered the following delivery methods and approaches.

SITE AND SERVICE

The site-and-service method will be used primarily in the informal settlements. A bulk refuse container (a so-called skip) will be placed on an accessible open piece of land for use by the community. In each case, the community is to be consulted on where to locate the skip. The intention is to have people in the community place their refuse and unwanted material in the container and to have the container periodically emptied. The problem with this approach is that refuse is blown out of the bulk container by the wind. The area around the container is usually heavily littered, and often the refuse in the container is set on fire and smoulders, causing air pollution and a further fire hazard. To prevent this, the skip approach requires that the community itself take responsibility for ensuring that refuse is placed in the container. However, the GJTMC and the MSSs have had no intention of doing anything other than placing the skip and removing it when it is full. Without the necessary investment of time, resources, and personnel for the purpose of building the awareness of the community, the chances of success for this approach are very low.

213

CONTRACTOR

The *Solid Waste Bylaws* stipulate that no person may render a refuse-collection service to a service user without the written consent of the GJTMC. The GJTMC may also appoint an agent or contractor to render a refuse-collection service but retains accountability for this service to the electorate and to the higher levels of government. The process of appointing such an agent or contractor must comply with the financial regulations.

The contractor approach aims to enhance the economic participation of people in the community. A contractor is contracted to collect the refuse from a given community for a fee. The contractor then distributes refuse bags throughout the community and has the choice either to pay anyone who returns the bag filled with refuse or to collect the refuse directly. All litter and refuse are collected by the contractor and placed in a bulk refuse container (skip) that is owned and serviced by the GJTMC. The cost of transporting the skip to and from the site and disposing of the refuse in a landfill is not recovered from the community and must be funded, therefore, by the GJTMC or its MSSs, or both.

Although the main advantage of this approach is that it provides aspirant black business people with an opportunity to go into this type of business, supported by local government, it has several problems. First, it requires a high level of cross-subsidization that better-off constituencies may well resent and therefore oppose. Second, the skip is the main collector of refuse, and the same problems occur with litter as in the site-and-service approach, albeit they are diminished because of the role of the contractor. Third, the contractor, not the GJTMC, is responsible for the service within the local community, and there is concern that this could undermine political accountability in the use of taxpayers' money for the delivery of a service that neither the GJTMC nor its MSSs directly manage.

214

COMMUNITY-BASED WASTE MANAGEMENT

Community-based approaches seek to use resources and labour drawn from the local community. This is what distinguishes the community-based approach from the contractor approach, because the contractor does not necessarily come from the local community.

The GJTMC has considered a community-based approach, whereby people in the community collect and transport the refuse from their area to a selected bulk-storage site or a disposal facility. A method of payment is then negotiated within the community, as well as between the community representatives and the GJTMC. The standards and frequency of service are determined by the community, and this service is rendered with the support of the community. A service like this would be unusual in that the labour is done, not by employees of the GJTMC, but by members of the community, and they are rewarded through a public-works program.

Clearly, the main advantage of this approach is that it introduces an economic incentive for high levels of participation in waste collection. It has, however, several problems. First, unionized municipal workers may see it as a threat to their jobs and as an attempt to undercut wage levels. Second, the skip remains the primary collector of refuse, and the same problems occur with the litter as in the site-and-service approach, albeit they are diminished because of the role of the community. Third, as people must collect their own refuse, it may contradict the principle that each and every residential unit in Greater Johannesburg is entitled to a refuse-collection service. Fourth, because the community representatives are responsible for the service within the local community, and not the GJTMC, this can undermine political accountability, as in the contractor approach.

TRADITIONAL SERVICE

Policymakers see the traditional-service approach as the one most consistent with the Solid Waste Directorate's policies and principles. The traditional-service approach is premised on the notion that the local government must provide storage capacity at each residential site and a door-to-door collection service, with universal frequency and standards determined by the GJTMC. This service is all inclusive and can in theory be adjusted to meet the demands of the community. In practice, the costs may be prohibitive. The tariff is set by the GJTMC or the MSSs, or both, and all service users are bound to pay the charges. This should enable the GJTMC to cross-subsidize payment to disadvantaged communities. When, however, the majority find it difficult to afford these tariffs and budget cutbacks prevent cross-subsidization from other services, this financial approach may prove problematic. Nevertheless, a standardized product delivered to individual residential units according to standardized procedures and routines is far easier for the new political leaders to understand and accept. It is also favoured by officials, who find routinely administered systems easier to deal with than complex community dynamics and development processes.

215

Those who favour the traditional-service approach argue that it takes account of development imperatives and community needs. Selected aspects of the service, they argue, can be contracted in terms of community-based collection systems, use unconventional transportation hired from local contractors, deploy local labour in local communities, and have various other community inputs. Retaining the service under the centralized control of the solid-waste departments can, it is argued, ensure political accountability, sound financial management, and equitable levels and standards.

At present, the majority of service users in Greater Johannesburg are serviced a minimum of once a week, with two bin liners per service. This service falls in line with systems in developed countries and is traditionally implemented in local authorities based on the British local-authority service-delivery model. It assumes that the local authority has a sustainable tax base and that budget reprioritization will not undercut the capital and operating requirements of the traditional waste system. These assumptions, however, are already being questioned, thus forcing the Solid Waste Directorate to consider other options.

COMMUNITY INVOLVEMENT

At present, the Keep Johannesburg Beautiful Association, an NGO, has specific mechanisms to involve the public in policy formulation. This is done via village committees, which monitor solid-waste collection. It has been suggested that Cleansing Forums be established in every place where they are practicable, using the village-committee principle, and that the GJTMC support these committees. Areas for urgent ongoing public involvement will need to be identified and prioritized, and existing organizations will need to be included in this process. This method also includes the community in the decision-making process by allowing these committees to comment on matters affecting their environment and to communicate these comments to the relevant committees of the GJTMC. In other words, the communities would have input into policy-making, and the local authority would play the role of watchdog over adherence to the policies by the service provider. This could lead to the greater involvement of small businesses in the waste system.

By the end of 1994, the various solid-waste administrations had reached no consensus about the approach or combination of approaches to most effectively deal with the challenges. As a result, the GJTMC still has no overall change-management strategy to transform the existing racially fragmented system of waste management into a two-tier metropolitan system.

Nevertheless, GJTMC has approved the principle that the cost of services in poorer areas can now be cross-subsidized. This is very significant because, for the first time, the authorities no longer regard services in the poorer areas as self-financing. Virtually all residential units in both formal and informal residential areas are now serviced in one way or another. The debate, therefore, is not about the quantitative extension of the system but about its qualitative restructuring to ensure a uniform approach across the metropolitan area, in line with the overall political imperative to deracialize the city.

It is necessary to evaluate the debate and options reviewed in this section from the point of view of the conception of governance we developed earlier in this chapter. We argued that a governance approach should take into account democratic accountability, capacity to manage (including organizational structure and

216

culture), relations of trust, and the space for reciprocity. The following subsections describe the general state of the debate and its broader context, rather than specific elements.

Accountability

Democratically elected nonracial local governments at metropolitan and local levels were a necessary condition for taking a local-governance approach in Greater Johannesburg. This achievement, however, was marred by two problems. First, although consensus had been reached on the need for a two-tier metropolitan approach, the failure to reach agreement on the distribution of powers and functions between these two levels has made it impossible to proceed with a detailed change-management strategy in the solid-waste sector. Consequently, the old JCC Solid Waste Directorate, which became that of the GJTMC, has had to drive the process without knowing whether it was to be a metropolitan-level department in the making or whether it and the other preexisting solid-waste departments were about to be restructured into four MSS solid-waste departments, attached to a small solid-waste directorate at the metropolitan level. This kind of strategic uncertainty undermines accountability and effective management. Second, no agreement was found on the need for a creative mechanism to bring small businesses into the waste-service sector, using the contracting approach, or to bring communities into self-help schemes, using the community-based approach. The persistence of a conventional conception of governmental accountability is the underlying reason for the continued adherence to this limited approach to service delivery.

217

Capacity

Under apartheid, Black Local Authorities were unable to generate the resource base needed to build up the managerial, organizational, and technical capacities to plan and develop an adequate level of service and to maintain and operate the infrastructure at a high standard. The establishment of the two-tier metropolitan system in Greater Johannesburg is clearly a necessary condition for resolving this problem. The centrality of the former JCC Solid Waste Directorate in the equation suggests that it is an institutional resource with considerable potential to meet the needs of the metropolitan area. However, two unresolved issues might prevent its being used. First, although the JCC Solid Waste Directorate and the preexisting solid-waste departments have the technical competence, staffing levels, and infrastructure to meet needs both during and after the change to a two-tier government, they may be unable to switch from a traditional, Fordist, routinized approach to mass service delivery, using standardized procedures, to a development approach requiring direct relationships with the clients via unconventional contracting methods and postmodern management procedures. It is going to take time for a development culture to take root and develop. Bringing development workers in who previously worked for NGOs may assist in making this happen. Second, as budgetary constraints become a reality, the future solid-waste departments at the municipal and submunicipal levels may well be forced to focus resources on the maintenance and operation of the existing infrastructure, rather than contemplate the extension of their services to the informal settlements where service payments are both inadequate and erratic.

Reciprocity

The sustained involvement of organized civil society and private-sector stakeholders in local-level negotiation processes between 1989 and 1994 helped to create a political culture and operating environment premised on the stakeholder approach to policy formation and implementation. To this extent, the space for reciprocal stakeholder participation exists. Senior officials of the solid-waste departments have attended numerous community meetings to discuss service-delivery problems, and dozens of forums have been established to discuss alternative service approaches with small-business operators who believe that the new dispensation will automatically favour contracting out and even full-scale privatization. Three factors, however, may tend to narrow the space so far achieved. First, the absorption of many local leaders into local government and the funding cutbacks that many NGOs are currently experiencing have severely weakened CBOs and nonprofit organizations. Second, the bureaucratic culture of municipal departments that evolved from apartheid tends to discourage reciprocity. It is simply much easier to make assumptions about service needs than to have to spend a lot of time communicating and negotiating. This culture removes incentives for participation. Third, a number of large-scale multinational and national companies with extensive experience in privatized public-service delivery are beginning to muscle in on the game. They have the resources to hire effective lobbyists, and their arguments are given serious attention. Major companies are already involved in solid-waste management, and they have an interest in increasing their involvement. If the GJTMC and its MSSs promote this, then the primary beneficiaries of reciprocity will be these companies, rather than the people in the communities and the small contractors, whereas the government has the greatest need to secure the participation, trust, and cooperation of precisely these people.

219

Trust

It is probably fair to say that low levels of trust are the greatest challenge facing all public-service managers, particularly solid-waste managers. Given the legacy of apartheid, it is unsurprising that relationships between officials and local communities are still fraught with tension. Officials want communities to pay for services, but people in the communities do not believe this will lead the officials to upgrade existing services or develop and extend them to unserviced areas. The officials may overcome these people's mistrust with promises in the short term. But in the long run, promises can lead to disillusionment, if raised expectations remain unmet. This is the cycle of postindependence Africa, and it may continue in South Africa if vote catching and budget constraints combine to trigger expectations and retard delivery.

In summary, although the negotiated transition to democratic, nonracial local government in Greater Johannesburg was a remarkable achievement, municipal authorities still have a long way to go to achieve a consolidated system of democratic local governance.

POLICY OPTIONS AND RECOMMENDATIONS

This section sets a recommended policy perspective for changes in Greater Johannesburg's system for solid-waste management. The GJTMC needs to consider four institutional options in implementing some combination of waste-management methods:

- *Metropolitanization of the traditional method* — This would entail the expansion of the existing administration at metropolitan and submetropolitan levels within the traditional institutional framework. The focus here would be on using the existing technology, an expanding pool of capital goods, and an increased labour force. Officials would develop the policy, and politicians would approve it. It would be implemented through routine procedures, timetables, and reporting. This would require a hierarchically structured administrative arrangement, with a cascading level of command. Given that community involvement in delivery of service would be limited in this option, community participation in the governance of the waste system would be restricted to policy-consultation forums or limited outsourcing.

- *Community contracting* — This would involve contracting community-based profit and nonprofit businesses to take responsibility for certain aspects of the waste stream, such as collection from residential sites and delivery to disposal sites; collection of certain wastes, such as organic materials; or even processing waste for certain purposes. This option would succeed only with an extensive program to build enough local management capacity to handle the contracting procedures. It would also require highly developed computerized contract-support systems and project monitoring to ensure sustainability. Policymakers would find it unacceptable to allow the quality of the service to depend on an unstable organizational and management capacity.

- *Labour-based collection* — This would be similar to the metropolitanization of the traditional method, but it would mean massively expanding the labour force at the delivery end for the purposes of job creation. Possibly using funds from the national public-works program, this approach would involve employing people nonpermanently or semiformally (for example, paying them per bag of refuse or at daily rates). If this option is preferred, for reasons related to employment creation (that is, for reasons exogenous to waste management per se), then it may lower the cost of the expansion of capital goods. In other words, this option would reinforce community-based involvement in delivery but subordinate it to the management processes of the

220

solid-waste departments. It would thus favour the interests of unemployed people, rather than profit or nonprofit entrepreneurs.

- *Privatization–commercialization* — This would involve either the complete sale of the waste service to a private-sector company or the establishment of a nonprofit utility owned by the local authority. The aim would be to secure community involvement via share ownership, linked to subcontracting. If large-scale borrowing from private financial institutions is going to be required to expand the service, it may well be necessary to consider this option, given the demands of these institutions to link lending to access to attachable assets.

221

The current trend in policy thinking is to view it as easier to develop the traditional system and level of service and extend it to the disadvantaged areas. The methods used in rendering the service, it is argued, must be labour intensive to promote job creation. Whether this is sustainable with a stagnant tax base and other service demands taking precedence for budget allocations is a moot point. The hard policy choices will only become apparent when extensions of the service translate into the costs of capital equipment, labour, and landfill management. Extending the system to service new areas is possible; the real tension in the system is only going to be felt farther down the line.

The recommended policy option should comprise the following elements:

- *An integrated metropolitan solid-waste system* — This would make the GJTMC's Solid Waste Department responsible for overall strategic management, bulk services (landfills, recycling, etc.), and development facilitation and innovation for unserviced areas, and the solid-waste departments of the MSSs would be directly responsible for the local services.

- *A combination of traditional service and labour-based collection* — This would mean having the traditional-service approach but with labour-based collection in poor areas and contracting out as much as possible.

- *The implementation of a change-management strategy* — This would be aimed in particular at the transformation of existing organizational cultures and management approaches, with a view to building a development ethos and postmodern management practices, such as working in teams and rewarding performance, rather than adherence to the rules; accountability in terms of a mission; information-based project management; and close linkages between monitoring and strategic management.

- *A review of existing approaches, technologies, and methods* — This review would take as its model a sustainable-resource approach, which aims to transform the existing linear conception of the waste stream, viewing waste as unproductive, to a circular conception of the waste stream, viewing waste as a productive input into new waste-based industries, including everything from recycling to composting.

This latter policy perspective rests on the assumption that the solid-waste service would be improved through having the active participation of citizens, CBOs, NGOs, and local businesses in policy formation and delivery. When it comes to statements about participation, however, this is often merely rhetoric. The difficulty is figuring out what participation means in practice. As already indicated, political leaders, community groups, and officials understand participation in diverse ways. Whereas the newly elected political leaders consider themselves the only authentic leaders of the community (supported in this self-concept to some measure by high polls in the founding elections), support is less than enthusiastic for formalized participatory processes. Despite this, we make the following recommendations to establish a framework for structured participation at different levels:

- Establish a Metropolitan Solid Waste Forum for policy formation and review, comprising organized civil-society and private-sector interests, the solid-waste departments from the metropolitan and local levels, and elected political representatives;

- Design a contract-management system to enhance outsourcing without undermining accountability;

- Design and initiate a community-based education and awareness-raising campaign, based on a low-cost community-organizing approach, rather than a high-cost private-sector marketing approach, to increase the general understanding and appreciation of the importance of waste management in the communities; and

- Promotion of a network of capacity-building organizations to provide training programs for local-government officials, NGOs, CBOs, and local businesses involved in labour-based or community contracting programs.

Finally, a review should be conducted of the management of the entire solid-waste stream from the perspective of sustainable resource use. Now that South Africa is signing international agreements as a responsible member of the United Nations, it is simply a matter of time before national government starts to encourage local governments to conduct their activities according to Agenda 21 guidelines. There is no reason why this should not start in Greater Johannesburg. This can be done by adopting the following approach:

223

- Commission a study to review international experience and draw out lessons applicable to Greater Johannesburg;

- Via the Metropolitan Solid Waste Forum mentioned above, collectively formulate a policy perspective for adoption by the GJTMC and the MSSs to guide medium- to long-term institutional reorganization and a resource-reallocation program for sustainable resource use; and

- Establish an interdepartmental unit within the GJTMC to link a sustainable approach to resource use in solid-waste management to similar initiatives in other departments, such as the use of sludge from the water-treatment works for composting or a requirement that new development proposals contain environmental-impact assessments.

CONCLUSIONS

This chapter has provided a framework in which to pose questions about the ways municipal-service policy will be managed in future. The discussion of governance suggested that severe resource constraints have given rise to a shift from state-centric notions of welfarist service provision to one of shared responsibility, according to which the responsibility for the governance of service provision is somehow shared between state agencies, the private sector, and civil society. This suggests four interpretations of what governance means in practice:

1. Cutting down state involvement in service provision by privatizing services and transforming administrations into efficient and competent managers of a service-oriented regulatory environment;

2. Increasing political democratization to make the state more accountable and responsive to a majority, rather than to an elite;

3. Developing institutional arrangements whereby state agencies, the private sector, and community-based profit and nonprofit businesses share responsibility for the governance of service; and

4. Removing the state from service provision by increasing privatization.

At the moment, the local-government transition in South Africa is essentially premised on the second conception of governance, that is, democratization and deracialization of local governance are intended to establish a framework for extending municipal services to everyone. This assumption was tested through an analysis of the waste-management system. Although existing policy bears this contention out, financial and economic pressures may force local governments to rethink the traditional methods of service delivery and consider options that fit more into the first and third of these conceptions of governance. This would certainly reinforce the multistakeholder, participatory approach to local-government transition that has already given rise to the new local governments.

In short, this chapter has provided a framework for thinking about governance in new ways. The South African local-government transition has provided a unique opportunity for testing some approaches to governance. Waste management, in particular, is an area in which tensions are most clearly revealed between the traditional approach to extended service provision, via expanded administrative delivery, and partnership-based approaches that bring other economic players into the management of the waste stream. It is still unclear how these tensions are to be resolved and by which pressures and trends they are influenced. It is too early to precisely judge their future dynamics, but not too early to start rethinking these issues in the light of the shift in international conceptions of governance.

225

Chapter 6

Synthesis and Recommendations

A.G. Onibokun

Synthesis

The review of waste management systems in four cities in this volume reveals many common features, as well as some peculiarities. This chapter summarizes the findings to draw lessons for Africa.

Waste governance and local-government evolution

The governance of waste management in Africa has been closely associated with the evolution of local-government systems, and each phase has had its own influence on waste-management systems. The seeds of the apparent chaos in the governance of waste in many African cities were laid during the colonial period. In Nigeria and Tanzania, for example, this was a time of racial segregation, with colonialists and natives confined to different quarters of cities. The segments inhabited by the colonialists were well planned and had basic infrastructural facilities provided either free or at heavily subsidized rates, whereas the native areas were left more or less on their own. But more importantly, despite many ordinances the colonialists put in place to strengthen urban administration, they regarded towns and cities as accidents of geographic expansion and, therefore, made no serious efforts to resolve the emerging problems, particularly not those of sanitation.

Despite the policy of assimilation adopted by the French in their colonies, segregation between the colonialists and the natives was also evident in these colonies, as was the difference in the levels of infrastructural facilities. In South Africa, apartheid policy governed the entire structure of cities, which were divided into four racially segregated areas: for whites, for Africans, for coloured, and for Indians. These areas were governed and administered separately, and they each had their own system for solid-waste management.

The uneven distribution of resources for service delivery has persisted, despite recent political changes in these countries. In Johannesburg, the massive differences in the quality of service between the black and the white areas continue. In Ibadan, Abidjan, and Dar es Salaam, despite the redefinition of roles of the different tiers of government and the fact that the areas formerly inhabited by colonialists have largely been taken over by indigenes, discrimination between segments of the cities in terms of service delivery can still be observed. In Ibadan, the operations of the Ibadan Urban Sanitation Committee (IUSC), the major institution for solid-waste management in the city since 1991, covers only 5 of the 11 local government areas of the metropolis, with two-thirds of the population. Yet, the proposed landfill sites are earmarked for locations in the six local-government areas not included in the operations of the IUSC. Similarly, in Dar es Salaam, the privatization of solid-waste management, embarked on in 1994 under the auspices of the Sustainable Dar es Salaam Project (SDP), covered only 10 wards of the city (the central parts and the rich-resident suburbs) to the exclusion of the poorer segments of the metropolis, which are earmarked for the landfill site. Such discrimination also occurs in Abidjan.

The other major features of the historical development include the following:

- There has been continuing shifting of responsibilities among agencies and the various tiers of government and between these and the private sector. Many actors are now active in waste management. Although waste management is now generally considered a local issue, central governments and national institutions play big roles and bear considerable responsibilities. In Dar es Salaam, apart from the National Environmental Management Council and apart from the Prime Minister's Office (PMO), which oversees local-government authorities through the Ministry of Local Government, four major central-government ministries play big roles in waste governance. The same is also true of the other cities. In Abidjan, the Ministry of Environment sets policies on public health; the Ministry of Interior supervises local governments; the Ministry of Economy and Finance sees to the payment of the contractors handling waste in the city; and Direction et contrôle de grands travaux (DCGTx, department of major public works) offers technical support to the Ministry of Environment.

  229

  Furthermore, these government institutions and teams are noted for their instability, and the executing agencies are often very volatile. Each reduction or enlargement of the government team has entailed a redefinition of competencies and organizational charts and quite often the appointment of new persons to head the structures.

- Whatever the types of arrangement between the different tiers of government, the higher tiers definitely dominate the lower ones. Thus, the local governments greatly depend on, and are usually controlled by, the central governments. This is particularly so for access to resources and political manoeuvrability. In Abidjan, power is concentrated in the hands of a unit in the PMO (earlier in the President's Office), the DCGTx. During the decentralization era of 1971–82 in Tanzania, the regions and districts usurped most powers of local government (administrative and financial), and the central government began to appoint senior personnel and approve the bylaws of local urban authorities. In Nigeria, local governments depend on the federal government for most of their revenue, and the ministries of local government in the states have been abolished, although a supervisory arm of the Governor's Office remains to monitor the activities of local governments. In South Africa, the *Group Areas Act*, of the early 1950s, ensures that developments in cities emanate from the central government.

■ The central governments have often intervened in waste (particularly solid-waste) management during crises. In Abidjan in 1991, for instance, faced with the problem of unauthorized refuse dumps and the protests of indignant people, the state mobilized supplementary resources by approving a special grant, managed by the Ministry of Environment, and the requisition of equipment and machinery from the Ministry of Public Works to carry out periodic refuse-collection campaigns. In the same way, the central government in Tanzania intervened to clear a backlog of waste in Dar es Salaam in 1994, when the management crisis reached alarming proportions. In Ibadan, after the military regime took power on 31 December 1983, environmental days have been organized on the Saturday of every second week to improve sanitation in the city.

■ Usually, institutions for waste management are in conflict with the city (local) governments (particularly, if waste management has been privatized). This often leads to politicization of waste management and reduces the local authority's opportunities to monitor and evaluate activities. In Ibadan, some of the local governments involved in the IUSC have made subtle attempts to opt out and manage their own wastes as they deem fit. Because of the politicization of waste-management issues in Abidjan, the Société industrielle des transports automobiles africains (SITAF, private solid-waste management operator), employed during the privatization period of 1953–90, laid off about one-third of its staff immediately after its contract was reviewed in 1990. Politicization also inhibited the performance of the private company, Multinet, appointed in 1994 to manage solid waste in the 10 districts of Dar es Salaam. Similarly, in the black township of Soweto, which adjoins Johannesburg, the contractor

230

employed to remove waste since 1987 was unable to perform because of the antagonism of the local authorities,
which was based on the fact that the contractor is a white
man and the bulk of his employees came from outside the
locality. As the allocation of the Greater Johannesburg
Transitional Municipal Council's (GJTMC's) solid-waste
service is still based on the previous apartheid racial divisions, discrimination against some groups of people
persists.

231

- Both the central and local governments lack democracy,
  transparency, accountability, and cooperation with the
  public in their operations and processes and in their relationship with civil society. This is largely due to the inadequacies of the people in political office. In Tanzania,
  elected councillors have proven to be ill-equipped to shoulder their responsibilities: they have been poorly educated,
  have had little knowledge of the purpose and practice of
  local government, and have been uncertain of their roles
  as councillors. In Nigeria, up until now people in political
  office have been selected, rather than elected; they have
  had little regard for the feelings of the people and have
  only tried to satisfy the whims and caprices of the people
  in the higher tiers of government who were instrumental
  in appointing them. In Cote d'Ivoire, as a result of too
  much politicking among people in political office, they
  have been too unfocused to tackle the city's problems. The
  South Africa waste-management system has remained
  unrepresentative, undemocratic, exclusive, and discriminatory. In all cases, it was difficult for these people to promote other stakeholder interests. In addition, a high
  turnover of both political and executive leadership has
  denied the various local-government councils the continuity in leadership needed to build up a stable management
  tradition.

- Many institutions and modalities have been tried and discarded. The current systems are still very fluid and, to a
  large extent, ineffective and inefficient. The roles of many
  institutions are often ill-defined, and the interactions
  among them are often marred with conflict and antagonism. The Cleansing Section of the Preventive Services

Subdepartment of the Health and Social Welfare Department manages solid waste in Dar es Salaam but completely lacks autonomy, even in crucial matters like the purchase of fuel and spare parts. It does not have a separate budget, and any money it collects goes to the Dar es Salaam City Council's (DCC's) general revenue. In Johannesburg, although the local-government transition program transferred all the functions of the solid-waste departments from the disbanded local authorities to the GJTMC, solid-waste management has retained the previous racial divisions, and the division of functions between the GJTMC and the four Metropolitan Sub-Structures (MSSs) remains unresolved.

■ In both Nigeria and Tanzania, waste disposal is clearly given relatively little priority among the functions that local-government authorities think they are expected to perform.

WASTE-GOVERNANCE SYSTEMS

Some salient aspects of the waste governance systems in the four cities are shown in Table 1. The systems vary from the highly privatized one in Abidjan to the highly public one in Johannesburg, with the Ibadan and Dar es Salaam systems lying between the two extremes. Overall, however, the participation of the private sector is still very low. Even in Abidjan, where the system was privatized between 1953 and 1990, the situation was more or less an arrangement with a government-owned company, as the city assisted SITAF in setting up business, paid a fee for services, and, in the event of a deficit, helped to balance its budget. Furthermore, the company employed since September 1992, ASH International, has had to be buoyed up by the DCC (with technical and financial assistance) to perform satisfactorily.

In Johannesburg, waste collection, transportation, and disposal are done primarily by the staff of the Solid Waste Directorate, using capital equipment paid for by the local authorities. However, over the past 10 years, some aspects of the system have been contracted out to private contractors in certain black areas where staffing has been a very great problem (for example, Soweto since 1987). But the contractor in Soweto has been unable to effectively execute the project because of local people's antagonism toward the firm. Another aspect of the system in Johannesburg is the use of the community-based approach, whereby the community leaders work with officials to select persons from within the community (the informal settlement or squatter camps) to collect and remove refuse to designated collection points. Where this is the approach, these persons are then paid to do this work, either through an employment contract or through donations.

Only Johannesburg and Dar es Salaam have a system of house-to-house collection. The problems associated with collection points led Multinet in Dar es Salaam to adopt the door-to-door collection system. The contractors in Abidjan and the public agency in Ibadan only remove garbage from refuse dumps (or collection points) to the landfill sites. In these two cities, the house-to-house collection is done primarily by households, small-time precollectors and sorters, and small contractors, in most cases employed by the residents. In Abidjan and Dar es Salaam, the residents are pleased with the activities of the small-time precollectors and sorters but have been very antagonistic toward the big contractors, accusing them of indiscriminate dumping. This antagonism complicates the contractors' operations. At a certain point, the contractor in Abidjan decided to close the transfer station, owing to problems with the precollectors, and move the refuse directly to the dump in Akouedo. Table 1 summarizes modalities for governance of waste in the four cities.

At the refuse dumps, skips are used to store the refuse. But only in Johannesburg are the refuse dumps and skips adequate; even there, a lot of waste is dumped indiscriminately around them, although not to the extent that it occurs in the other three cities. Except in Dar es Salaam, where manual loading of tippers and lorries is employed, transfer of wastes from the refuse dumps is done mechanically, with the skips or bins emptied into refuse compactors by means of a lifting mechanism. Mechanical transfer reduces litter and spillage, but it is an expensive method. Ideally, refuse dumps are cleared at least once a week, but this happens only in the white areas of Johannesburg, whereas it takes 2–3 weeks in the black areas of Johannesburg and much longer in the other cities.

Waste is generally transferred to designated landfills. Johannesburg has seven sanitary landfills, and the other cities have one each (although another three are being planned for Ibadan). The

Table 1. Modalities for governance of waste, Abidjan, Ibadan, Dar es Salaam, and Johannesburg.

	Abidjan	Ibadan	Dar es Salaam	Johannesburg
Waste-storage methods	Not standardized: mostly drums, plastic bags (introduction of refuse bags in 1995, but not popular)	Not standardized: buckets, plastic pails and bags, drums	Many types: paper and plastic pails and bags, bamboo baskets, etc	Standardized in white areas: refuse bags (2 per refuse bin): not standardized in black areas
Transfer from homes to refuse dumps and land-fill sites	By contractor employed by city council: also, small contractors employed by residents	By residents; also by firms employed by residents	By the residents; also by either the city or the contractors, depending on the location	Collected from refuse bins and transferred to refuse-collection points by the city or by private firms
Refuse-dump management	Transfer stations located in different parts of the city. At some point closed by the contractors, ASH International, which moved refuse directly from homes to landfills	50 skips located at major road junctions (provided by the IUSC)	Use of skips in a few places: few and far between, giving rise to unauthorized dumping grounds	500 000 refuse-collection points, mostly in the former white suburbs Use of 240-L wheeled bins Managed by the city In the informal settlements, 5.5-m^3 bulk refuse container for every 200 shacks, provided by the city
Transfer of wastes	Crusher trucks; fork lifts with loading bins	Loaded mechanically into refuse-compactor vehicles (skip eaters) Litter spillage cleared manually	Manual loading of tipper lorries mostly (a lot of litter spillage) Use of skip eaters in a few places	Mechanical loading Bins emptied into the back of compactors by means of lifting mechanism (little litter spillage)

Frequency of removal	Supposed to be weekly but sometimes every 2–3 weeks	Supposed to be weekly but sometimes once a month	Very irregular Only small proportion of wastes cleared	Weekly in white areas, every 2–3 weeks in black areas
Disposal of wastes	1 landfill site (more or less a refuse dump because no sanitary treatment or diversion of biomedical materials takes place)	1 landfill area (3 others planned)	1 landfill site (in reality, not a sanitary landfill but a dumping ground)	7 sanitary landfill sites
Recycling	Negligible: neither organized nor recognized	Negligible	Negligible	Negligible
Overall waste-governance setting	Mostly privatized	Primarily state run; some privatization	Privatization of a few areas since 1994; some state run	Mostly state run; some privatization in black townships; community-based approach

Source: Field surveys in the four cities, 1995–96.
Note: IUSC, Ibadan Urban Sanitation Committee.

landfill sites in Abidjan and Dar es Salaam are more or less refuse dumps, rather than sanitary landfills, because no sanitary treatment or diversion of biomedical waste takes place. In these two cities, environmental hazards have increased in the neighbourhood of the sites, and residents have become antagonistic to the contractors. In Johannesburg, although the seven existing landfill sites are adequate for the needs of the immediate future, the most serious problem is that this city has no adequate approach to the disposal of hazardous industrial waste. Attempts to use existing landfill sites for industrial waste have resulted in numerous grass-roots conflicts between the companies concerned and the residents of nearby suburbs.

To date, approaches to solid-waste disposal in all four cities have been directed more to efficient disposal than to sustainable resource management. This is reflected in the fact that very limited recycling of wastes takes place. The recovery network of scavengers and recyclers is neither organized nor recognized, and appropriate laws to regulate their operations have yet to be put in place.

Furthermore, most of the emphasis for waste management has been on solid waste. Attempts at liquid-waste management in Abidjan started only after the cholera outbreak of 1962, which prompted the city to draw up a master plan. Even now, only 40 % of households are connected to the central sewerage system. This is in sharp contrast to Dar es Salaam and Ibadan, where less than 5 % and 0 %, respectively, of households are connected to a central sewerage system. The emphasis in industrial-waste management in all cities has been on the enactment of appropriate laws, which, as observed in Ibadan, have not been seriously implemented. Despite the concentration on solid waste, as of 1997 only a small proportion of the solid waste was removed — 10 % each in Dar es Salaam and Ibadan and about 55 % in Abidjan.

FINANCIAL AND TECHNICAL CONSIDERATIONS

In general, urban management in the four cities has not been conceived in terms of economic considerations. Starting from the colonial period, governments installed infrastructural facilities and services in the low-density (high-income) areas, with little consideration of the cost. These services were provided either free or at subsidized rates, whereas possible revenues were kept artificially low. Even in Abidjan, which has an elaborate system of taxes and levies, such as the drainage tax levied on landed property, state subsidies sustain most programs. Only 30 % of the cost of waste management is recovered in Abidjan, compared with 5 % in Johannesburg and much less in Ibadan and Dar es Salaam. As a result, the waste-management systems have proven unsustainable. Except in South Africa, therefore, the lower tiers of government saddled with waste management rely on higher tier(s) of government, particularly the central governments, to sustain their programs, and when the allocations fall far short of the needs, as they usually do, great problems arise.

237

Waste management in all the cities, except in the white areas of Johannesburg, where a reasonable amount of capability has been built over the years, faces a general dearth of qualified personnel, which is not unconnected to the low esteem and low wages of waste-management personnel. In addition, most machines and equipment for waste management are not in good working condition because of insufficient maintenance, which is due primarily to difficulties in procuring spare parts. At the time of the surveys (1995–96), 68 % of the machines and equipment in Abidjan were working; 33 %, in Ibadan. In Dar es Salaam, the situation was different because more than 20 % could and did work, but the city could only afford to fuel 20 %. It is therefore not a surprise that in most cases, only a small proportion of the waste is disposed of. In many of the African countries, governance adopts a fire-fighting approach; that is, when things get really bad, the upper tier(s) of government come to the rescue of the waste-management agencies.

CITIZEN PARTICIPATION

Another salient aspect of governance of waste management in the four cities is the limited involvement of civil society (through formal representation in policy formulation and executing bodies); the limited citizen participation in operation and maintenance; and the limited involvement of small contractors in the execution of projects. Households have no influence on solid-waste management systems, as they are rarely consulted about the system to be adopted by the central authorities. This is partly because only a few citizens take an interest in the city's affairs — attending meetings, interacting with officials, and taking them to task or even participating in elections.

In terms of commitment and awareness of their responsibilities, it is only in the white sections of Johannesburg where citizen participation is high. In the black areas of Johannesburg, as well as in the other cities studied, irregular and inadequate services, constantly changing collection systems, poor relations between citizens and council officials, a high level of corruption among council officials, and failure to mobilize the citizens through proper education have led to low levels of commitment to the activities of the councils and widespread ignorance and apathy. Also, people have a lack of confidence in public institutions and their activities. Even when taxes and levies are imposed, there is a general unwillingness to pay.

Community-based organizations (CBOs) and nongovernmental organizations (NGOs) are playing significant roles in other areas of urban life but have not been involved in waste management to any reasonable degree. It is only recently, prompted by the dismal failures exhibited by the existing systems, that they have started to show an interest, many of them with funding from donor agencies.

LAWS AND REGULATIONS FOR WASTE MANAGEMENT

The four reports show clearly that the governments of the various countries have taken adequate legislative steps to tackle environmental problems, including waste management. Abidjan has a master plan for the retrieval and removal of solid waste. Dar es Salaam has 58 pieces of legislation dealing in one way or the other with the environment. The same situation exists in Nigeria. The failure of the system is therefore largely due to the weakness of the enabling legislation and related agencies and the inability or unwillingness of officials to enforce such laws. Thus, much of the legislation goes unenforced, and some of it is completely out of date, especially in terms of provisions and sanctions to deal with those who flout them. This situation is particularly grave because there is a general lack of voluntary compliance with laws by the public in most of the cities.

238

FOREIGN ASSISTANCE OR INTERVENTION IN WASTE MANAGEMENT

Foreign governments and donor agencies have been active in waste management in the four cities. Their involvement has come in different forms, including feasibility studies, a master plan, donations (in cash and in kind), emergency cleanups at the peak of solid-waste crises, and the prompting and sponsorship of CBOs and NGOs. In Abidjan for example, the United Nations Development Programme and the World Health Organization assisted in drawing up a drainage master plan, and a Canadian consulting group (Roche International), supported by the Canadian International Development Agency, prepared a comprehensive master plan for waste management. The Japanese intervened in Dar es Salaam in 1987, financing studies on waste generation and management, and followed this up with donations of waste-management equipment. The Italians donated trucks in 1991. The emergency cleanup of Dar es Salaam in 1993–94 was carried out with foreign funding, and the SDP, which is foreign-sponsored, is overseeing and formulating waste-management policies and encouraging civil society to participate in waste management. Examples of such interventions in Ibadan and Johannesburg can also be given.

239

Although such interventions have helped to alleviate the waste problems in these cities, they have also brought their own problems, including the following:

- They have created a dependence syndrome;

- Because equipment and machines are sourced from different countries, problems of maintenance have arisen;

- Sometimes the strategies proposed and adopted by the city authorities have been inappropriate; and

- The emphasis has not been on sustainable and appropriate small-scale technology.

LESSONS

What are some of the lessons we can learn and some of the conclusions we can draw from the cases reviewed in the volume? As explained in the first chapter, one of the objectives of the four studies was to identify best practices for other countries. Below are therefore some of the lessons.

GOOD GOVERNANCE

The reports from the four cities amply demonstrate that lack of good governance is at the root of most of their urban problems, particularly in waste management. Therefore, appropriate structures are urgently needed to ensure good governance.

Experience from all over the world has shown that the institutionalization of good governance hinges on democratization and participation. This entails bridging the gulf between the rulers and the ruled and increasing trust, interdependence, reciprocity, responsiveness, and accountability in governance. Therefore, present efforts in South Africa and Nigeria aimed at restoring full participatory democracy should be encouraged. Efforts should also be made to strengthen the existing democratic systems in Tanzania and Cote d'Ivoire. The people's commitment to democracy should be strengthened through

- Cultivation of a new political culture that emphasizes commitment, honesty, dedication to duty, and service to humanity of municipal councillors and officials;

- Education to help people understand the need to participate fully in electoral processes and show more interest in the ways their elected representatives govern; and

- Appropriate mechanisms to ensure that high-quality leadership is elected for purposeful government.

CITIZEN PARTICIPATION

Good governance requires the cooperation of the people. A lot of improvements can be made if urban managers and the populace sit together to find ways and means of solving urban problems. People should also be encouraged to establish local-community organizations to enhance urban governance. Central governments should encourage local governments, by example and by regulation, to operate more transparently and accountably, both to themselves and to the citizens.

If systems for solid-waste removal are to be efficient, citizens need to know their daily responsibilities, the routines, the collection timetables, the standard procedures, and the locational factors. An elaborate system of public education should therefore be called for, with a focus on critical issues, such as methods for waste collection, storage, and delivery to the refuse dumps and the inherent dangers of giving inadequate or no attention at all to waste.

To ensure a higher level of commitment from the citizens, facilities for solid-waste management should be shared equitably within cities. Just as efforts are now being made in Johannesburg, all parts of cities must be covered, irrespective of income, race, geography, etc. The target should be to remove at least 90% of all wastes, and this target should apply in all parts of the city. Waste management should be recognized as a public good and a public responsibility. Any resident should be able to enjoy the benefits of the service.

241

THE REVENUE BASE OF LOCAL GOVERNMENTS

The experience from the four cities reveals that no system of waste management can be effective without an effective revenue base. The revenue base of most municipal governments in Africa is very poor. Cities need to enhance their collection of local revenue and to manage available finances more beneficially. Furthermore, more power should be devoted to local governments, and statutory responsibilities should be made to match the requisite resources so that local governments can perform the duties assigned to them.

It makes no sense to assign a number of responsibilities to local-government councils without their having corresponding sources of revenue. As noted in the Nigerian case, the Constitution assigns responsibility for 45 municipal functions to the local-government tier. However, the local government in Ibadan can effectively perform less than a quarter of these functions because it lacks a good revenue base. Consequently, although waste management is the responsibility of the local government, the state government has very largely assumed responsibility for it because the local government cannot bear the costs. This is because the federal and state levels of government control about 80% of nationally generated fiscal resources, and they control almost all feasible sources of revenue in the country. As a result, local governments in Nigeria depend too heavily on federal allocations. Until the revenue-allocation formula reflects the importance of local government in governance, waste management, together with other local-government responsibilities, will continue to suffer. The path critical to follow is the devolution of power to local governments and the meaningful decentralization of the resource base.

STREAMLINING OF RESPONSIBILITIES

At present, a major impediment to good governance is the fragmentation of governance, that is, the tendency among the various tiers and agencies of government to pursue their programs and projects with little or no collaboration. This has resulted in confusion, collision, and inconsistency. Therefore, a more holistic view should be taken of urban planning, including waste management. All types of land use, housing, transportation, marketing, water supply, waste generation and disposal, etc., should be regarded as subsystems of a larger planning system, each impacting on the others. Furthermore, the institutional framework, particularly that for solid-waste management, must be reviewed, with a view to reducing the number of institutional actors and clarifying their responsibilities. The institutional actors who remain should bring themselves together and streamline their powers and roles, with a view to improving performance.

This will be possible only if African governments believe in true democracy, decentralization, and devolution of power. Abidjan's institutional setup provides a model for improving local governance in other cities. The Johannesburg experience also illustrates what can happen if local governments are allowed to operate as an effective tier of government.

PRIVATE-SECTOR INVOLVEMENT IN WASTE MANAGEMENT

In view of the financial constraints and limited infrastructure relative to needs of the public sector, the private sector should be involved in a reciprocal stakeholder-participatory approach.

Experiences in Abidjan, Ibadan, and Dar es Salaam have also shown that the private sector, despite the various problems confronting it, has been more efficient and effective in the management of waste than the public sector. Even in Johannesburg, where the public sector has proven effective in the white areas, indications are that this system is coming under stress as the scope of operations is widened to incorporate other parts of the city. In view of this, efforts should be made to ensure a higher level of participation from the private sector. In cities where the private sector is now involved, governments should streamline their regulations to make them more relevant to local problems and more enforceable and sustainable. In addition, small-scale operators should be encouraged to get involved, particularly at the levels of house-to-house collection and transfer of waste to refuse dumps. Currently, more stress is put on increasing collection than on reducing generation and disposal problems. Small-scale operators also need regular training and capacity-building, as well as being encouraged to share expertise, experience, and facilities to enhance their individual capabilities.

LAW ENFORCEMENT AND INSTITUTIONAL HARMONIZATION

Governments in the four cities studied have put in place several laws, policies, and programs to monitor and protect the environment. But it is well known that governments in African countries are long on policies and short on implementation. To reverse this trend, the governments of African countries should reexamine their laws and regulations to determine their currency, appropriateness, and applicability and then strictly enforce those that are relevant.

Attention is required in the following areas:

- Where local-government bylaws on refuse disposal exist, they are somewhat uncoordinated, both among themselves and with the state laws. There is a need for the harmonization of local and state solid-waste management regulations and functions.

- Strategies should be developed to ensure more effective enforcement of all laws. Such strategies should include provision of economic incentives, such as tax relief for operators, social facilities for communities, and enlightenment campaigns conducted through various media channels.

COST RECOVERY

Waste-management systems in the cities studied have proven unsustainable. A major reason for this has been the limited capacities of the responsible public agencies and institutions to recover their operating costs. In Abidjan, which has the highest level of efficiency among the four cities in this respect, only 30% of the cost of waste management is recovered. In the other cities the recovery rates are 5 % or less. As waste-management institutions and agencies in African cities will find it increasingly difficult to source funds from elsewhere, cities such as these need to take a critical look at this situation and set measures to substantially raise the levels of cost recovery through funds and taxes, such as the Fond national de l'eau (national water fund) in Abidjan and waste-management taxes in developed countries.

Experience from other parts of the world (including Egypt and Zimbabwe, just to mention a few in Africa) has shown that people are prepared to pay for waste services if they are efficient and a good mechanism is put in place for revenue collection, along with a penalty for defaulting. A lesson from the cases reviewed is that government should increasingly encourage privatization of waste management, particularly collection, transportation, disposal, and recycling. Experience has shown that a mixture of waste collection in both the rich and the poor areas should be allocated to one private-sector establishment to ensure effective coverage of the entire city (including both the rich and the poor areas). This can introduce an element of cross-subsidy, as the richer areas pay higher rates than the poorer ones.

AFFORDABLE AND SUSTAINABLE TECHNOLOGY

Another reason for the unsustainability of waste-management systems in these African cities has been their capital-intensiveness, arising largely from heavy reliance on large-scale imported technology, without local capacities for maintenance. This trend must stop, and more emphasis should be placed on the use of small-scale, locally available technologies, such as hand-drawn carts, manually operated devices, and wheelbarrows. The heavy reliance on imported equipment in the cities studied leads one to conclude that the UN International Decade of the Environment (1970–80), with its manuals and training on small-scale, low-input waste-collection technologies, has had little effect. It has not altered the picture.

Although heavy conventional machinery is still required for transfer from collection points, and from individual points in outlying areas, to dump sites, it has become unaffordable in terms of both capital and maintenance costs. Although such specialized equipment is certainly required, the greatest problems in all countries are those posed by collection from overwhelmingly inaccessible communities (from household to dump points, from dump points to collection points) and by recycling, where the issues are those of sorting, grading, shredding, drying, digesting, pulverizing, pelletizing, and gasification. All these problems have created the dire need for local construction of practical, effective, and sustainably affordable equipment through the application of appropriate technology, ranging from manual to modestly mechanized bins, carts, custom-built vans, shaker–sorters, dryers, badgers, drum digesters, and gasification chambers.

245

A recent study in Nigeria (CASSAD 1998) revealed that competent public-sector design and production-engineering agencies can manufacture affordable equipment, including the Nigerian Institute for Oil Palm Research, Benin; the Project Development Institute, Enugu; the Federal Institute of Industrial Research, Oshodi, Lagos; the National Centre for Agricultural Mechanisation, Ilorin; and the Centre for Automotive Design and Development, Zaria.[1] The study in Nigeria (CASSAD 1998) also identified competent private-sector engineering, design, and fabrication companies, including Systemax Foundries and Engineering Works, Benin; Aminex Industrial Machines Limited, Enugu; Engineering Express Enterprises Limited, Enugu; Nigeria Machine Tools Limited, Osogbo; Addis Engineering Limited, Isolo, Lagos; FOBA Engineers Limited, Ibadan; Mesba Engineering Company, Ilorin; and Arewa Metal Containers Limited, Kaduna. For the highly specialized area of engineering services, such as foundry and furnace operations, finishing, and testing, the study named the African Regional Centre for Design and Engineering Manufacture, Ibadan.

Similar in-depth studies in other African countries would certainly reveal untapped opportunities in Africa for reducing the overdependence of African countries on imported equipment. The potentials in each country should be identified, and a concerted effort should be made to tap such potential.

WASTE-RECYCLING PRACTICES AND OPTIONS

Experience from the four countries studied has revealed that a major part of the waste-management problem is that waste is still regarded as waste, not as an asset. As a result, waste is currently

---

[1] These firms and those that follow are given as examples, and this is not intended as an endorsement by the author or IDRC.

recycled in the four cities at a very skeletal and low-key level. Government agencies have not even addressed the issue of recycling. Some private-sector businesses already do recycling in varying formats and intensities, through informal efforts of individual scavengers. In every major district of the four cities, the activities of scavengers have become very prominent. These scavengers, or pickers, move from one refuse dump to another, removing useable items from the dumps, which they sell to members of the public and to the few industries that have sprung up for industrial recycling of waste.

In Nigeria, the National Directorate of Employment (NDE) encourages the activities of these scavengers. The NDE advised the pickers to form a cooperative society to receive a loan package from the NDE; this would also ensure easy recovery of any loan disbursed to the members. The pickers have a union, known as the Raw Material Waste Collection Association. Encouragement for industrial recycling of wastes is urgently needed in Africa. The industrial recycling of waste is gradually taking route in Africa, with two main thrusts: manufactured products (plastics, textiles, glass, scrap metals) and organic materials (biomass, food leftovers, animal dung, bone, blood, etc.).

Considerable informal and modestly formal trade occurs in municipal solid waste (scrap-metal iron, aluminium, alloys, glass, plastics, polythene) and livestock waste (blood, horn, hoof). There is potential for entrepreneurship in biomass (the aquatic weeds water hyacinth and water lettuce), which can be a useful source of energy and a fibre substitute in the paper industry. Composting (for the production of organic fertilizers) and biogas production (from vegetable matter, animal dung, poultry droppings) have been almost entirely neglected. They can reduce deforestation from fuelwood harvesting, and organic fertilizers and methane gas produced by these means are environmentally friendly.

Evidence from Cairo in Egypt, Manila in the Philippines, and Ibadan in Nigeria (UNCHS 1986, 1989; Al-Mahdi and Mashhur 1989; Assaad 1991; CASSAD 1998) shows that industrial recycling of waste can be a profitable venture. All levels of government and the development agencies operating in Africa actively support and promote such ventures. Apart from achieving a cleaner environment, effective recycling of waste is a feasible strategy for employment creation, income generation, and poverty alleviation. Government, through its various economic-development programs, should give priority to private initiatives and proposals to recycle industrial wastes.

Recycling of industrial wastes should also be actively pro- moted by the development agencies, such as the United Nations Development Programme, the United Nations Industrial Develop- ment Organization, the United Nations Children's Fund, the United Nations Fund for Women, the United Nations Fund for Population Activities, the International Labor Organization, and the Ford Foundation. NGOs and the private sector should be encouraged, through microcredit programs, to create small-scale industries for industrial-waste recycling. A recent study conducted by the Centre for African Settlement Studies and Development of the feasibility of waste recycling in Nigeria (CASSAD 1998) revealed that the volume of waste generated in Nigeria would sup- port more than 5 000 waste-recycling industries. All that is needed to make this possible are incentives, microcredit for seed money, a policy to facilitate the process, and the good will of both the public sector and the civil-society organizations.

247

Concerted community participation is needed to achieve effective waste recycling in African cities. The key issues include waste-management policy, reduction of the amount of waste, max- imization of the practice of separating at source, promotion of small-scale waste-recycling industries, and integration of resource recovery into formal waste management. Minimization of waste is a prerequisite for the effective recycling and reuse of waste. The key actors dealing with these issues should be identified, and lev- els of implementation should be planned. Public-awareness cam- paigns, mobilization of community participation, incentives, and training and promotion are the key inputs. A document from Habi- tat (UNCHS 1986), an outcome of a regional workshop, contains some guidelines for promoting community participation.

The economic assessment of recycling and reuse is a difficult task. Some of the economic benefits are difficult to quantify. Indi- rect economic benefits, such as reductions in health and pollution costs, are also difficult to quantify. Industries gain direct, quantifiable benefits. Recycling of solid waste is labour intensive. Urban centres in developing countries have relatively high num- bers of migrant workers and a workforce that is either unskilled or has low levels of skills, and these assets can be effectively tapped to increase employment and reduce poverty.

Recycled products have a low environmental impact. The quality of the urban environment is directly related to the general public-health status of the residents. People involved with waste recycling and reuse are a high-risk group. They often suffer from a variety of ailments, such as eye irritation, respiratory diseases, illnesses resulting from smoke, dust, airborne pathogens, and parasites, and skin diseases.

A large number of small-scale industries depend on recyclers and scavengers for their cheap raw-material supply. The starting point for understanding the social dimensions of this form of waste recovery is a recognition of the centrality of waste recycling in the lives of the poor. The various groups of people involved with waste recycling are householders, door-to-door collectors, formal waste collectors, street scavengers, and dealers and traders in waste. Scavengers are the poorest, and they are the most dependent on intermediaries, who exploit them. The scavengers are the victims of discrimination, often branded as thieves and delinquents. A study conducted by Habitat revealed the annual income distribution of various groups (in United States dollars): scavengers, 44; street peddlers, 60; workers in the small-scale, cottage-based waste-recycling industry, 100; and dealers, 385. This distribution is inequitable, and it is estimated (UNCHS 1989) that about 1% of urban dwellers make a living on recycling. Upgrading the recycling sector would double employment and improve working conditions.

Community participation and mobilization efforts should therefore address some of the following key issues:

- *Waste minimization* — This can be accomplished by changing consumption patterns and life styles, using more recyclable materials, and banning waste imports.

- *Maximization of source separation* — This can be accomplished by mobilizing, sensitizing, and supporting the households and the informal sector to embark on simple waste-recycling projects. This approach will create new jobs while also promoting a cleaner environment.

- *Promotion of small-scale waste-recycling industries* — This can be accomplished by improving performance, increasing levels of knowledge, and improving the marketability of waste.

■ *Integration of recycling and formal waste management* —
This can be accomplished by improving communication,
increasing management capabilities, and developing monitoring instruments.

The key actors in the field are

■ *Domestic consumers and industry* — They influence the
amount and the nature of waste.

■ *Government* — It sets priorities through regulations and
laws for consumers and industry.

Levels of intervention should address the following:

■ *Creation of awareness* — Greater awareness of environmental and public-health issues would help to promote
structural improvements and environmentally friendly
behaviour. The main actors would change their behaviour
and attitudes. This would encourage more community
participation in recycling and reuse.

■ *Use of incentives* — Incentives may be used to encourage
people and the community to adopt best practices in waste
management. Such incentives could include prizes and
certificates of recognition awarded to communities,
NGOs, and CBOs that excel in waste-management innovations and practice.

■ *Restrictive legislation* — When creation of awareness and
use of incentives fail, legislation is the option. This also
demands monitoring and sanctions, and it costs the government substantially.

■ *Public-awareness campaigns* — These reduce waste generation and promote recycling and reuse. Effective methods
include the use of traditional and modern channels of
community communication, targeting the younger people,
who are prone to be attracted to changes in life styles;
mass media; and neighbourhood workshops and meetings.
These campaigns should be organized at the beginning of
a scheme and throughout the project period. The
campaigns should include education and information.
Local politicians and policy makers should be involved in

these programs. Government, NGOs, and educational institutions might be the facilitators.

- *Mobilization of community participation* — This will promote waste separation and effective waste collection, which can achieve short- and medium-term results. Workshops, neighbourhood communication sessions, and financial incentives encourage better participation. Some of the questions to be kept in mind in formulating the instrument are Who should participate? What is expected of them? To what extent should they contribute? Support should be obtained from the formal waste-management authority. People should be involved right from the start. One of the outcomes would be the establishment of neighbourhood associations. General-education level in a community should be high to encourage the practice of separating wastes. Community participation can only be achieved with understanding and appreciation. Community participation should be initiated in the neighbourhoods, but always coordinated under the auspices of local authorities. In low-income areas, separation of waste in households is very profitable. The city can organize door-to-door collection of useable materials, or the residents can bring their collected paper, glass, and plastic bottles to the transfer depots, where dealers might have their shops or market stands.

- *Training and promotion* — Transfer of local know-how should be an important component of these programs, and they should include training on recycling techniques, organization, marketing, communication, and health. People who operate or initiate small-scale waste-recycling industries generally lack information, and therefore information is needed. The success of recycling depends on the marketability of the product, as people favour products made from new materials. This will change only if services are adequately provided, and the local authority should play a major role in this. Training and promotion should lead to action plans, and the required inputs for these activities are facilities for pilot projects, long-term assistance, short-term assistance, and financial support.

250

HEALTH, SAFETY, AND PREVENTIVE MEASURES

As explained earlier, scavenging is assuming an important dimension in waste-recycling practices in Nigeria. Scavenging has many advantages, including the following:

- It provides a decent livelihood for scavengers from the sale of the salvaged items;

- It reduces the volume of solid waste;

- It reduces the cost of collection and disposal of solid wastes;

- It sustains some industries that use salvaged items as raw materials;

- It provides jobs to unemployed youth; and

- It creates the potential for sophisticated recycling plants to be established.

251

However, scavenging has some detrimental effects on the health of the scavengers, who suffer from eye irritation; respiratory diseases, with coughing, sneezing, etc.; skin diseases, especially scabies; minor injuries from stepping on broken bottles or sharp objects in the refuse; headaches from working in the sun; and backaches from bending down most of the time.

Because scavengers help to manage waste,

- Government should assist this group financially;

- The scavengers should form a cooperative society so that members can secure loans through such a society;

- Government should recognize the scavengers' union and give it legal backing;

- The scavengers should be trained to go about their business in a way that maximizes profit;

- The scavengers should be trained to wear a type of uniform, such as overalls, jungle boots, gloves, helmets, and nose masks, which would further enhance their dignity; and

■ The scavengers should receive basic health training (first aid) to learn how to take care of themselves in case of any minor injury.

Human beings can come into direct or indirect contact with solid waste at several stages in its handling and processing. The groups at risk are populations of unserved areas (especially school children), waste workers, workers in facilities that produce infectious or toxic material, people living close to disposal or recycling facilities, and people living in the dumping areas. Some common health hazards are the following:

■ *Infections* — These include skin and blood infections resulting from direct contact with waste and from infected wounds; eye and respiratory infections resulting from exposure to infected dust; zoonoses resulting from bites by wild or stray animals feeding on wastes; and enteric infections transmitted by flies on wastes.

■ *Chronic diseases* — These include chronic respiratory diseases and cancers resulting from exposure to dust and hazardous compounds.

■ *Accidental injuries* — These include skeletal disorders resulting from the handling of heavy containers; infected wounds from contact with sharp items; poisoning and chemical burns resulting from contact with small amounts of hazardous chemical waste mixed with general waste; and burns and other injuries from occupational accidents at waste disposal sites or from methane-gas explosions at landfill sites.

Preventive measures at various workplaces should include the use of gloves, long boots, face masks, headgear, and eyeglasses. Under certain circumstances, a change of machinery to avoid excessive heat or use of heat-preventive devices may be helpful. Inhalation can be reduced through use of portable oxygen cylinders or protective face masks. Change in shift time would also be useful, depending on the type of exposure.

Appendix 1

CONTRIBUTING AUTHORS

Koffi Attahi is an Ivorian planner trained in Canada, where he obtained his doctorate in urban planning from the University of Montréal. He was previously in the Department of Geography at the University of Abidjan and was the director of its Centre de recherches architecturales et urbaines. He is currently the regional adviser at the regional office for Africa of the United Nations Development Programme (UNDP, with the UNDP–World Bank Urban Management Programme in Abidjan, Côte d'Ivoire). He has carried out extensive research on urbanization and urban management in francophone sub-Saharan Africa and has worked as a consultant for the United Nations Centre for Human Settlements (Habitat), the World Bank, and the overseas development agencies of Canada, Germany, and the United States. He has contributed to two of Habitat's monographs on urban management — *Metropolitan Planning and Management in the Developing World, Abidjan and Quito* (1992) and *The Management of Secondary Cities in Sub-Saharan Africa* (1991) — and to *African Cities in Crisis* (1986), edited by Richard Stren and Rodney White.

David Hutt is the acting director of the Solid Waste Department, Greater Johannesburg Transitional Metropolitan Council, Johannesburg, South Africa.

J.M. Lusugga Kironde holds an MSc and PhD in Economics, with specialization in land economics. He is at present a lecturer in land economics at the Ardhi Institute, Dar-es-Salaam, Tanzania. Dr Kironde has been an adviser to the Government of Tanzania on urban development and land use.

254

J.A. Kumuyi, a regional-development expert, is a program director at the Centre for African Settlement Studies and Development (CASSAD), a nongovernmental organization (NGO). Professor Kumuyi obtained his BA and PhD in geography from the University of Ibadan. After many years of consultancy service in the private sector, he joined the Nigerian Institute of Social and Economic Research (NISER) as a senior research fellow, where he rose to become a research professor in 1989. He was the head of the Business and Industrial Consultancy Department of NISER for many years and a consultant to federal and state governments in Nigeria on economic-development and urban-management issues.

Adepoju G. Onibokun holds an MA and PhD in urban and regional planning from the University of Waterloo, Waterloo, Canada. His extensive professional contributions in the urban field include participation on many Nigeria federal- and state-government advisory committees on urban matters. He is the first Nigerian professor of urban and regional planning and has taught at a number of universities in Nigeria and elsewhere, including for many years teaching as professor of urban planning at the University of Illinois at Urbana and at the University of Ibadan, Nigeria. He has also served as consultant to the World Health Organization, the World Bank, and the United Nations on matters related to urban and regional planning, infrastructure development, and institution building. Professor Onibokun founded and is chief executive officer of CASSAD. He has written more than 200 books and articles.

Mark Swilling is the director of the School of Public and Development Management, Faculty of Management, University of Witwatersrand, Johannesburg, South Africa. He was a development-project worker in Planact, and earlier he was a lecturer in the Department of Political Studies, University of the

Witwatersrand, and a research officer in its Centre for Policy Studies. His achievements include participation in the design and establishment of Planact, the School of Public and Development Management, the Community Bank, the Metropolitan Chamber, and numerous development NGOs involved in the delivery of mass housing. He has published several books and more than 50 articles on the nature of the South African state, community movements, the politics of the independent trade-union movement, the South African local-government system and policy alternatives, the management of urban transition, transport policy, South Africa's international relations, and the dynamics of nonrevolutional transitions to democracy. He recently completed a PhD in the Department of Sociology at the University of Warwick, United Kingdom. His thesis was entitled "Urban Control and Changing Forms of Political Conflict in the Western Cape with Special Reference to Uitenhage, 1979–1986." His work is now focused on the management of change in state administrations and the structuring of new forms of democratic governance in the public and community sectors.

Appendix 2

ACRONYMS AND ABBREVIATIONS

ARNUM   African Research Network for Urban Management

CASSAD   Centre for African Settlement Studies and Development
CBD   central business district [South Africa]
CBO   community-based organization
CIAPOL   Centre ivoirien anti-pollution (Ivorian antipollution centre)
CWRSC   Cemtral Witswatersrand Regional Services Council
         [South Africa]

DAI   Département d'Assainissement et d'Infrastructure (depart-
         ment of sanitation and infrastructure) [Côte d'Ivoire]
DCC   Dar es Salaam City Council [Tanzania]
DCGTx   Direction et contrôle des grands travaux (department of
         major public works) [Côte d'Ivoire]
DFR   Durban Functional Region [South Africa]
DSSD   Dar es Salaam Sewage and Sanitation Department
         [Tanzania]

EIA   environmental-impact assessment

257

EPC   Environmental Protection Commission [Nigeria]

FEPA   Federal Environmental Protection Agency [Nigeria]
FNA   Fonds national pour l'assainissement (national sanitation fund) [Côte d'Ivoire]
FNE   Fonds national de l'eau (national water fund) [Côte d'Ivoire]

GDP   gross domestic product
GJTMC   Greater Johannesburg Transitional Metropolitan Council [South Africa]
GRA   government-reserved area [Nigeria]
GURI   Global Urban Research Initiative

IDRC   International Development Research Centre [Canada]
IUSB   Ibadan Urban Sanitation Board [Nigeria]
IUSC   Ibadan Urban Sanitation Committee [Nigeria]

JCC   Johannesburg City Council [South Africa]

MLHUD   Ministry of Lands, Housing and Urban Development [Tanzania]
MOE   ministère d'Environnement (Ministry of Environment) [Côte d'Ivoire]
MSS   Metropolitan Sub-Structure [South Africa]
MTI   Ministry of Trade and Industries [Tanzania]
MWEM   Ministry of Water, Energy and Minerals [Tanzania]

NDE   National Directorate of Employment [Nigeria]
NEMC   National Environmental Management Council [Tanzania]
NGO   nongovernmental organization
NISER   Nigerian Institute of Social and Economic Research
NLGNF   National Local Government Negotiating Forum [South Africa]
NUWA   National Urban Water Authority [Tanzania]

PMO   Prime Minister's Office [Côte d'Ivoire; Tanzania]

RCC   refuse-collection charge
RDC   refuse-disposal charge
RDP   Reconstruction and Development Programme [South Africa]

SDP   Sustainable Dar es Saalam Project [Tanzania]
SETU   Société d'équipement des terrains urbains (state land-development agency) [Côte d'Ivoire]
SIIC   Service d'inspection des installations classées (classified installations inspection service) [Côte d'Ivoire]
SITA   Société industrielle des transports automobiles (industry group for automobile transportation) [France]

SITAF   Société industrielle des transports automobiles africains (private solid-waste operator) [Côte d'Ivoire]

SODECI   Socété des eaux de Côte d'Ivoire (Côte d'Ivoire water company)

TEOM   taxe d'enlèvement des ordures ménagères (tax for household-refuse removal) [Côte d'Ivoire]

TLC   Transitional Local Council [South Africa]

TMC   Transitional Metropolitan Council [South Africa]

BIBLIOGRAPHY

Akintola, F.O.; Agbola, T. 1989. The magnitude and composition of waste water in selected settlements in Nigeria. Department of Geography, University of Ibadan, Nigeria. Mimeo.

Al-Mahdi, A.; Mashhur, A. 1989. The informal sector in Egyptian cities. CNRSC, Cairo, Egypt.

Ame, A.M. 1993. Recycling of solid waste in Dar es Salaam city. Ardhi Institute, Dar es Salaam, Tanzania. Diploma project.

Assaad, R. 1991. Les Zabbalin. Peuples méditerranées, 41–42, 181–92.

Barkan, J.D.; McNulty, M.L.; Ayeni, M.A.O. 1991. "Hometown" voluntary associations, local development, and the emergence of civil society in western Nigeria. Journal of Modern African Studies, 29(3), 457–480.

Blunt, P.; Jones, M. 1992. Managing organizations in Africa. de Gruyter, Berlin, Germany; New York, NY, USA.

Bratton, M; Rothchild, D. 1992. The institutional bases of governance in Africa. In Hyden, G.; Bratton, M., ed., Governance and politics in Africa. Lynne Rienner, Boulder, CO, USA. pp. 263–284.

Bratton, M.; van de Walle, N. 1992. Towards governance in Africa: popular demands and state responses. In Hyden, G.; Bratton, M., ed., Governance and politics in Africa. Lynne Rienner, Boulder, CO, USA. pp. 26–47.

Brenner, J. 1992. Johannesburg's informal economy. Planact, Johannesburg, South Africa. Mimeo.

Bukurura, L.H. 1991. Public participation in financing local development: the case of the Tanzanian development levy. African Development, 16(3–4), 75–100.

261

Byekwaso, A. 1994. Community based organisations in land servicing. Ardhi Institute, Dar es Salaam, Tanzania. Diploma project.

CASSAD (Centre for African Settlement Studies and Development). 1994. Managing sustainable/healthy growth and development of Ibadan: environmental profile of the metropolitan area. CASSAD, Ibadan, Nigeria.

———— 1998. Feasibility of industrial waste recycling in Nigeria. Report of a project commissioned by the Federal Environmental Protection Agency, Abuja, Nigeria.

CFD (Caisse française de développement). 1995. Étude des filières de récupération des différents types de déchets. CFD, Abidjan, Côte d'Ivoire.

Chaligha, A.E. 1987. Financing local government sources for economic development. *In* Stiftung, F.E., ed., The financing of local government in eastern and southern African countries. Prudential Printers; Kul Graphics, Nairobi, Kenya. pp. 52–67.

Chazan, N. 1992. Africa's democratic challenge. World Policy Journal, 9(2), 279–308.

Chazan, N.; Mortimer, R.; Ravenhill, J.; Rothchild, D. 1988. Politics and society in contemporary Africa. Lynne Rienner, Boulder, CO, USA.

Christie, P.; Lessem, R.; Mbigi, L., ed. 1993. African management. Knowledge Resources, Johannesburg, South Africa.

Coetzee, S.F.; de Coning, C. 1992. An agenda for urban research: South Africa in the 1990s. Paper presented at the Workshop on Urban Research Agenda for Southern Africa, Jun 1992, Johannesburg. University of the Witwatersrand, Johannesburg, South Africa.

Cranko, P.; Wooldridge, D. 1995. Transforming public sector institutions in South Africa. *In* McClennan, A.; Fitzgerald, P.; Munslow, B., ed., Managing sustainable development in South Africa. Oxford University Press, Cape Town, South Africa.

CRI (Cabinet Roche International). 1987. Plan directeur de récupération et d'élimination des déchets de la ville d'Abidjan. United Nations Development Programme; World Bank; Canadian International Development Agency, Ottawa, ON, Canada.

DAI; VA; DCGTx (Département d'Assainissement et d'Infrastructure; Ville d'Abidjan; Direction et contrôle des grands travaux). 1991. Étude de la gestion des ordures ménagères de la ville d'Abidjan. DAI, Abidjan, Côte d'Ivoire.

Daily News. 1991. MPs raise concern over education standards. Daily News, 22 Apr, p. 5.

DCC (Dar es Salaam City Council). 1992. Environmental profile of the metropolitan area. Report prepared for the Sustainable Dar es Salaam Project, Dar es Salaam, Tanzania. Unpublished.

———— 1995a. A survey of solid waste generation in Dar es Salaam. Report prepared for the Sustainable Dar es Salaam Project, Dar es Salaam, Tanzania.

———— 1995b. Waste generation in Dar es Salaam. Health and Social Welfare Committee, DCC, Dar es Salaam, Tanzania.

DCGTx; AUVA (Direction et contrôle des grands travaux; Atelier d'urbanisme de la ville d'Abidjan). 1990. Atlas de l'occupation duè sol d'Abidjan. DCGTx, Abidjan, Côte d'Ivoire.

Dryden, S. 1968. Local administration in Tanzania. East African Publishing House, Nairobi, Kenya.

Egunjobi, L. 1986. Problems of solid waste management in Nigerian urban centres. *In* Adeniyi, E.O.; Bello-Imam, I.B., ed., Development and the environment. Nigerian Institute of Social and Economic Research, Ibadan, Nigeria. pp. 74–92.

FEPA (Federal Environmental Protection Agency). 1990. *Federal Environmental Protection Act.* 1988 Cap 131 (1990, LFN), as amended by the *Federal Environmental Protection Act* 1992, No. 59.

Ferrari, M. 1988. Statement presented at the International Workshop on the Goals and Guidelines of the National Environmental Policy for Nigeria, 12–16 Sep. Federal Environmental Protection Agency, Lagos, Nigeria.

FGON (Federal Government of Nigeria). 1978. The 1976 local government reform. Federal Ministry of Information, Lagos, Nigeria.

———— 1979. The Constitution of the Federal Republic of Nigeria 1979. Federal Ministry of Information, Lagos, Nigeria.

Gboyega, A. 1983. Local government reform in Nigeria. *In* Mavwood, P., ed., Local government in the Third World: the experience of tropical Africa. John Wiley, Chichester, NY, USA. pp. 225–247.

GOCI (Government of Côte d'Ivoire). 1980. Recensement national de la population et de l'habitat. Direction de la statistique, Abidjan, Côte d'Ivoire.

Gossi, C. 1994. Community based waste management, Department of Environmental Engineering. Ardhi Institute, Dar es Salaam, Tanzania. Diploma project.

Halfani, M. 1995. Urban governance in East Africa. Paper presented at the Global Urban Research Initiative Conference on African Urban Governance, 14–15 Jan, Dar Es Salaam, Tanzania. The Ford Foundation, New York, NY, USA.

Halfani, M.; McCarney, P.; Rodriguez, A. 1998. Towards an understanding of governance: the emergence of an idea and its implications for urban research in developing countries. *In* Stren, R., ed., Urban

263

research in the developing world. University of Toronto Press, Toronto, ON, Canada. (In press.)

Hardoy, J.; Satterwaite, D. 1992. Environmental problems in Third World cities. International Institute for Environment and Development, London, UK.

Harsch, E. 1993. Accumulators and democrats: challenging state corruption in Africa. Journal of Modern African Studies, 31(1), 31–48.

Haskoning and Konsadem Associates. 1994. Ibadan Solid Waste Project: institutional and management study. Final report prepared for the Oyo State Government, Ministry of Finance and Industry, Ibadan, Nigeria.

Haskoning and M-Konsult. 1987. Study on solid waste management and pollution caused by sewerage systems in Dar es Salaam. Vol. 1: Technical proposals. Report prepared for Dar es Salaam City Council, Dar es Salaam, Tanzania. Unpublished.

———— 1988. Study on solid waste management and pollution caused by sewerage systems in Dar es Salaam. Draft main report: solid waste management. Dar es Salaam City Council, Dar es Salaam, Tanzania. Unpublished.

———— 1989. Staged action plan on pollution management for Dar es Salaam. Report prepared for the Ministry of Water, Energy and Minerals, Dar es Salaam, Tanzania.

Hyden, G. 1983. No shortcuts to progress: African development management in perspective. University of California Press, Berkeley, CA, USA.

———— 1992. Governance and the study of politics. In Hyden, G.; Bratton, M., ed., Governance and politics in Africa. Lynne Rienner, Boulder, CO, USA.

Jorgenson, T.B. 1993. Modes of governance and administrative change. In Kooiman, J., ed., Modern governance. Sage Press, London, UK.

Kaseva, M.E. 1995. Integrated solid waste management strategy in Dar es Salaam. Report prepared for the International Labour Organization, Geneva, Switzerland. Unpublished.

Kironde, J.M. Lusugga. 1994. The governance of urban development in Tanzania. Paper presented at the Workshop on the Governance of Urban Development in East Africa: A Research Perspective, 1–2 Aug, Dar es Salaam, Tanzania. African Regional Network for Urban Research, Dar es Salaam, Tanzania.

———— 1995. The evolution of the land use structure of Dar es Salaam 1890–1990. University of Nairobi, Nairobi, Kenya. PhD thesis.

Koehn, P. 1992. Decentralization for sustainable development: constraints and opportunities. Paper presented at the Economic Commission for Africa Regional Conference on Development Management in

Africa, 9–13 Nov, Addis Ababa, Ethiopia. Economic Commission for Africa, Addis Ababa, Ethiopia.

Kooiman, J., ed. 1993. Modern governance. Sage Press, London, UK.

Kulaba, S.M. 1989. Local government and the management of urban services in Tanzania. *In* Stren, R.E.; White, R., ed., African cities in crisis: managing rapid urban growth. Westview Press, Boulder, CO, USA; London, UK. pp. 203–246.

Kyessi, A.; Sheuya S.A. 1993. The role of the community based organisations (CBOs) and non governmental organisations (NGOs) in squatter upgrading. Paper presented at the 5th International Seminar on Construction Management for Sustainable Selfhelp Housing in Habinet Countries, 22–26 Nov, Dar es Salaam, Tanzania. Government of the Netherlands, The Hague, Netherlands.

Landell-Mills, P.; Serageldin, I. 1991. Governance and the development process. Finance and Development, 28(3), 13–24.

Leftwich, A. 1993. Governance, democracy and development in the Third World. Third World Quarterly, 24(3).

Maclaren International Ltd. 1970. Master plan for wastes disposal and drainage, Ibadan. Vol. V. Report prepared for the Ministry of Works, Ibadan, Nigeria.

Maliyamkono, T.L. 1995. Who votes in Tanzania and why. Eastern and Southern African Universities Research Programme, Dar es Salaam, Tanzania.

Mbago, J.L. 1985. Local government and development in Tanzania: case study of the Dar es Salaam City Council. University of Dar es Salaam, Dar es Salaam, Tanzania. MA thesis.

Mbembe, A. 1989. Economic liberalisation and the post colonial African state. *In* Carter Centre, ed., Beyond autocracy in Africa. Carter Centre, Atlanta, GA, USA. pp. 42–58.

Mbyopyo, G.M.S. 1993. Peoples' participation in sustainable selfhelp land servicing in Dar es Salaam: case study of Changanyikeni. Ardhi Institute, Dar es Salaam, Tanzania. Mimeo.

MCAL (Manus Coffey Associates Limited). 1992. Brief study of solid waste proposals for Dar es Salaam. Report prepared for the Dar es Salaam Sustainable Cities Project, Dar es Salaam, Tanzania. Unpublished.

———— 1993. Managing the sustainable growth and development of Dar es Salaam: solid waste management. Report prepared for the Sustainable Dar es Salaam Project, Dar es Salaam, Tanzania.

———— 1994. Negotiation for start up of the privatisation of solid waste collection. Report prepared for the Sustainable Dar es Salaam Project, Dar es Salaam, Tanzania.

———— 1995. Managing the sustainable growth and development of Dar es Salaam. Vol. 2: Solid waste disposal. Report prepared for the Dar es Salaam City Council, Dar es Salaam, Tanzania. Unpublished.

McClagan, P.; Nel, C. 1995. The age of participation. Barret Coehler, San Francisco, CA, USA.

McClennan, A.; Fitzgerald, P.; Munslow, B., ed. 1995. Managing sustainable development in South Africa. Oxford University Press, Cape Town, South Africa.

Mgana, S. 1993. Baseline environmental study and preliminary design guideline proposals for the proposed Vingunguti landfill site. Report prepared for the Sustainable Dar es Salaam Project, Dar es Salaam, Tanzania. Unpublished.

Mkongola, N.E.K. 1988. The administration of development levy collection in Tanzania: the case of Mwanza urban districts. University of Dar es Salaam, Dar es Salaam, Tanzania. MA thesis.

Mpinga, M.A. 1993. Design of solid waste transfer stations: case study — Ilala district (Dar es Salaam). Ardhi Institute, Dar es Salaam, Tanzania. Diploma project.

Mwapachu, J.V. 1995. Who should next lead Tanzania? Change, 3(1–2), 2–11.

NEST (Nigerian Environmental Study Action Team). 1991. Nigeria's threatened environment — a national profile. NEST, Ibadan, Nigeria.

NISER (Nigerian Institute of Social and Economic Research). 1988. Socio-economic survey of Ibadan city: report of a survey commissioned by the Ibadan Metropolitan Planning Authority. NISER, Ibadan, Nigeria.

NPC (National Population Commission). 1992. Nigerian 1991 census (provisional). National Population Commission, Lagos, Nigeria.

Nye, J.S. 1967. Corruption and political development: a cost benefit analysis. American Political Science Review, 62(2), 418–426.

Obadina, O.A. 1995. Summary of proposition paper for issue No. 1: solid waste. Sustainable Ibadan Project, City Consultation on Environmental Issues, Ibadan, Nigeria.

O'Donnel, G.; Schmitter, P.; Whitehead, D. 1986. Transitions from authoritarian rule. Johns Hopkins University, Baltimore, MD, USA; London, UK.

Ola, C.S. 1984. Town and country. Planning and environmental laws in Nigeria. Oxford University Press, Ibadan, Nigeria.

Olowu, D. 1981. The administration of social services in Nigeria: the challenge to local governments. Local Government Training Programme, University of Ile-Ife, Ile-Ife, Nigeria.

———— 1994. Bureacracy and the people: the Nigerian experience. Obafemi Awolowo University, Ile-Ife, Nigeria. Monograph.

Olowu, D.; Akinola, S.R. 1995. Urban governance and urban poverty in Nigeria. *In* Onibokun, A.G.; Faniran, A., ed., Governance and urban poverty in anglophone West Africa. Centre for African Settlement Studies and Development, Ibadan, Nigeria. CASSAD Monograph Series 4.

Oluwande, P.A. 1983. Some aspects of effective urban solid waste management in developing countries. Department of Preventive Medicine, Ibadan, Nigeria. Mimeo.

Onibokun, A.G. 1989. Urban growth and urban management in Nigeria. *In* Stren, R.E.; White, R., ed., African cities in crisis. Westview Press, Boulder, CO, USA.

———— 1997. Governance and urban poverty in anglophone West Africa. *In* Swilling, M., ed., Governing Africa's cities. Witwatersrand University Press, Johannesburg, South Africa.

Onibokun, A.G.; Faniran, A., ed. 1995. Governance and urban poverty in anglophone West Africa. Centre for African Settlement Studies and Development, Ibadan, Nigeria. CASSAD Monograph Series 4.

Onibokun, A.G.; Kumuyi, A.J. 1996. Urban poverty in Nigeria: towards sustainable strategies for its alleviation. Centre for African Settlement Studies and Development, Ibadan, Nigeria. CASSAD Monograph Series 10. pp. 1–2.

PAI Associates. 1983. A sector plan for managing the Nigerian environment: progress report. Federal Ministry of Housing and Environment, Lagos, Nigeria.

Picard, L.; Livega, A.; Nkya, E. 1999. Politics, the bureaucracy and the local state: local government in southern Africa. *In* Picard, L.; Garrity, M., ed., Local government in southern Africa. International Institute of Administrative Sciences, Brussels, Belgium. (In press)

Planact. 1990. The Soweto rent boycott. Planact, Johannesburg, South Africa.

Rubindamayugi, M.S.T.; Kivaisi, A.K. 1994. Employment creation and livelihood improvement through waste collection and recycling: a demonstration and test pilot project in Hannah Nassif, Dar es Salaam, Tanzania. Report prepared for the International Labour Organization, Geneva, Switzerland. Unpublished, Nov.

SDP (Sustainable Dar es Salaam Project). 1995. Managing the sustainable growth and development of Dar es Salaam. SDP Office, Dar es Salaam, Tanzania. Unpublished, May.

Sridhar, M.K.C. 1996. Turning waste to wealth: a strategy for urban poverty alleviation in Nigeria. Department of Preventive and Social Medicine, University of Ibadan, Ibadan, Nigeria. Unpublished report.

Starr, S.F. 1990. Soviet Union: a civil society. *In* Macridis, R.C.; Brown, B.E., ed., Comparative politics: notes and readings. Brooks–Cole Publishing, Pacific Grove, CA, USA. pp. 194–197.

Stren, R. 1992. Large cities in the Third World. *In* United Nations Centre for Human Settlements, ed., Metropolitan planning and management in the developing world: Abidjan and Quito, Nairobi. United Nations Centre for Human Settlements, Nairobi, Kenya. pp. 1–30.

Stren, R.; et al. 1992. African urban research since the late 1990s: response to poverty and urban "growth." Urban Studies, 29(3–4), 533–588.

Stren, R.; Halfani, M.; Malombe, J. 1994. Coping with urbanization and urban policy. *In* Barkan, J.D., ed., Beyond capitalism vs. socialism in Kenya and Tanzania. Lynne Reinner Publishers, Boulder, CO, USA.

Stren, R.; White, R., ed. 1989. African cities in crisis: managing rapid urban growth. Westview Press, Boulder, CO, USA.

SWD (Solid Waste Directorate). n.d. Mission statment of the Solid Waste Directorate. SWD, Greater Johannesburg Transitional Metropolitan Council, Johannesburg, South Africa. Pamphlet.

Swilling, M.; Cobbett, W.; Hunter, R. 1991. Finance, electiricity costs and the rent boycott. *In* Swilling, M.; Humphries, R.; Shubane, K., ed., The apartheid city in transition. Oxford University Press, Cape Town, South Africa.

Swilling, M.; Johnson, K.; Monteiro, O. 1995. Building democratic local urban governance in southern Africa: a review of key trends. Paper presented at Global Urban Research Initiative Meetings on Urban Governance, 2–5 Oct, Mexico City, Mexico. The Ford Foundation, New York, NY, USA.

Swilling, M.; Van Zyl Slabbert, F. 1989. Waiting for a negotiated settlement: South Africans in a changing world. Africa Insight, 19(3), 138–146.

SWMWG (Solid Waste Management Working Group). n.d. Solid waste management report of the Solid Waste Management Working Group. SWMWG, Dar es Salaam, Tanzania.

Tanzania. 1979. The Dar es Salaam masterplan. Marshall Macklin Monoghan, Toronto, ON, Canada.

———— 1991. Taarifa ya Kamati ya Kuimarisha Serikali za Mitaa Na.2 [the Bomani report]. Dar es Salaam, Tanzania. Unpublished report.

———— 1992. Report of the Presidential Commission of Inquiry into Public Revenue and Taxation [the Mtei report]. Dar es Salaam, Tanzania. Unpublished report.

UNCHS (United Nations Centre for Human Settlements) 1986. Community participation in low-cost sanitation. UNCHS, Nairobi, Kenya.

———— 1989. Solid waste management in low-income housing projects: the scope for community participation. UNCHS, Nairobi, Kenya.

United Nations. 1990. Practical measures against corruption. United Nations, New York, NY, USA. A/CONF.144/8, 29 May.

————— 1995. World urbanization prospects. United Nations, New York, NY, USA.

Uyanga, J. 1982. Towards Nigerian national urban policy. Ibadan University Press, Ibadan, Nigeria.

Weigle, M.A.; Butterfield, J. 1992. Civil society in reforming communist regimes: the logic of emergence. Comparative Politics, 23(4), 1–23.

World Bank. 1989. Towards sustainable development in sub-Saharan Africa. World Bank, Washington, DC.

————— 1992. Governance and development. World Bank, Washington, DC, USA.

————— 1993. Federal Republic of Nigeria: poverty assessment indicators. Federal Office of Statistics–World Bank Resident Office, Lagos, Nigeria.

Wraith, R. 1964. Local government in West Africa. George Allen and Unwin, London, UK.

Yhdegho, M. 1991. Urban environmental degradation in Tanzania. Environment and Urbanisation, 3(1), 147–152.

269

About the Institution

The International Development Research Centre (IDRC) is committed to building a sustainable and equitable world. IDRC funds developing-world researchers, thus enabling the people of the South to find their own solutions to their own problems. IDRC also maintains information networks and forges linkages that allow Canadians and their developing-world partners to benefit equally from a global sharing of knowledge. Through its actions, IDRC is helping others to help themselves.

About the Publisher

IDRC Books publishes research results and scholarly studies on global and regional issues related to sustainable and equitable development. As a specialist in development literature, IDRC Books contributes to the body of knowledge on these issues to further the cause of global understanding and equity. IDRC publications are sold through its head office in Ottawa, Canada, as well as by IDRC's agents and distributors around the world. The full catalogue is available at http://www.idrc.ca/books/index.html.